AF552919

MYTHS AND REALITIES
of
SECURITY & PUBLIC AFFAIRS

MYTHS AND REALITIES
of
SECURITY & PUBLIC AFFAIRS

Arvindar Singh

Ocean Books Pvt. Ltd.

ISO 9001:2008 Publishers

Published by
Ocean Books (P) Ltd.
4/19 Asaf Ali Road,
New Delhi-110 002 (INDIA)

ISBN 978-81-8430-112-0
Myths and Realities of Security & Public Affairs
by **Arvindar Singh**

Edition
First, 2011

Price
Rs. 350.00 (Rs. Three Hundred Fifty Only)

Printed at
Bhanu Printers, Delhi

Dedicated to
the Memory of My Parents
Late Lt Gen Mohindar Singh, AVSM
and Mrs Marjorie Singh
who taught me
the invaluable principles of life
which made me
what I am today

Acknowledgements

I would like to acknowledge that various writings in this book have been published courtesy– The Himachal Times, The United Services Institution of India, Defence Watch, Uday India Dehradun Classified and Bhavan's Journal.

Preface

This work has been for me in many ways a culmination of an idea which had occurred to me some years ago when I realised that I done a fair bit of writing on certain subjects and I thought it may be an interesting idea to put these between two covers. I do not claim to be person of much scholarshi p but have throughout my life applied my mind and given to what I have read some deep thought. I have also over years read up a fair amount on current events and historical subjects which led me to take up writing as a free lance scribe. It has been said in an oft repeated cliché that "man proposes, God disposes" in my writing career I have felt that this saying could not have been more true, thus I have undertaken bringing out this anthology. Life's experiences have taught me some precious lessons which remain imprinted on my mind. In the Guru Granth Sahib, the holy book of the Sikhs, Guru Nanak says, "*Make contentment thy earnings Modesty thy begging bowl and pouch; Contemplation thy ashes.*" Guru Nanak also made the following observation pregnant with wisdom *"Truth is the highest virtue; higher still is truthful living."*

On the question of true happiness the Bhagvat Gita opines that true happiness can only be accomplished by being fully content and surrendering all desire for mammon. One of our saints said long ago, *"food, sleep, fear and sexual relations are common to men and animals. Only Dharma or religion distinguishes men from animals. Those who have no dharma will behave like animals."* Professor Dil Mohammad Princi pal of the Islamic College wrote in his lucid transalation of the Gita "*Gita is one of the greatest spiritual books in the world. It explains to us what man is, what God is, what Love is, what knowledge is, what is the way to work."* The Holy Koran says in its verse, "*I follow what is revealed to men from my Lord:this is nothing but light from your Lord, and guidance, and mercy for any who have faith."* (The Holy Koran 7:23) Likewise the Bible states, on the everlasting presence of God" *So God created in his own image, in the image of God created he him; male and female created he them."(The Holy Bible;Gensis 1:27)* While the above mentioned passages bring great peace and solace to the mind and from them I have learnt much from them when the going is sometimes been ardous in more respects than one,but one has learnt to over come difficulties and in some cases "stoop to conquer" when required.

The various chapters of the book have been arranged according to a certain groupings for the ease of the reader.

I have deliberately tried to give importance to those themes like the defence of secular fabric of our country priorities in the section entitled as well issues of Defence and Security of which I have been writing for a considerable period under the title "National and Defence".

The section on "personalities" deals with a wide specturem of individuals from various walks of life who have made an impact on our public life as well as other walks of existence. In a work like this I felt it was necessary that the lives of these renowned persons whom I have written on gets reproduced.

The section dealing with "miscellany" addresses general topics which are both relevant and of literary value as it gives the jest of various books I have reviewed among other things.

Some chapters have been written specifically for the book and therefore do not have any reference to any publication. The chapter on Dehradun the city which has been my home for more than 25 years is one such example. It has been said that the place you live in, your occupation and the person whom you take as your partner for life is your destiny and nothing can alter it. In my case the first two have been decided and the third still remains in the realm of possibility as I approach the fifth decade of my life! Therefore I thought it only fitting that I pay tribute to the city which took me into its bossom.

The chapters "Those whom I Have Known" and "The Madras Regiment and Lt Gen Mohindar Singh" are also chapters which have been exclusively written for this volume. In the chapter "Those whom I have known" I have given a bit of an autobiographical glimpse of some eminent personalities and some who have played an important role in my life's experiences in various ways. A tribute to my father an outstanding officer of the Army in his own right, and a descri ption of the famous regiment he was a part of would in place in a volume of this nature according to my way of thinking.

Some glimpses of Uttarakhand and its personalities was inevitable as my home State has formed a definite niche on my writings over the years, and indeed our small State has produced many a man or woman of substance. Dehradun has often been refered to as the intellectual capital of northern India. With its lush greenry, interesting book-shops and well stocked Libraries there is no doubt that the city has become a hub for the "thinking man" or "thinking woman"(I add the latter least I be accused of male chauvinism!) Being a resident of this valley has also inculcated in me a love for nature *"the silence that is in the starry sky, the sleep that is among the lonely hills."* Something about the place you live wears of on you, and I can only hope that in my case the effect has been positive.

I would be failing in my duty if I did not acknowledge the help and assistance I received from various people during the period that I was working on getting this work together. I cannot mention everyone here but I would like to mention particularly Ms Jehanara Wasi who is a well known editor, Mr Upendra Arora of The Green Bookshop Dehradun. The late Lt Gen R.K. Jasbir Singh had also given me very valuable advice on how this volume should be brought out, and it is to my most profound regret that he could not live to see this book come out.

ARVINDAR SINGH

Contents

MISCELLANY

NATION & DEFENCE

1

40th Anniversary of the Sino-Indian Conflict: A Historical Perspective

"I hope that I am not leaving you as cannon fodder for the Chinese....."

General K.S. Thimayya, in one of his farewell speeches on the eve of his retirement in 1961

Forty years have gone by since the fateful morning of October 20, 1962 when the People's Liberation Army of Communist China launched a massive offensive in the Namka Chu Valley on the Kameng Frontier Division of the North East Frontier Agency (NEFA)*, to begin a bloody and one sided battle which was to end with the unilateral cease-fire a month later on November 20, 1962, after which India claimed that the Chinese were in possession of 33000 sq. kilometres of Indian territory.

In that autumn of great significance in India's political and military history, many myths were shattered. The Himalayas could no longer be considered impregnable; Jawaharlal Nehru's policies both international and domestic lay shattered around him leaving him a broken man with only 18 months to live; the Indian Army was sufficiently disgraced as a force devoid of even the basic weaponry and supplies, the "Higher Direction of War" in the Ministry of Defence had come a cropper, the policy of "Panch Sheel" or peaceful coexistence was now in the dustbin of history; V.K. Krishna Menon, the "intellectual" Defence Minister, would finally take his bow from ministerial office and above all, an atmosphere of gloom and despair would envelope a defeated nation. While considering the events before and after the gigantic debacle we should also consider the lesson it holds out which is relevant to the present day. "Those who forget history; are condemned to repeat it" is a saying that has special meaning with regard to the situation in present-day Arunachal Pradesh.

At the Shimla Conference held between the British and Chinese representatives in 1914, the McMahon Line was demarcated. Captain McMahon (who represented the British) had earlier been associated with the demarcation of the Durand Line. The British wanted India to have complete dominance over Tibet while China was to be left with only nominal suzerainty over an autonomous Tibet. Given the complex nature of the talks things did not work out according to this formula of the British administration. The Chinese delegate Ivan Chen,a seasoned diplomat proved a hard nut to crack. The British agreed to divide Tibet into two zones of inner and outer and while Chinese suzerainty would hold sway over the entire country, China would have no say in the administration of outer Tibet which would in effect be a buffer state between both countries. Though Ivan Chen initialled the treaty, the talks ended in a stalemate with the Chinese government later denouncing Chen for his action. An Anglo-Tibetan accord on the above mentioned lines did take place, however, at Shimla in a rather deceptive atmosphere with Ivan Chen being sent into another room at the time of the signing. Though he was aware of what was happening, he was not aware of the nitty-gritty of the accord, which remained under wraps for many years.

In the immediate aftermath of the establishment of the People's Republic of China in October 1949, China issued a statement clearly giving vent to their intention to militarily overrun Tibet at short notice, which in fact took place later in October 1950. New Delhi voiced an angry protest over the invasion, only to receive a sharp retort from Beijing, "Tibet is an integral part of China, and the problem of Tibet is entirely a domestic problem of China. The Chinese People's Liberation Army has entered Tibet to liberate the Tibetan people and defend the frontiers of China." Thus Beijing had sent its blunt and clear message to New Delhi, "lay off" was the sum total of the cryptic communiqué. It was rumoured that President Truman had offered India help to liberate Tibet at this juncture but our "lofty idealism" was still holding sway over the foreign policy. Extremely dubious also was the role of the then Indian Ambassador to China, K.M. Pannikar who was, according to a contemporary source said to have substituted the word "sovereignty" for the word "suzerainty" in the diplomatic messages of New Delhi on the Tibetan question. Sardar Vallabhbhai Patel then Deputy Prime Minister wrote a very critical letter, as is well known, to his Premier on the Chinese occupation of Tibet, shortly before his death in the winter of 1950. In substance he meationed that K.M. Pannikar had been in effect "brainwashed" by the Chinese administration. Describing the final act of the Chinese as "a little short of perfidy" he went on to express his hunch that India was dealing with a "potential enemy", He also spoke of "a long term consideration of our defence needs and assurance of arms ammunition and armour to deal with the double threat in the North and East." Obviously the Sardar was in a prophetic mood. Nehru`s reply to the Sardar is not known and it can be quite clearly deduced from the events that followed that the sage advice of the Deputy Prime Minister had fallen on deaf ears. The Sardar unfortunately died on December 15, 1950. Nehru admitted in Parliament in 1951, "I saw no reason to discuss the frontier with the Chinese government because, foolishly if you like, I thought there was nothing to discuss." India's backdoor had thus been opened to a large, powerful, and expansionist China.

After the 1954 accord with Nehru in Beijing the Chinese did not lend agreement to their Indian counterpart's view that the McMahon Line had been virtually recognized by their government. They did,however,include in the treaty the Panch Sheel principles of mutal respect for each other's sovereignty and integrity, non-aggression, non-interference in each other's internal affairs, mutual benefit and peaceful coexistence. According to the 1954 Agreement India relinquished all extra territorial rights and privileges in Tibet which was a legacy of the British government, it virtually recognized Tibet as a part of China. In his talks with Prime Minister Nehru at Delhi in 1956,Zhou En Lai did not make any reference to Aksai Chin and confined his discussion to the eastern border. Only after the construction of the Aksai-Chin road in 1958, was this to become an issue of discussion. The 1956 visit was at the peak of the *"Hindi-Chini bhai-bhai"* era during which Nehru was in a buoyant mood. He accepted at face value Zhou's assurances on the McMahon Line without going into the details. Even though Beijing accepted certain facts further negotiations would be required for proper alignment of the boundary. India's protest on certain Chinese maps of the eastern border was met by an assurance from Zhou that these were old maps of the Kuomintang regime which the new government had not yet revised.

In October 1958, came the bombshell that China had built a highway through what was undisputedly Indian Territory in the Ladakh region of Aksai-Chin. Angry protests followed and Zhou claimed that the Sino-Indian border had not ever really been delimited. In 1959, the revolt took place in Tibet which resulted in the Dalai Lama fleeing the country and taking asylum in India. Close on the heels of this came the Longju Incident when the post in NEFA was taken over by Chinese Border Guards. Relations between the two countries were now openly inimical. In the spring of 1960, Zhou-En-Lai visited India for a week long summit. This meeting was held in a rather frosty atmosphere where Zhou many of Indian political leaders. The summit, however, was destined to fail. China did offer a 'barter deal' under which Aksai Chin would be leased out to Beijing and on the eastern border the McMahon Line would remain as the status quo. Since it was a rather vague proposal and Indian public opinion would have been wildly hostile to it, this was rejected without much ado. At the press conference, immediately after seeing off the Chinese premier, Jawaharlal Nehru made out "that the whole context of the talks had been China's aggression." Zhou was not amused,and described it as "an atttitude not to be taken with guests...we are very much distressed by the attitude as we respect Prime Minister Nehru." It was decided that officials from both sides would continue a dialogue.

On the eve of the border war, the military and political establishments were not in a state of cohesion? In August 1959, General K.S. Thimayya tendered his resignation but withdrew it on being beseeched to do so by Nehru who said he would iron out his differences with the acerbic Krishna Menon. Later Nehru castigated Thimayya in parliament making out the whole affair to be a storm in a teacup and classifying Timmy's (as the late General was popularly known) action as 'trivial' and 'peculiarly unwise'. The issue of the out of turn promotion of Lt General B.M. Kaul was said to be the chief cause of this issue. There were major ideological differences between Krishna Menon and the right wing Finance Minister Morarji Desai which led to the army being starved of weapons,clothing and equipment resulting in the troops being at heights of 15,000 feet in cotton clothing and canvas shoes, also using the archaic .303 Rifle of World War I vintage. The troops were also unaccclimatized. In his statement to the Lok Sabha about 10 months after the war, on September 2, 1963, the Defence Minister Yashwantrao Chavan was to say, "It is axiomatic that an unacclimatized army cannot be as fit as one which is. It has been revealed that despite this our troops stood the rigours of the climate although most of them were rushed at short notice from the plains." A word about the much hyped "Forward Policy". The author of this was Lt General B.M. Kaul who had virtually no battle experience and was an Army Service Corps (ASC) officer who was at that time Chief of General Staff at Army Headquarters. He had spent the Second World War in charge of a drama troupe to entertain troops, but somehow Nehru thought highly of this officer despite his manifest shortcomings. Of Kaul, General K.S. Thimayya had said, 'Every sepoy in the army knows that he has never been a combat soldier. You can't hide that sort of thing in the army. The officers don't respect Kaul.' The "Forward Policy" which entailed increasing drastically the number of patrols and posts in Chinese held Indian Territory obviously failed as we did not have roads or proper back-up for the forward posts. Lt General S.D. Verma, Corps Commander of the 15th Corps in Jammu & Kashmir, protested in 1961 saying that the Prime Minister's assurances had no relation to the ground situation.The trouble began with the attack on September 8, 1962 on Dhola Post south of the Namaka Chu river which had been established under the "Forward Policy" in June 1962. Despite a feedback from our formations on the ground about our inadequacies, New Delhi issued orders to 'evict the Chinese'. It must be noted that through most of September, Prime Minister Nehru, his number two Minister Morarji Desai, and Defence Minister Krishna Menon were out of the country.

On October 3, Lt General B.M. Kaul was rushed into the front as Commander of the newly created 4th Corps at Tezpur. When the Chinese inflicted heavy casualties on Indian troops at Tseng Jong with mortar fire on 10th October, Kaul's first reaction to Brig Dalvi was, "Oh my God, they mean business". On 11th October, Kaul had a high level meeting with Prime Minister Nehru and all the top brass. Even though he has denied it in his memoirs, there is evidence to suggest that he induced Nehru to issue his infamous statement to the army to "throw the Chinese out" while proceeding to Sri Lanka on 13th October. At that juncture it was calamitous to talk in this vein.

On 20th October came the massive onslaught at Namka Chu with the superior strenghth of five to one. The 7th Brigade put up a valiant fight but was soon outmanned and outgunned. General Kaul was rushed to Delhi as he had fallen ill with oedema. Nobody was in charge of the ill fated 4th Corps, as Lumpu and Tawang fell on 21st and 25th October respectively. In the northern sector also,the Chinese launched an attack and overran the Chip-Chap Valley of Ladakh. However, our retreat was much better organized in this zone.

During Kaul's illness, Lt General Harbaksh Singh took command of the 4th Corps and had he continued in command the history of the battle may have been diiferent, but, in a few days Kaul was back in the chair. The withdrawal from Sela and Bomdi La was uncalled for and caused exaggerated panic. According to Major General D.K. Palit, Director of Military Operations, the GOC of the 4th Division at Sela Major General A.S. Pathania was given an ambiguous set of instructions by Lt General B.M. Kaul on the evening of 17th November. This fiasco at the peak of the battle, when withdrawal was not dreamt of by the troops on the ground, would not have taken place had the doughty Harbaksh been at the helm of affairs. Notes D.R. Mankekar in the *Guilty Men of 1962,* "I have come across many young officers involved in the Sela and Bomdi La fighting who insisted that they received orders for withdrawal at a moment when they were locked in battle and were flinging back the enemy, giving and taking causalities without a thought of retreat." Stocks left behind at Sela sustained 25,000

Chinese troops for nearly two weeks. This was the magnitude of the debacle.The stiffest resistance the Chinese had to face in NEFA was at Walong in the Lohit sector where 15 attacks were repulsed by the11th Brigade and about 5000 casualties were inflicted thus significantly slowing down the pace of the Chinese. The unilateral cease-fire on 20th November came a few hours after Nehru made a fervent appeal for aid to President Kennedy in the shape of fighter and bomber squadrons. He even specified the number required –15. This was to remain unknown to the Indian public for a few years till it was revealed in parliament. American C-130 Transport aircraft had already reached Calcutta on 3rd November. When Ambassador B.K. Nehru presented this appeal for help to Kennedy's aide Carl Keysen in Washington he was met with the biting words, "So your spirit couldn't stand even a minor attack for two weeks. Churchill went on single-handed without any help from anybody for two whole years; you have collapsed in fifteen days." B.K. Nehru was to describe it as his most humiliating moment as Ambassador. Kennedy, it must be noted though, was more than willing to help India, and would have concluded a $500 million Defence deal with India had his life not been tragically cut short.

It remains a mystery till date as to why the Indian Air Force was not used in the Battle of 1962. The Chinese would probably not have used their Air Force on such a long range and our Air Force would have given crucial support to our army on the ground. Our aircraft like the Hunters were of a much higher calibre than those possessed by the Chinese Air Force. Krishna Menon, the much maligned Defence Minister had according to certain sources advocated the use of air power but he was overruled by Nehru who was fearful of an attack on Calcutta. It is a pathetic commentary on the lop-sided and dis-organized "higher direction of war." It is an undisputed fact that China had many pressing reasons for the border war in the fall of 1962. Mao Zedong wanted to cut this Democratic Asian power to size, and at one stroke virtually undermined the position of Jawaharlal Nehru on the world stage. A vibrant democratic and powerful India was a danger to this dictatorial communist regime.

The Henderson Brooks Report, alleged to be a condemnatory document against the then government, remains to date unpublished by the Government of India for reasons best known to it. It is rumoured that the British journalist Neville Maxwell has a copy of it. In his foreword to D.R. Mankekar's book which was republished in 1998, the then Defence Minister George Fernandes has said, "there was no serious effort at introspection to find out why and how the proud Indian Army was made to bite the dust by the Chinese." It would be eminently in the interest of the Defence forces as well as the nation as a whole, if this comprehensive document is made public even if it is 40 long years after the event.

Four decades after these dramatic events in the border war, we have to, as a nation consider deeply our perception of this affliction to our national pride. As things stand now there is a distinct possibility of China intervening in an Indo-Pak skirmish given Beijing's covert assistance to the Pakistan Nuclear and Missile programme and particularly if America remains neutral. Also an uprising in Tibet cannot be ruled out as the populace of this state is distinct from the Han (the vast majority of the Chinese race). All these are predictions for the future.

(Published in USI Journal Last Quarter 2003)

□

2

Gujarat: Where Do We Go From Here?

The Parliamentary debate on Gujarat generated much interest among the thinking public and the "opinion makers". Parliament is our highest debating forum. It carries the precious cargo of our people's hopes and aspirations. Though the government won the numbers game in the Lok Sabha it had to concede the first place to the opposition in the Rajya Sabha by accepting its resolution "unanimously". Many points in the debate rankle in one's mind. Sadhvi Uma Bharati`s rather weak defence that the Gujarat affair was nothing but the Congress's desire for power; her rather shocking hypothesis that those who disagree with a certain viewpoint are almost traitors so to speak; why blame poor Chandrashekar for calling her a Nazi? Anyone who can perceive the basics of political thought will come to the same conclusion – I do not think that grey matter is so scarce. Then we had George "the giant killer" (he won the appellation after defeating Congress boss S.K. Patil in Mumbai in 1967) going into the nuances of rape victims. Something churned within me when I heard him speak thus; something that gave one a feeling that everything is going wrong. Our great parliamentarians like Nehru, Morarji Desai, Azad, Kidwai, Nath Pai and Madhu Limaye must be turning in their graves. I thought I would mention the last two deliberately as they belonged to George's school of thought or his launching ground into politics, the Praja Socialist Party. Venkiah Naidu showed a total loss of depth when he said "only numbers matter in a democracy, not sentiments".

Where does one go from here? Have we lost the moral moorings in our public life? Have we reached the nadir in every sphere of our existence as a democracy? Has moral responsibility of a government ceased to be an issue as BJP men in parliament and outside continue with rhetoric that only the "people of the state should decide who the Chief Minister should be". Why have so many ministers and even Chief Ministers resigned in the past? Jayaprakash Narayan is quoted by those in authority. Anyone even to a slight degree familiar with his ideological moorings would know that the Lok Nayak could never in his wildest dreams be on the same side of the party which has allowed the death dance and shameful events to take place in the last two and a half months in a state considered one of India's most prosperous. Let us remember that it was Jayapraksh Narayan who through his Nav Nirman movement brought about the fall of the Chimanbhai Patel government in 1974, and the Jan Sangh was a part of this movement; at that time "moral responsibillity" was obviously an issue worth believing in. "India can be governed firmly or not at all", said Lord Wavell, the illustrous Viceroy. Is this the firmness in administration that we have shown since the last two months? The government must indulge in deep introspection to save the situation and remove a Chief Minister who has violated the constitution; all democratic norms and indeed all norms of decency.

To come back to the Parliamentary debate and its implications one cannot help feeling that the time has come for all parties to pick up the pieces of the shattered edifice of the basic values of our democracy. But the onus of this lies on the government; they must concede some points of the opposition's demand; remove this hated figure who has indulged in the worst type of bigotry ever seen in the land of Gandhi and Patel; both of whom were two sides of the same coin. Then only can a meaningful effort to heal the wounds of the people begin. The opposition has not only to be taken into confidence; they have to have sufficient confidence in the government of the day. Otherwise even a 100 K.P.S. Gills will not have the desired result. The pseudo-patriots (to use Julio Ribeiro's interesting phrase) must learn that "Sarve Dharma Shambhava" is not a mantra to be chanted to act as a mask, but must be put into actual practice. Well-known writer Arundhati Roy in a recent piece has warned of fascism being fuelled by national disillusionment. We must act against these tendencies before it is too late.

I would like to end this article with the wise words of the Mahatma which has immense relevance as the country finds itself in the midst of a grave national crisis:

> "Gather together under one banner, all men from all religions and races of India and infuse into them the spirit of solidarity and oneness to the utter exclusion of all communal and parochial sentiments."

(Published in The Himachal Times April 2002)

□

3

Indian Military Academy: 70th Anniversary Celebrations

The Indian Military Academy at Dehradun situated against the backdrop of the exquisitely picturesque snow-capped Garhwal Himalayas was on December 10, 2002, the venue of an event momentous in its rather sublime history. It was celebrating its 70th Anniversary. The guest of honour was India's first Field Marshal S.H.F.J. Manekshaw, MC or "Sam Bahadur" as he is popularly known, (the nickname habit is an off-shoot of the American Army) who does actually belong to the very first batch of 40 gentlemen cadets who were commissioned from the Academy in December 1934. This batch is known as the "Pioneers".

The Field Marshal's "Dinner Night" at the Academy on 9th December was unique both in the history of the Academy as also the Indian Army as both Field Marshal Sam Manekshaw and General S. Padmanaabhan, Chief of the Army Staff were present. Toasts were proposed to the President, the Indian Military Academy and to Sam Bahadur. The grand old soldier was the focus of all eyes throughout the evening in the wooden panelled lounge of the Officers Mess.

One is most conscious of the British Empire while visiting an Officers mess, which can justifiably be called the empire's last outpost. A dinner night at an officers mess encompasses a combination of chivalry and decorum and echoes with Sandhrust accents and bristles with martial mostaches. One expects to find Kipling scribbling in some quiet corner and Gunga Din serving up a tot of whisky. The mess is a museum of Anglophilia whose ethos has permeated every nook and cranny of the Indian Army. The Dinner Night at the Academy mentioned here was conducted with clock-work precision.

The toasts drunk on the occasion of the 70th Anniversary Dinner Night were in the form of army custom. The President of the Mess Committee ascertained for himself that all glasses were charged before knocking the table thrice to ensure silence and addressed the Vice President of the Mess Committee with the words, "Mr. Vice, the President." The Vice President now followed with the words, "Gentlemen the President" now all guests assembled stood up and intoned the words "the President" and drank the toast. The same procedure was followed for the other two toasts mentioned.

Seeing the great old soldier of yore present at the Dinner Night brought to the surface of the mind, the following verse from Kipling which he seemed to say to the Indian Army:

I've eaten your bread and your salt,
I've drunk your water and wine,
The deaths ye died I've watched beside,
and the lives ye lived were mine.

The Staff serving the dinner were attired in the traditional Indian turban and Indian cap bearing the colours of the Indian Military Academy. On the occasion of the Academy Dinner Night the officers were dressed in black Jodhpur coats with matching trousers and golden embossed badges of rank. The outfit is without doubt macho in its appearance. Sam Bahadur had a dark green Jodhpur on; this is because Officers of the Gorkha Regiment wear dark green instead of black. India's first Field Marshal belongs to the Indian 8th Gorkha Regiment. Upon commissioning into the army he did his attachment (a period of a few months which is given to a junior officer to familiarize himself with army traditions) with the 2nd Battalion the Royal Scots. It so happens that the first British Field Marshal George Hamilton, the 1st Earl of Orhnay who was bestowed the rank by King George II in 1736 also belonged to the 2nd Battalion the Royal Scots. A remarkable coincidence indeed!

The dining hall where the academy dinner nights is a long hall which can seat more than 200 hundred people on formal occasions such as this. The Academy silver is also displayed on such occasions and being an institution which has completed four score and ten, the silver collection of its Mess is undoubtedly vast and varied. It may be interesting to point out that the commencement of dinner is called by a loud announcement in the national language by the Mess Sergeant to the President of the Mess Committee.

An Officers' Mess like the one at the Indian Military Academy is established as per military tradition to promote cordiality, comradeship and *espirit-de-corps.* It is home to all military officers and as an institution has a great influence on an officer's life. Mess customs and traditions instil in officers a strong sense of loyalty and co-operation.

On December 10, the Parade Ground in front of the hallowed drill square with the Passing Out Cadets lined up in navy blue tunics facing the distinguished audience carried an air of the ultimate martial practice about it. A thunderous applause went up as Sam Bahadur arrived in the prestigious four-horse carriage presented by the erstwhile Maharaja of Patiala to the Academy. He looked smart and crisp on that cold December morning carrying all his 89 years with immense dignity.

After receiving the compliments of the parade with a General Salute which he returned with the customary raising of the Field Marshal's baton, he proceeded to review the Passing Out Parade in the four-horse Patiala coach to the playing of martial tunes by the Academy band, accompanied by the Commandant of the Academy mounted on a charger. The serenade of youth and valour was in tune with the best army traditions. The enormously impressive drill square in front of the imposing Chetwode Building (named after Field Marshal Sir Philip Chetwode, Commander-in-Chief of the British Indian Army) is a feast for the eyes on a Passing Out Parade Day. The Field Marshal's review was followed by a march past in quick time.

In his address to the cadets about to receive their commission, Manekshaw said,

"Many changes have taken place since I was a cadet, we had horse and mule for transport. Today you have the motor vehicle. We were armed with the good old .303 Rifle. Today you are armed with the finest gun in the world. When I was a Lieutenant, I was sent at night across the enemy lines to find out their gun positions, their barbed wire fences and minefields. Today the satellite cameras do it for you.

But one thing remains the same and that is your task and you duty. You are required to ensure the security of this country against any aggression. This means that you will have to fight and fight to win."

The Field Marshal's clear voice boomed across the parade ground, "If you lose don't come back, you would have disgraced your country, the people won't look at you." he rasped. And then in a style typical of him, Manekshaw sounded the ultimate warning to the young officers, "Even your 'Garhwali` (wife) will despise you! The audience roared its approval.

After the address, Manekshaw presented the awards such as the "Sword of Honour" gold, silver and bronze medals to cadets who had excelled themselves. The Parade culminated with the cadets trooping into the Chetwode Building to the strains of "Auld Lange Sanye". The Parade was followed by the "Piping Ceremony" which implies the "piping" of stars to the new graduates of the Academy. Field Marshal Sam Manekshaw piped the stars of cadets from friendly foreign countries who had graduated. This was followed by the oath taking ceremony, rendering of the Academy song and playing of the National Anthem which brought the curtain down on the day's festivities.

The Indian Military Academy, known as the "Indian Sandhrust" was set up in 1932, 15 years before India attained Independence after consistent demand for the setting up of an academy to train Indians for the army by the national leadership. After the Round Table Conference in 1930, a committee headed by Field Marshal

Sir Philip Chetwode, GCB, GCSS, CCMA, DSO Commander-in-Chief of the Indian Army was appointed to arrange the setting up of the "Indian Sandhurst". The committee submitted its report in July 1931 and selected the buildings of the Railway Staff College at Dehradun as suitable to house the new Academy for the Army. The Academy began functioning on October 1, 1932 and was formally inaugurated by Sir Philip Chetwode on December 10,1932. Among those invited to the inaugural function were a large number of national leaders who had demanded the establishment of this academy. The first batch of 40 cadets included apart from Manekshaw, Cadet Smith Dunn and Mohammed Musa who rose to be the Chiefs of the Armies of Burma and Pakistan respectively.

In 1934 the Academy received colours from the Viceroy Lord Willingdon on behalf of the King Emperor and later from the Indian Presidents S. Radhakrishnan and Fakhruddin Ali Ahmed in 1962 and 1976 respectively. The Indian Army has been described as one of the finest and oldest armies of the world. Of the Indian Army,Field MarshalSir Philip Chetwode remarked at inauguration of the Academy, in 1932, "No better material exists in the world and they have proved it on many stricken fields." Sir Phillip Chetwode while inaugurating the academy also gave it its **credo** which is as follows,

"The safety, honour and welfare of your country comes first always and every time, the honour, welfare and safety of the men you command come next, Your own ease, comfort and safety comes last always and every time."

Napoleon had said that "every subaltern joining the army has in his knap-sack a Field Marshal's baton. It is up to him to achieve it through his efforts." Sam Manekshaw lived up to this Napoleonic ideal.

The Academy has trained about 50,000 officers for the Indian Army which is a fairly large number by standards of various developed countries the world over. It is divided into four battalions named after Sam Bahadur and other famous Generals of the Indian Army including Lt General Parminder Singh Bhagat, a Victoria Cross winner, who was awarded the Victoria Cross for unparalleled bravery and inspiring leadership in January 1941 on the road to Gondar, Abyssinia. Among other things, the Academy inculcates qualities of leadership,discipline,adventure,initiative,endurance and intelligence in tactics of modern war.

Over the years a number of dignitaries from India and abroad have visited the Academy. Successive Presidents, Prime Ministers and Ministers for Defence have reviewed the Passing Out Parades. Apart from preserving the old colours, the Academy museum houses a treasure trove of memorabilia as well.

The City of Dehradun where the Indian Military Academy is located is one which dates back to the great Indian epic the *Mahabharata.* It is a township in the lap of a valley about 250 Kms from the capital, New Delhi. Since the year 2000 it has been the provincial capital of India's newest state, Uttarakhand and is at the foothills of the Himalayan ranges. It is also a gateway to the holy pathway to Badrinath, a sacred pilgrimage spot. This vibrant land of the Himalayas is a tourist's paradise.

(Press Release December 11, 2002)

□

4

The Madras Regiment and Lt General Mohindar Singh

Wellington, a small cantonment nestled in the Nilgiri Hills of Tamil Nadu is famous for more reasons than one. It is home to the prestigious Defence Services Staff College known popularly as the 'Mecca of Military Learning'. Therefore, what Mecca is to the practising Muslim, the DSSC is to the officers of the defence forces. Also alongside this college of international repute is the Madras Regimental Centre, the training centre of one of the oldest regiments of the Indian Army. Raised in the year 1758 by the British government of Madras in anticipation of the Anglo French war, the Madras army received its baptism by fire against the French forces in the battle of Chengam in North Arcot District. Colonel Smith, the commander of the Madras soldiers observed, 'I never saw men behave with more resolution and intrepidity than those I have the honour to command.' Other significant achievements of the Madras infantry were the conquest of Puducherry (earlier known as Pondicherry) in 1792; Ceylon in 1795–96, of much momentousness also was the capture of the fort of Serirangapatnam on May 4,1799 against the forces of that mighty warrior Tipu Sultan. In his book *The History of the Madras Regiment,* Lt Colonel E.G. Phythian Adams, OBE notes, " As soon as the ramparts were cleared, a detachment was sent to secure the palace, which was also the treasury and to protect the family of the sultan, but they had been anticipated by the 8th Madras Infantry which had been sent across the river by Colonel Wellesley. After some delay in parleys, General Baird who had great difficulty in restraining the indignation of the soldiers at the murder of the prisoners taken during the siege was admitted into the palace and the sultan's two younger sons surrendered to him. Tipu's fate was unknown till his body was found under a heap of slain soldiers after nightfall".

The Author's father Lt Gen Mohindar Singh, AVSM presents a memento to President N. Sanjeeva Reddi on behalf of the Defence Services Staff College, Wellington, 1981. He was Commandant of this institution for nearly four years

The medal for the battle of Serirangapatnam was announced in the year 1808, but in fact not distributed to the surviving victors till 1811. The obverse of the medal showed the storming of the breach with the meridian sun denoting the time,and an inscription in Persian, 'The fort of Serirangapatnam the Gift of God, May 4, 1799.' The reverse of the medal shows a lion subduing a tiger with the words 'The Lion of God the Conqueror.' This medal was given in gold to high ranking Officers, in silver gilt to Field officers, and in silver to Captains and Subalterns, while the Non-commissioned officers received it in bronze and Privates in 'pure graven tin.' The conquest of Serirangapatnam (situated on the Bangalore–Mysore highway) heralded the end of the hegemony of that great warrior, Tipu Sultan.

It would be pertinent to mention here that the Madrasi soldier was also to prove the vanquisher in the Battle of Assaye against the Maratha confederacy led by Sindhia in the Second Maratha War of 1805. Major General Wellesley, the future Duke of Wellington, led this campaign. He said of the forces participating, "Our troops behaved admirably. Our sepoys astonished me". The 8th Battalion of the Madras Infantry became a favourite of Wellesley at the commencement of his career in India and accompanied him on every service. This Battalion was commonly known as 'Wellesley ka Paltan'. The Assaye elephant became a part of the crest of the Madras Regiment after Independence when the British crown was removed from it. On the anniversary of the Battle of Assaye colours were presented to the newly formed training centre in 1942. The Madras Infantry was to see action in the Third Burma War of 1885–89, and in the invasion of Tirah in the North West Frontier in 1895–98. For this campaign the 21st Madras Infantry (Pioneers) was awarded the battle honours *Punjab Frontier and Tirah.*

During World War I (1914–19) the 61 and 63 Pioneers and PLI were deployed in East Africa and the units particularly the 61 won laurels. Another Madras battalion 75 CI was on service at Aden from April 1916 to December 1920. It was engaged in the capture of Jabri and Handley Hill. In the post armistice period the Turkish commander (of the rival army) commented that his men feared the 75 CI more than any Indian formation, "because they were not afraid to go in with the bayonet", words that speak for themselves.

The Moplah rebellion in Malabar in 1921-22, was the result of fanatical mullahs spreading the word that the British were at the point of winding up their rule in India, and they began seizing arms of the police stations, blocking roads, blowing up railway lines and bridges as well as cutting off telegraph poles. The Moplahs were determined to convert those who did not belong to their faith to Islam. In the crushing of this revolt the 64 Madras Infantry Pioneers from Bangalore and the 83 WLI (Walijhabad Light Infantry) of the Madras troops took part in and acquitted themselves well in action. His Majesty was pleased to order the Medal Malabar1921–22 to be given to all ranks who partici pated in this action. Awards for gallantry were also made.

During World War II the Madrasi soldier was to make his mark on the Burma Front. At the "shark" piquet near Moreh Capt (later Lt General) R.S. Naronha (of the 4th Battalion) held out for 16 days and inflicted heavy casualties on the Japanese forces. Capt. Noronha was awarded the Military Cross and four other ranks received military medals and a number of others received Certificates of Gallantry. The 4th Battalion was also the first Battalion to cross the Chindwin in the ultimate offensive towards Rangoon. Later on in the attack on Mandalay river, Major Norohna was awarded a bar to his MC and Jamedar Thomas was also to be similarly awarded. 1 Madras also played a crucial role in clearing the city Surabaya (Indonesia) during 1945–46. Between November 1945 to April 1946, the paltan had lost 20 men and 52 were wounded, whereas the enemy lost 608 personnel. Major C.P. Menon was awarded the Military Cross and Lance Naik Perumal received the IDSM.

The Battalions 2 and 4 Madras were deployed on internal security duties in Delhi during Independence and Partition of the subcontinent. By all accounts they discharged their duties setting a high standard. Of them, Governor General Lord Louis Mountbatten said, while addressing an attestation Parade at Wellington on April 27, 1948, "They carried out the most difficult duty a soldier can be called upon to perform, namely, that of internal defence, in the most exemplary manner as I can personally testify since I visited their posts." It was recorded that once while returning from an evening function Mountbatten's car was challenged by a sentry from 4 Madras, as the driver did not stop the car, the sentry opened fire without causing damage. The next day Lord Mountbatten sent a letter of appreciation to the Commanding Officer commending the prompt action of the guard at the Viceregal Lodge. 1 Madras provided security to the Father of the Nation, Mahatma Gandhi during his stay at Kolkata in July–August 1947.

8 Madras was also in action during 'Operation Polo' when the government sent forces to Hyderabad state as a result of the Nizam of Hyderabad declaring independence with the support

of the Razakars. 1 Madras was deployed at Kathua in Jammu region of the LOC and was involved in skirmishes with Pakistani forces in 1947–48. Unfortunately it lost its Commanding Officer Lt Col CPA Menon in an ambush on April 26, 1948. The Battalion won one Mahavir Chakra and three Vir Chakras.

A Madras regiment battalion (4 Madras) was involved in the UN Force in the Congo in 1962–63. This was to curb the secessionist moves of the mercenaries led by the Katanga leader Moise Tshombe. The battalion was responsible for capturing Jadotville town from the mercenaries. In the action the battalion received 1 Vir Chakra, 4 Sena Medals, 10 mentioned in Dispatches and 1 VSM. Brigadiers K.A.S. Raja and R.S. Norohna of the regiment were commanders of the Indian Brigade group in the Congo and both were awarded the PVSM. The formations of 2, 16, 17 Madras saw action during the Sino-Indian Conflict of 1962. In the 1965 campaign against Pakistan, the Madras troops (3 & 4 Madras) stormed Maharajke in the Sialkot District in West Punjab State of Pakistan. 4 Madras received one Maha Vir Chakra, three Vir Chakras and three Mentioned in Dispatches.

Mention must also be made of the heroic role of the Thambi in the 1971 war with Pakistan. In the intense action in the battle of Basantar in the Western sector 16 Madras was a key player and played a heroic part. The Commanding Officer Lt Col VP Ghai was martyred and won a well deserved Maha Vir Chakra. The Battalion won a total of two Maha Vir Chakras, five Vir Chakras, and two Sena Medals. The Battalion 26 Madras won the Battle Honour 'SIRAMANI 1971' for the battle of Siramani in the Khulna Sector of Bangladesh. Capt S.S. Walkar of 18 Madras also won the MVC posthumously in the battle at Hingoro Tar (Sind). Apart from these awards the regiment won numerous other awards in the western and eastern theatre. Post 1971 the Thambis have given a good account of themselves in Operation Pawan as a part of the IPKF operation in Sri Lanka, in which seven battalions of the regiment were deployed. Two Battalions (3 and 25) received COAS citations for combating insurgency in Punjab and Jammu & Kashmir.

My father Lt General Mohindar Singh served the Madras Regiment for thirty-six years. He carried out his regimental duties with rare dedication and was a loyal *thambi.* He went out of his way to render help to any officer or soldier of the regiment particularly those in distress. During the 1971 Indo-Pak conflict he was commanding 19 Infantry Brigade in Jammu. He was assigned the task of attacking the enemy who had well organized defences between the rivers Chenab and Chandra Bhagah. The Chandra Bhagha meets the Tawi further down, both Chandra Bhagha and Tawi merge in Pakistan near abouts the Marala Headworks which provide the entire irrigation and power supply for what was then West Pakistan, and lay adjacent to this strip of land called "Chicken`s Neck" which was thus very crucial for Pakistan.This strip of land earlier called 'the dagger' was renamed "Chicken's Neck" by Brig Mohindar Singh who felt that the name 'dagger' jutting into Indian territory was a misnomer, and it should be called a "duck or chicken's neck, which could be rung at will" The mission involved 170 sq kms of Pakistan Territory. He planned the attack of his Brigade in a meticulous and efficient manner, timing and rehearsing his battalions with zeal and vigour. His bold plan in surprising the enemy in a wide outflanking movement jeopardized the enemy defence plans and forced it to vacate the area in great panic leaving behind large quantities of arms,ammunition and equipment. The remaining pockets of Pakistani territory were mopped up with lightning speed and determination, clearing up the entire area. He was awarded the AVSM for this action.

According to Lt General JS Rawat, PVSM, VSM who commanded 3/5th Gorkha Rifles (Frontier Force) during the Chicken's Neck Operations the operation plan was prepared after deep discussion in March/April 1971, and the final plan was drafted by the three commanding officers in the Commander's Office over whisky and dinner. The plan had been war-gamed and discussed meticulously and the Battalion Commanders were fully convinced about viability of the plan. General Rawat says, "One of the greatest qualities of our Commander was his ability to sell his ideas to his subordinates and make them feel that it was their idea." For example, he told General Rawat 'that yours is the most difficult task' thus giving a boost to the ego of his Commanding Officer and ensuring high morale. An amicable relationship prevailed which was one of the key elements of the success. According to General Rawat the commander gave the battalion CO's full freedom in day-to-day functioning and was with them when required. Brigadier Mohindar Singh did not interfere with the plan, and said that he was confident of the ability of his battalion commanders in the matter of following the basic guidelines laid down by him. 3/5 Gorkha Rifles as General Rawat remembers, was given the task by Brig Mohindar Singh, to man the border with CRPF in the months running up to the battle, at that time Rawat was a little surprised at the task assigned to his battalion but, later he understood when the actual campaign was to commence that the intention of his Commander was to make the battalion fully familiar with the terrain they would encounter in battle. The helicopter reconnaissance was upto the Naik level in 3/5 Gorkha Rifles, so thorough was the planning. As per the plan authored by the Commander Brig Mohindar Singh, it was decided that 11 Guards Commanded by Lt Col (later Lt General) JM Singh would launch a frontal attack on the Chicken's Neck and 3/5 would soon after launch a massive attack from behind to surprise the enemy. The attack by 11 Guards was thus to be a diversionary tactic. Later 11 Guards launched the assault on village Phuklian which was taken 18 hours ahead of schedule. Village Khoje Chak was the goal set for 3/5 GR. Also they were to secure the two ferries near Marala Headworks. 7/11 Gorkha Rifles were to prepare a launching pad at one stage for 3/5 GR but got delayed as they were searching for the enemy which had already been mopped up by 3/5 Gorkha Rifles. The Commander told Rawat on the radio "consolidate but don't be in a hurry to take Khoje Chak." Sound advice, as snipers could be present in the tall 25 feet *sarkanda* grass. Unfortunately due to lack of clarity at the Corps and Command level 3/5 GR and other battalions were not given the go ahead to bomb the Marala head-works which would have resulted in the flooding of West Pakistan.

The Pakistan battalion, 36 Punjab, which had been deployed by the Pakistani army was routed. The CO of 3/5 Gorkha Rifiles Col Rawat asked to launch his assault as early as possible and was granted his request. More than 800 men, para commandos and armoured corps column moved silently in the dead of night through thick sarkanda grass, 1400 yards of white tape was provided to the men so that nobody lost his way in the dark. On many occasions shelling and firing ensued in the dead of night. The smooth and cordial relations which existed between the Divisional Commander Major General ZC Bakshi, PVSM, MVC, VRC and the Brigade Commander Brig Mohindar Singh contributed in no mean way to the success of the operation, both were cool and non-interfering in their approach. "Throughout the battle", says General Rawat, my Brigade Commander was with me when I needed him and he joined the battalion during the action on many occasions. Casualties on our side were very low unlike on the Pakistani side where the casualties were close to a 100. 3/5 Gorkha Rifiles for example, had only 2 casualties.

Veteran broadcaster Melville DeMellow, said in his programme 'Remembered Glory', broadcast on All India Radio,

The battle for Chicken's Neck is over. But somewhere in the tall sarkanda grass is the gash of 1000 lb. bomb or a tawny stain where a man once crouched and fell – or two men came to terms with life and then fought fiercely with each other. Somewhere an empty helmet lies, mouth open in a mine field, its wearer long since dead. And so when people talk of easy victories, they sometimes forget that for some it is never easy, for in the easiest victory someone dies in the line of duty, someone is trapped in a minefield and someone stops a bullet with his number on it, so that the charging line may hold and go straight on to the final objective and victory. The Battle of Chicken's Neck was a great victory and we honour those who fought it and particularly those who gave their lives while fighting to achieve the victory, remember that:

He does not die,
That can bequeath-
Some influence-
To the land he knows.

But also remembering, that the garlands we offer to their memory must never be allowed to wither."

Subsequently Mohindar Singh was posted as Brigadier General Staff of a Corps and Deputy Commandant of the Indian Military Academy, Dehradun. He was posted to command 20 Mountain Division in Binnaguri (West Bengal) in 1976 in the rank of Major General. In 1978, he was designated Commandant of the Defence Services Staff College and held this office for 3 and a half years and was promoted to the rank of Lt General in 1981 while holding the same appointment. In 1982 he assumed charge as Director General of Military Training at Army Headquarters and in that capacity was Chairman of the Joint Training Committee of all three services. He retired from the army in 1984, settling down in Dehradun. He passed away in 1998.

Undoubtedly it can be said of him that he had an inspiring character and outlook and his proficiency as a soldier was of a unique nature.

□

5

Siachen Glacier: The Costly Standoff

As we prepare for another round of peace talks following thePrime Minister's initiative which began at the now famed rally at Srinagar, one of the most important and demanding issues to be resolved is the bone of contention of the presence of the Indian Army in the Siachen Glacier and the resultant high altitude deployment by Pakistani troops. Siachen represents a colossal waste both in man and material for both our countries. Defence Minister George Fernandes has reportedly informed Parliament that a whopping Rs 1095 crore per annum is being spent on the armed presence in this god forsaken land, where even a minor tooth ache implies a costly evacuation by helicopter, as the helicopter is the only link with the outside world. It has been estimated that a Cheetah helicopter costs about Rs 20000 an hour to fly at the height of the glacier. Equi pment failure at these heights of 21000 ft is a persistent problem in this bleak environment as equi pment of any type is not designed for operation at heights such as these. According to knowledgeable sources the above figure quoted by Fernandes is a conservative estimate.

To understand the logic of this impossible and often unbelievable conflict we have to travel back to the early 1980s when Mrs. Gandhi was feeling increasingly insecure politically given the volatile atmosphere in Punjab and Assam as well as other political issues. The military leadership at the time gave her an opportunity to score what was perceived as a massive scoring point against Pakistan, which was domestically speaking a political master stroke for her in her 'Durga' image. Based on the support of 'evidence' provided by mountaineers with little operational or military knowledge and the opinion of a particular general who had ambitions to head the Indian army, the occupation of Siachen began on April 13, 1984, by the landing of a platoon of soldiers on the glacier. Pakistan was quick to respond and forced its occupation along the 80 km Saltoro range at the glacier. At the time it was made out as a vast tactical gain for the Indian Forces. In fact, it was one of the most disastrous military decisions of the political leadership since independence. No strategist worth his salt will see any value in launching an offensive in this harsh terrain unfit for man or beast. It is clear as daylight that a 'phony' war had been foisted on both countries for well nearly two decades.

At the time of the delineation talks held in 1972, after the Shimla Accord, the joint survey group marked off the border to point NJ9842 with the ambiguous statement "and thence northward to the glaciers". This could be the bench-mark for the final settlement of this issue. What kind of life prevails for the troops at Siachen? Life at minus 50 degrees Celsius has to be seen to be believed. An immense toll on the biological functions, appetite, sleep and metabolism, loss of body heat in excess of the body's capacity to remain warm due to the wind chill factor as well as frost bite are only some of the hazards in these inhospitable parts of the world. Approximately 500 casualties have so far occurred in this meaningless war, and many troops have been maimed for life through frost bite. Snow storms and avalanches take their terrible toll of casualties as well as the crevasses. Winds of the astronomical speed of 150 km/h blow across the glacier which at a length of 77 kms is a record in non polar glaciers. Yet political conditions have not permitted a halt to this exercise in futility. It has been pointed out by various sources on the Siachen issue that there is growing feeling, in the junior ranks of the army, that the senior hierarchy and political leadership has forced the rank and file into this inconsequential effort of high altitude warfare. This has been reflected in certain articles in military journals. This is not a happy augury for one the most disciplined fighting forces of the world.

Another point to ponder is the issue of catastrophic proportions that environmentally speaking, the occupation of the glacier by the army causes. Used artillery shells, empty fuel containers, tetra packs, aluminum foil and human waste dumped into the crevasses may result in the drying up of the rivers like the Ganga, Brahmaputra and Indus, which are the main lifelines of both India and Pakistan. We owe it to our future generations that such a disaster is avoided. The Pakistan presence on Saltoro range results in a ding-dong battle continuing almost every day. At times a post is captured, only to be recaptured by the Indian forces. Much blood is shed in the bargain. Twice in the past, in 1989 and 1992 India and Pakistan have been close to a pact to settle the issue but dithering on both sides prevented it coming about. In 1989 it was the parliamentary elections in India which made Rajiv Gandhi hold back, and in 1992 Narasimha Rao feared hostile reaction from the principle opposition party, the BJP. Pakistani leaders also were weary of hardliners in their country. Vajpayee's statesmanlike attitude irrespective of the 'invisible and sometimes visible' American 'hand' in the peace moves must bring about a covenant on the Siachen Glacier. This can also be a monumental confidence boosting measure (CBM) to "walk the high road to peace" paraphrasing Vajpayee's message to Musharraf in the summer of 2001 in the run up to the Agra Summit.

Many suggestions have come forth on what shape a final agreement should take. One such has been the establishment of a 'peace park' of the kind which exists in many areas of the world, like between Greece and Turkey on the banks of the Evros river, or the La Amistad Peace Park between Costa Rica and Nicaragua. It may be also pertinent to think of a simple de-militarization of the entire glacier area without any strings attached. The danger of Pakistan occupying the glacier after our withdrawal, as some skeptics suggest, should be of no great concern to us tactically as it would be a harebrained initiative and it is extremely doubtful if they would do so given the present global scenario.

A highly decorated general of the Indian Army who has had vast battle experience in Jammu and Kashmir once said that "India should welcome Pakistan if they want to occupy the Siachen Glacier, nothing would be so debilitating for their armed forces as this." A unilateral and phased withdrawal should be under the active consideration of our government for it would show to the world the genuineness of the meaning of the Vajpayee initiative as befitting of a large nation like India on the chessboard of international politics. India has much to gain and nothing to lose by such an initiative. On the Pakistani side also many voices of sanity are making similar appeals. It has been wisely said,'opportunities multiply when seized, and they die when neglected.' The Siachen tangle is one such opportunity waiting to be seized.

In local Balti language the word Siachen means rose. May an agreement on Siachen have the same significance of offering a bouquet of roses between our two nations.

(Published in Defence Watch June 2003)

□

6

MIG-21 Crashes: What Ails the IAF's Warhorse?

MIG–21 the oldest Aircraft of the Indian Air Force which constitutes 60 per cent of its fleet has been in the news for all the wrong reasons. A recent spate of crashes, the last one at Bagdogra on November 14, has led to a considerable deal of speculation in the media, both print and electronic as well as in parliament regarding the airworthiness of this fighter jet which has rather uncharitably been called a 'flying coffin and a 'widow maker.' According to the Defence Minister Mr George Fernandes fifty-three Mig 21 aircraft have crashed since 1998, killing 30 pilots (apart from civilians like in Jalandhar in May 2002), and causing a loss to the tune of Rs 143.82 crores to the exchequer. He disclosed this in the Rajya Sabha on November 21, 2002. The minister further informed the house that three Russian experts would soon be visiting the 3 divisions of HAL to ensure more stringent quality control measures, he clarified that failure of the R–25 engine had been the chief cause of the crashes. Going back somewhat further, as many as 80 pilots and 185 aircraft have been lost in the last 10 years. In a press interview Mr Fernandes went on to state about the MIG 21, "I am told these are excellent aircraft but very demanding and this seems to be one of the causes for accidents. We will be phasing out the first lot of MIGs this year. We are getting other aircraft into our inventory. We hope the situation will improve."

The Public Accounts Committee of Parliament in its report

on March 21› this year has recommended that this jet be phased out. But this per se, seems a rather simplistic solution which may not be feasible. Firstly the aircraft accounts for 60 per cent of the fighter fleet of the air force the number of these aircraft being 400, and the argument that it is old and somewhat obsolete does not hold good, as even older aircraft like the American B–52 Bomber, which saw action in Afghanistan during 'Operation Enduring Freedom' last year, are still very much in use. The aircraft is however quite unsparing as far as pilot errors are concerned.

The object should not be to sensationalize the issue but to find a solution so that no more precious lives are lost and the taxpayers money is not wasted apart from lowering the morale of one of the finest air forces of the world. The then Defence Minister Mr. Jaswant Singh was voicing this school of thought when he stated in 2001, "The government does not agree with this kind of sensationalizing of a security related issue. These aircraft remain fully airworthy and continue to carry out all the tasks as planned in the first induction."

It has been stated in the Russian daily *Izvestia* that India has of late been buying *substandard and uncertified* spares from former Warsaw Pact countries in Eastern Europe and splinter states of the former Soviet Union. The Russian Aircraft Corporation "MIG" has alleged that the Indians *procured* a number of twin seater MIG 21 jet trainers from Kazakhstan, Moldova and Romania in 1995–97 through a British Company, they allege that the MIGs involved in the unfortunate accidents were *not supplied* by the Russian Aircraft Corporation and that certified quality spares imported from Russia *were being re-exported by* HAL to Algeria and Vietnam. Also the Russians have raised a charge of *cannibalization* with the front of the aircraft picked from one country, wings from another and engine from a third. Such planes according to these sources were delivered to the Air Force from Romania and some were overhauled on the IAF's orders by HAL. These allegations will have to be gone into by the government with the objectivity they deserve. They may be grossly exaggerated, but the air must be cleared.

However, one must keep in mind the historical background of this fine aircraft before arriving at an analysis on the issue in its entirety. The MIG 21 was developed by the Russian Aircraft Corporation in 1955 as two prototypes 'faceplate' and 'fishbed' ultimately the 'fishbed' was selected for mass production. It has been the most successful aircraft of the former Soviet Union in terms of numbers built and exported. Its popularity spread fast among Soviet allied countries and it was pressed into service in various countries from Afghanistan to Yugoslavia. China manufactured an unlicensed version called J–7, which it sold to Pakistan, Bangladesh, Sri Lanka and Albania. It was inducted into the IAF in 1965 and did take part in the Indo–Pak conflict that year, though not with much success as our pilots were still unfamiliar with its working. However it gave an excellent account of its self in the 1971 war with its short take off length and good maneuverability.

India has not yet inked the deal for the acquisition of the Advanced Jet Trainer 'Hawk' from Great Britain, said to be one of the principle causes of the high accident rate. In an interview to *The Indian Express* on November 24, 2002 Mr. George Fernandes threw light on the Advanced Jet Trainer (AJT) issue when he said, "The AJT story started in 1982 and it is indeed unfortunate that we have not yet acquired it. I have taken steps to ensure that we make some headway and that something that has already taken twenty years be concluded soon. There are many who would say that fighter trainers are crashing because we have no AJT (though there may really be no co-relation). These crashes began in 1971 but very little or no attention was paid to AJT. It is now that we are trying to procure it and perhaps because of the emphasis that I have laid on this procurement those others have started talking about it. The delay is not because of any lack of will but because of the insistence on going through a process that ensures that the country has an AJT that is the best available."

It can, therefore, be hoped optimistically that the government is giving top priority to the AJT deal. It is eminently in the national interest that no further delay takes place on this issue.

As a further word on the AJT issue, it is pertinent to point out that the La Fontaine Committee headed by the former Chief of Air Staff had brought out the failure of the Air Force establishment to train pilots adequately. Indian fighter pilots are trained on the subsonic aircraft like 'Kiran' and, therefore, it is a qualitative jump to fly Mach 2 speed aircraft such as the various variants of MIG 21. Former Air Chief Marshal S.K. Kaul had expressed his view, "The government's lack of action on the AJT is nothing short of crass disregard for the force's vital needs." Three years back in 1999, the then Chief of Air Staff A.Y. Tipnis had blamed poor training facilities for the high level of crashes. It is learnt from reliable sources that India may only buy about sixty trainer aircraft whereas UK and France have gone in for about one hundred and fifty such trainers with one squadron in reserve. This is an extremely relevant point to ponder on as we acquire insufficient trainers it may hardly solve one of the main complications facing the IAF today.

The phasing out of the MIG 21bis (original version of the plane) must be taken up speedily, as the problem of metal fatigue given the high landing speed of aircraft is something to be kept in mind. The MIG 21MF or electronic warfare variant according to experts is a modern jet with a sophisticated ancillary system and powerful gearbox. Another problem is absence of a good MIG 21 simulator as the present simulator is of the old generation. Apart from this is the high cost of spares which has reduced the serviceability of MIGs from 60–75 per cent to 40–50 per cent, therefore pilots are unable to fly as much as they should. Ideally a pilot should get 750 hours on various types of lesser aircraft before graduating to the MIGs. With a befitting simulator and AJTs it can be brought down to 350 hours.

The question of the MIG crashes is one of the most momentous issues confronting the Ministry of Defence and the Government of India today.

(Published in Defence Watch December 2002)

□

PERSONALITIES

7

Walking Down Memory Lane with Maj General Ranbir Bakshi, MC

Maj Gen Ranbir Bakshi, MC is a man of many parts and an institution in himself. Ninety two summers have not dimmed his zest for life, and he is making a momentous contribution to the society at large as chairman of Raphael Ryeder cheshire Foundation which caters for the care of physically disabled, mentally retarded, and tuberculosis patients as well as victims of leprosy. He talked to me on a wide variety of subjects in a freewheeling interview:

1. Could you shed light on your early life and how you thought of joining the army?

I had a normal life in childhood. I changed a variety of schools. Interestingly, I had my primary education in a Mission School at Dehradun in 1919 for 6 months. After doing my 12th in the Punjab I was able to get admission into Government College, Lahore. I joined the Swimming Club in Lahore in 1931 as I had learned swimming as a young boy in my village. In 1931 the first Indian Olympic Swimming meet was held in Kolkata, all states from Central Provinces and Berar, Madras, to UP were represented. Others won all the events barring one. I won the backstroke event which created quite a sensation. In the year 1934 international services students meet was held in Germany for which I was selected on the basis of my sports qualifications. We were also to tour Europe. We went to London, and at India House we were received by senior British Civil Service Officers. At the function there an old man came up to us and began talking to us about our background and other things. He spoke some Punjabi as well, I told him I belonged to Rawalpindi. He asked if I was a Mohyal Brahmin, and I was shaken at his intimate knowledge of India and the Punjab. On his asking, I said I was interested in flying and becoming a civil pilot. He said "No, you should join the army." This old man, as I realized later was Field Marshal Birdworth. In 1934 I joined the Territorial Army in Ambala and in 1935 I was commissioned in the 10th pre-independence course of the army. One of my contemporaries was Field Marshal Sam Manekshaw who was serving in the same formation where I was commissioned.

2. In which operation did you receive the Military Cross?

I was the first Indian Artillery Officer to receive the Military Cross during the Burma Campaign and my NCO Makhan Singh was the first to receive the IDSM in Burma. The award was given to me by King George V (father of the present Queen) at Buckingham Palace, London. We had landed at Rangoon on March 3, 1942 and saw action that night itself. Only one battery of Artillery was giving support to 17th Division. I am still in contact with some veterans of the British Indian Army whom I knew in Burma, but most of them are unfortunately dead.

3. What were the salient features of your army career?

I had the honour of commanding my own regiment to which I was commissioned. I was Military Assistant to the Commander-in-Chief Gen Rajendrasinhji in 1954–55, I commanded the School of Artillery, I raised the new centre at Nasik, I served with the DRDO Organization where I designed the 'Prashant' gun and retired as Commandant of the National Defence Academy, Khadakvasla, Pune on August 9, 1966. As Commandant of NDA when I had to send some Cadets home it was a painful experience. However, when I met them later on they did not turn their backs on me and were doing well in other vocations. My career in the army was memorable in many ways.

4. How did you come to be associated with work for the handicapped, the children of a 'lesser God', and how has 'Raphael' progressed over the years?

I joined the 'Raphael' managing council in September 1973, at the request of the late John Martyn ex–principal of Doon School. In 1975, I became director of the institution. In 1980 I became Chairman and handed over the directorship to another ex-army officer. Raphael Ryder Cheshire Foundation has an interesting history. The late Lord Cheshire had requested Pandit Jawaharlal Nehru for land to set up a centre for TB patients, leprosy patients, and the mentally and physically handicapped. The land was given by the government of UP on a thirty year lease, which later in 1989 was extended for a further thirty years, with a proviso for extension for a further 30 years. The involvement of Lord Cheshire and Lady Cheshire was instrumental in raising large sums of money to run this place. Substantial contribution was made by the governments of Australia and New Zealand. The arrangement was that support from Australia was for 9 months of the year, and New Zealand for 3 months of the year. In 1979 we felt that we should have better classrooms and shelter for the mentally handicapped. We approached the Secretary Social Welfare, GOI a dynamic officer called Asa Singh who within three months sanctioned us an amount of Rs 2.5 lakhs for the purpose. Rs 5.5 lakhs was raised from Australia and New Zealand. This building is now known as 'Ava Vihar'. This is the only building built with government assistance in 'Raphael'. Seventeen of the girls who were children of 'Raphael' have been trained as specialized educationists of the handicapped. Children of leprosy victims had problems in getting admission into schools. But CNI (Church of North India) institutions were the first to take them in. Eleven of the boys were recruited into the army, and two went to the police. Other boys are working in various factories. Some of them work as staff and employees in 'Raphael'. There was a demand from the local parents of handicapped children to have some rehabilitation for them, 10 per cent of the population are estimated to suffer from some form of handicap or the other. With the help of a teacher in Doon School, Sheel Sharma and the headmaster we set up a day centre in the Doon School. From the UK we were able to raise Rs 16 lakhs to start a day centre at

'Raphael'. Talking about our efforts in treating TB we had three hundred and thirteen admissions to our hospital in the year ending March 31, as well as treated nine thousand eight hundred and ninety patients and suspected patients. Our Mobile Teams attend to an average of four hundred and seventy-five patients a month. Sixty-six patients of leprosy are in our care as of now. I have been with this institution for thirty years now. This year, I intend to ask the council to appoint an ex-officio chairman who can take over from me at a later stage.

5. Could you share with our readers some memories of the late Lord Cheshire with whom you were associated?

When I first met him, I was greatly impressed by his personality and simplicity, a highly decorated air force officer, so calm and collected. I asked him how he, as a military man got in the field of working for the handicapped and the terminally ill. He said there was a sergeant in the air force who fell terminally ill and the hospitals could not care for him. He said that Leonard Cheshire was the only one who could care for him, so Cheshire did a week's crash course in treating the terminally ill and took this man in his care into his house. That is how the Cheshire Foundation started. The first Cheshire Home was set up at Andheri, Mumbai and the second was in Dehradun donated by the Jind family. The charter of the Cheshire Foundation is to offer a bed to a terminally disabled person who has no one to look after him so that he may end his life peacefully. Sue Ryder, the wife of Lord Cheshire had also started a trust for the terminally ill in England, called the Sue Ryder Trust, but this institution is under another trust. A third trust called the Raphael Ryder Cheshire Foundation which is unique as it is probably the only NGO in the world which takes care of 4 disabilities under one roof.

6. What plans do you have for 'Raphaels' future?

Our future vision encompasses establishing a research and reference centre for the mentally challenged so that we can have accommodation for any parent coming, so that he or she may consult the neurologists, physiotherapists, doctors etc. This centre would provide for the entire Northern India and would be a great asset to the populace affected by these problems.

On July 9, a Vocational Centre for the mentally handicapped will be officially inaugurated by Sardar Surjit Singh Barnala, HE Governor of Andhra Pradesh and former Governor of Uttarakhand.

7. As a person who has completed a very useful 92 years of life, what would you express as a word of advice to the younger generation?

It is a difficult question to answer. Many of the younger generation whom I come across are excellent in various aspects. Youngsters tend to live on loans and get into habits which are not correct. I never took a loan in my life. Youngsters should improve themselves morally and care for the less fortunate in society.

(Published in The Himachal Times, Dehradun, July 2004)

□

8

Our Marshal in Air Force Blue

On January 26, 2002 the government conferred the rank of Marshal of the Air Force on Air Chief Marshal Arjan Singh, a doughty warrior of yore. This was a significant decision making him the first Air Force Officer and the third Indian after Field Marshals K.M. Carriappa and S.H.F.J. Manekshaw, to hold the Five Star Rank. Arjan Singh's name invariably brings to mind memories of the 1965 war, during which our boys in blue pounded the Pakistani Army and Air Force in Sialkot, Lahore and other sectors as well, thereby preventing to a large extent any penetration by the Pakistani Air Force on our vital installations. But the 83-year-old former fighter pilot has much more to talk about. Arjan Singh's remarkable career began in 1939 and apart from playing a pivotal role in building up the Air Force in the post-independence period he participated in many battles as the years rolled on. He was awarded the DFC (Distinguished Flying Cross) in 1944 by Lord Louis Mountbatten who flew specially to Imphal for the ceremony.

The octogenarian tea-totaller is still as athletic and handsome and full of the zest for life as ever. He wears the caps of Marshal of the Indian Air Force,former diplomat (where he even had a cordial relationship with Pope Paul II) and former Lt Governor of Delhi with disarming ease. It was a freewheeling conversation which ensued when I spoke to him at his artistically furnished, book-lined study at New Delhi's Kautaliya Marg. He mentioned he was born in a village in the Lyallpur district which is now in Pakistan. His early schooling after the primary class was in a village school, he was thereafter educated at a high school in a small town.

Subsequent to this he moved to a school in Montgomery District now known as Sahiwal which is also in Pakistan presently. This was a government high school with a very high standard and since he scored a first division in Matriculation he was able to get admission to Government College Lahore where he remained for three years from mid-1935 to mid-1938. Both at school and college he learnt a lot as the standard of teachers and professors was very high. Learning about discipline and being thorough with one's work helped him throughout his life. At college he was interested in sports and received three colours in the College itself in swimming, athletics and kabbadi. He was captain of the swimming teams of the College, University and Province (State) teams and was fond of athletics and free-style swimming. He was able to establish two all- India records in the one and a half-mile and one mile in swimming events.

There was no particular reason as such for joining the Air Force but as a youngster when he saw people in uniform he felt a great desire to put on one himself. He could have opted to join the police or the army but it just so happened that he used to see many airplanes flying over his village and over his school and thus thought that flying would be an interesting profession. When he got an opportunity to opt for the Air Force, he did so. He appeared in the All India Competition for the Army, Navy and Air Force and was selected for the Air Force and went to Cranwell in England to train for a period of two years. However, war started before the projected date of the culmination of his training, which was shortened to 18 months, and was commissioned in December 1939. He stayed in England for sometime, and then came back to India to join its only Squadron, No. 1 Squadron because there was a shortage of pilots. The Squadron was based in Ambala and he joined it, as far as he could remember in January 1940.

Arjan Singh first saw action in 1940. The Squadron was operating off and on in the North West Frontier Province where the British and Indian Forces where engaged in fighting against the Pathans. Now, the Pathans were a turbulent people creating law and order problems. But Arjan Singh thought it a good idea for preparing our troops and removing from their minds the fear of war. His plane, a Hawker Audax was once shot down by the Pathans and he force landed in a dry stream between two hillocks, right in the middle of a running battle between the British Army and the Pathans Arjan Singh's Gunner, Ghulam Ali was wounded and he waited till Gulam Ali could be evacuated safely. He remained in touch with Ghulam Ali who lived in Germany till a few years ago.

Arjan Singh took part in the actual attack which started in May-June 1944 on the Imphal front. The offensive concentrated on capturing the Valley that was surrounded entirely by the Japanese. The Valley was besieged, the only road from Dimapur via Kohima to Imphal was cut off, and no other road existed from Silchar or anywhere else through which communication could flow through. All supplies had to be made by air, and transport aircraft were not enough in numbers. Therefore, American transport aircraft which were flying to China to assist Chiang Kai-Shek over the hump were requested to divert in order to drop supplies like large quantities of fuel and ammunition and so on. Before the siege of Imphal most of the Army and Air Force units had moved out. All squadrons had been pulled out except No1 Squadron and another Squadron of the Royal Air Force. Arjan Singh was the Squadron Commander of No. 1 Squadron. As a squadron leader, his job and that of his squadron was primarily attacking the Japanese Army in support of our Army. So the attack consisted of striking tanks on the road, troops, guns, and also penetrating up to a hundred miles rearwards to the enemy. They also performed the very useful task of taking photographs of the Japanese camps, send aircraft on reconnaissance and come back and report. They cleared the entire area of the Japanese in about 3 months. This was achieved because of the army fighting on all fronts in the valley as well as the attacks of the Air Force were very successful near the Chindwin river, over Tamu and the Kabaw Valley.

Arjan Singh recalls that at one time the Japanese were so close to us that their guns started shelling the Indian airfield, and guns in those days did not have a very long range. These guns were perched on the surrounding hills. Fortunately they did not hit any worthwhile targets or do any damage. While going out on sorties the RAF always flew in twos. Two aircraft used to go out as one pilot could defend the other incase of trouble or in case he had to have a forced landing and also to join the attack. Once while returning from a sortie he observed several enemy troops moving down the hills towards the valley, behind the army's 4 Corps Headquarters. This threatened to be a very serious attack so he immediately reported it to the higher authorities and they were ordered to launch a fully armed offensive with all the 16 aircraft of the squadron. The aircrafts were fully armed with bombs and rockets and this was the most vital action taken in support of our army. It prevented a large strike by the Japanese Army on the ground.

When one attacks troops on the ground, he felt, it is difficult to tell from the air the number of casualties inflicted. Sometimes they used to go back to find out how much damage was done and sometimes not. Later he came to know that they inflicted a large number of casualties in this particular attack. One of the battalions coming in belonged to the INA of Netaji Subhas Chandra Bose. Arjan knew the Commanding Officer of this battalion in Singapore. The Japanese were very good fighters at the beginning of the battle, but subsequently the fight went out of them as they were woefully short of supplies, ammunition and medical cover. Also the local populace was hostile to them and the humid climate took its toll. But he felt he gained real battle experience fighting in Imphal. He flew every day for one year without a single day's holiday and has every single day's action recorded in his log book which is a huge book. The war in the air conducted by 221 Air Group of which No.1 Squadron was a part equalled the amount of devastation caused by the advance of the 14th Army and the battle for Imphal eventually proved to be a killing ground for the Japanese Army. Destruction of communications and logistics had a fatal effect. The army advanced on the wings of the Air Force.

(Note: The Imphal Plain lies 3000 feet up in the heart of the Manipur Mountains.)

He was awarded the DFC in May 1944; it was given to him at a special ceremony by Lord Louis Mountbatten who was at that time the Supreme Commander of the South East Asia Command based at Kandy in Ceylon (now Sri Lanka). He came specially for this purpose and pinned the honour on Arjan's chest. The ceremony was held in the squadron dispersal area in the middle of the jungles. Within the year, eight more people were awarded the DFC from No.1 Squadron. That was the largest number of DFCs any squadron got on the Burma Front.

According to an article in the *"Hindu"* dated February 12, 2002, Arjan was almost court martialled. He recalls the incident. Arjan was at that time located in Cannaore to take part in some exercises with the army, to give them training of preparation for an air attack, he was a young man, only a Pilot Officer, which is the first rank in the Air Force, and was operating from the parade ground and flying a Wapiti, which could land in a small space. They used to land on the parade ground and there was a fort nearby. He went back to the same place about 10 years ago and found it was still the same. His Corporal aircraftsman was a man called Bhaskran who ultimately retired as an Air Commodore. He belonged to a nearby town called Tellicherry and was very interested to fly over the town, Arjan told him with a chuckle, "come along I'll take you up and show you the town from very close quarters." It was a small town and they made quite a few rounds over the town and his house, flying at low levels, he recalls. The Sub Divisional Magistrate was a Britisher who reported the matter to Air Headquarters and they asked him for an explanation. The Squadron Commander was Squadron Leader (later Air Marshal) Mukherjee and he told him what to write to get out of it. He did so and nothing more was heard, says the Marshal of the Air Force. But at that time the punishment as mentioned was quite severe and one could be court martialled! In his opinion, every pilot with any courage has done low flying. Low flying is very enjoyable, it is very dangerous undoubtedly but is a great thrill and young people want thrills. He had often done low flying, but this was the only time he was caught!

Reflecting on the Sino-Indian conflict of 1962, Arjan Singh is also of the view that the Air Force should have been used. Probably the government did not want to enlarge the conflict. After all the decision to use the Air Force in any country lies with the government and normally by the head of government. The Air Force at that time was well prepared, he recalls and was in a good position and should have been used. The Chinese did not have much air support at all, and would not have been able to bring in jet aircraft at such a long range. We were, therefore, in a better position, but that is what happened, he says with tangible regret in his voice. Arjan Singh headed the IAF in 1965. I quizzed him about the operations. He said,"Actually the real first war in which the Air Force participated after independence was in the 1965 conflict. Pakistan sent infiltrators throughout August into the Kashmir Valley. This was known as Operation Gibraltar. They did not achieve much success there. It was only then that they decided to use their regular army in a big way, on the Line of Control (LOC).

Operation Grand Slam was unleashed in which they first struck at Chhamb Juarian on the LOC. Had their plan been successful it would have done us a lot of harm. They wanted to capture Akhnoor Bridge or destroy it; as that is the only link to the northern side cutting off Poonch, Rajouri and all the places north of Akhnoor and ultimately they may also have cut off the Jammu-Srinagar highway. On the whole for the Air Force it was a successful operation because we had only a few aircrafts, which were rather old. The attack took place just before dusk and it was very successful otherwise they would have taken Akhnoor according to the Army's estimate. We attacked them for two days running. Even though the Pakistan Air Force was well equipped with F-86 Sabre Jets,which had a very good reputation, our aircraft were Gnats, Hunters, Mysteres and Canberras which carried out attacks all over Pakistan. These planes attacked Rawalpindi, Peshwar, Sargodha and Kohat. The Canberras flew about 200 counter air and interdiction missions and did exceedingly well. On 7 September we launched a major attack on Sargodha, which was the largest and most important air base, well into the interior of Pakistani territory. During this raid by Mysteres and Hunters, we destroyed three F-86 Sabres and one F-104 Star Fighter. On 19 September a Hunter Squadron achieved a remarkable success in the Sialkot Sector by destroying a large column of Pakistani Tanks. We reached targets that were about 50 miles inside Pakistani territory and hit 72 of their trains which where transporting troops, supplies, ammunition, and other military items. This was very crucial. Pakistan could not hit any of our trains. It is always more of a success story to hit the installations or troops behind the fighting front because they are more complacent and do not have many defences. We did make a mistake in Chhamb-Juarian where we hit some of our own troops, these mistakes do occur in the heat of battle. We did destroy 70 Patton Tanks also and gave valuable support to the army on all fronts." I asked him about the mishaps at Pathankot and Kalaikunda where we lost 18 aircraft on the ground, he was very sad about these two big mishaps, he said. It must be realized that we had hundreds of aircraft and 18 are a very small number. When he enquired into the matter he found it was a failure of command, not of the staff on the ground. The PAF, however tried to attack our aircrafts on the ground at Ambala, Halwara and Adampur unsuccessfully. In Ambala they ended up bombing the church when they attacked at night. In Halwara we drowned quite a few Sabares. Such things will happen in war, as human beings are fallible.

The next query pertained to the lack of institutionalized joint Defence planning by which it is felt that our performance could have been better in 1965, as was borne out in 1971, when even though not institutionalized it was better coordinated. His views on this are quite explicit. "I have no doubt," he says "that the operations would have been much more successful had there been better coordination between the Army and Air Force. For example, I was not told by the Army the time of their attack on the Wagah front, which consequently was a major failure. The whole attack should have been planned and jointly carried out by the Army and the Air Force. It would have achieved better results."

Arjan Singh was not happy that we accepted the UN sponsored cease-fire in 1965 at the point of time that we did. First Pakistan accepted it and then we did it. The Air Force was just getting into its stride, our morale was very high and there was great confidence in the service. The whole tempo had risen and we could have achieved more success. I suppose the government has to take various things into consideration taking a long term view. Arjan Singh remembers of those momentous days, when the then Defence Minister Yashwantrao Chavan mentioned in his war diary that he walked like a peacock and was a real fighting Sikh! "Chavan's diary is a very authentic document because he was writing it every day in his own hand", said the Marshal of the Air Force.

Regarding structural changes during his long tenure of 5 years, he says he was more concerned in seeing to it that our units were fully operational,that the expensive equipment and aircraft were put to proper use. His whole emphasis was not to change too many things, but to improve the operational functioning of the Air Force and the operational ability of the pilots, which he tried to do in every way possible even by setting a personal example like taking part in firing and flying whenever possible which he felt would encourage junior officers. Holding forth on his experience as a diplomat in Switzerland and Kenya as well as Lt. Governor of Delhi, he says that as a diplomat, of course it is quite a different life from the services. The main thing is to ensure a positive image of the country abroad. Trade and economic affairs were and are very important. He liked Switzerland as he had first visited that country in 1938 and used to go skiing there. During his time in Kenya, Indians were welcome not like Idi Amin who was then driving the Indians out of Uganda. He knows Delhi well and has been living here for a long time, he says. Therefore, as Lt Governor of Delhi he felt that one should pay attention to the administration and get results. You must exercise your authority when required, you must trust people to do things, and you must delegate authority properly so that every part of the machine functions well. People must work properly and not pass the buck or be indecisive. Quite a few people hesitate to take responsibility in administration. He was Lt Governor for only about a year.

I then asked him on his vision of the IAF of the future, particularly in the post-Pokharan scenario with creation of Integrated Strategic Command which many believe is the first step towards the creation of the office of Chief of Defence Staff, to which he said that, "This is a good point and very relevant. Of late airpower has assumed much greater importance in warfare. It may not have been recognized as such but the Air Force played an important role in the second World War. The landing on Normandy could not have taken place without the intensive air action before hand. It was a joint operation. In the Gulf War also air attacks were carried out for three-four weeks before the ground troops went in and this cut down the number of land casualties. All vital targets were destroyed by air attacks which facilitated the land battle. Even of late in Afghanistan, America has used minimal troops against the Taliban and largely depended on air attacks. America is very hesitant to use much of its troops in war after the experience in Vietnam. About the future

I would say that I am clear that within the resources available, equipment must be kept up-to-date, if possible by indigenous production. Aircraft and missiles are expensive no doubt but this expense has to be borne for the security of the country. The post of Chief of Defence Staff can produce good results if properly initiated. However, we have to be careful about certain things. For example, the air defence of the country is primarily the duty of the Air Force to some extent assisted by the army. We can't mix these things. Again defence of Mumbai, Cochin and so on is a naval consideration. All this has to be recognized in the Joint Command, that certain areas will have to remain exclusively with a certain service. This will be taken care of, I'm sure, but the whole world is now following the concept of joint command, so we should not be left behind. However, one should not rush into it, and learn from the mistakes of certain other countries. The difference between our country and other countries, particularly America is that while we fight our battles on our own borders, they fight in other countries and places like Vietnam, Kosovo, the Gulf and Afghanistan for example.

Then the European countries have commitments in Africa. But our country is confined to defending our borders and shores. We have to keep in mind this crucial difference while making joint defence plans. Also we must use our resources to get the best results, which can only be done by a combined integrated effort. Take helicopters, for example, which the army also requires, one can economize on it in a combined effort. I 'm quite clear that good joint operational planning and combined training in peacetime will produce better results in any future conflicts at the minimum cost to the country with respect to all three services."

(An Interview with Marshal of the Air Force Arjan Singh, DFC published in Defence Watch April 2002)

□

9

Jayaprakash Narayan Centenary: 1902–2002

"Never again will anyone be able to claim that democracy is unsuited to any developing country or that the poor and the hungry do not value their rights."-The London *Economist* after the 1977 General Elections

Jayaprakash Narayan, widely known as "JP," will be remembered for a great many things, but the crowning glory of his selfless career will undoubtedly be the historic victory of the Janata Party in the spring of 1977. JP can undoubtedly be hailed as the architect of that victory which was an upheaval, the like of which this country has not seen again,as it was after 19 dark months of naked dictatorship under the emergency regime.

"Not since the time of Gandhiji has moral force, personified by a frail invalid triumphed so spectacularly over the forces of evil", said eminent jurist Nani Palkhivala, of Jayaprakash, immediately after the victory. "One life transformed the destiny of 620 millions. He changed decisively the course of history..." he went on to say in an emotionally choked voice at a public meeting.

Going through the panorama of achievements and ideals set out by JP during his life of 77 years one cannot escape being struck by the utter selflessness of this icon of our times. He was offered the Deputy Prime Ministership and even Presidency of India virtually on a platter. But he turned it down without a second thought, to work among the people as he thought best, be it through *Bhoodan* or 'total revolution'. His critics felt that he ran away from responsibility. But the purity of his intentions was never questioned.

His daring escape from Hazaribagh jail on the night of Diwali in 1942, along with six comrades was an example of his revolutionary spirit. When re-arrested in 1944, he was tortured badly in Lahore gaol where he has made to sit on ice slabs for hours together without any clothes and kept in a foul dungeon for months. He was interrogated night and day.

Among other things he will be remembered for is his dedication to the socialist ideology along with Lohia and Acharya Narendra Dev, as well as his efforts in the *Bhoodan* movement of Bhave. The memorable surrender of dacoits which he brought about in 1972 is another achievement. In April 1962 he had urged Nehru to 'retire and take up the leadership of the people like Gandhiji but by then he and Nehru had drifted apart, a far cry from 1948 when Nehru hailed JP as "the future Prime Minister of India."

1974, was the year when JP truly became the "Loknayak" or leader of the people. From Patna he launched the nation-wide agitation which brought about the great upheaval of March 1977. "Sampoorna Kranti ab nara hai bhavi itihaas hamaara hai" (total revoloution is our slogan; future history belongs to us) this was the slogan that reverberated throughout the countryside. So much so that even the Akali Dal raised the slogan "Patna sahib to aayi awaz Hind da neta Jayaprakash" (the call has come from Patna Sahib; Jayaprakash is the leader of the nation)

During the Emergency Jayaprakash's health was impaired and he would remain on dialysis for the rest of his life. "My world lies in shambles around me," JP wrote in the opening lines of his 'Prison Diary' in July 1975. The metamorphosis of 1977 was to change all that. His last two years saw him in frail health and disillusionment as the Janata government collapsed in mid-1979.

When JP received his graduation degree in 1928, from Columbus University in the United States, he had already been in that country for 6 years. To supplement his education and expenses, he worked on a grape ranch near Yuba city, a canning plant and a Chicago stockyard as well as a salesman for hair straightner and complexion cream in a Negro quarter in Chicago. He returned to India at the end of 1929 after taking a Master's from Ohio University, something rare for an Indian or an Asian. As General Secretary of the Congress he played an active role in civil disobedience in the fist half of the 1930s. He formed the Congress Socialist Party in 1934 and moved into the Communist movement later on.

American author Vincent Sheehan once noted that "JP had nobility in appearance, voice and manner." The public of our nation also had a similar opinion of him. The struggle for 'Total Revolution' was the largest mass movement after the freedom struggle. On Total Revolution he said, "A total revolution in India should mean a revolution from the village upwards to the largest urban concentration. There must be a total change in civic life, civic relationshi ps,civic institutions,and as we go beyond the sphere of civic life to enter the larger spheres of national life. According to my concept of total revolution the individual man would also undergo a revolutionary change. So it is the totality that undergoes a change including the individual."

(Published In Himachal Times, Dehradun, October 2002)

□

10

A Requiem to Madhu Dandavate

On an early winter evening of November 12, 2005, one of the stalwarts of the socialist movement of India left for his journey into the great unknown. Professor Madhu Dandavate was a man of many parts. Not for him was the politics of crass opportunism, not for him was the politics of enriching one's personal assets that one finds so prevalent in the present-day world, not for him was the politics of power which he believed was a means to an end instead of an end in itself. Throughout his long innings in the arena of public life nobody could ever caste aspersions on his spotless character.

His stints on the treasury benches were short-lived. But not too short to be remembered with great reverence long after they were over. His tenure as Railway Minister will long be looked back upon as the golden era in Rail Bhavan, so also his short stint of 10 months as Minister of Finance, in the National Front government of 1989–90, when the gentlemen of the opposition found themselves in power after the Rajiv Gandhi government lost the hustings.

Dandavate was born at Ahmednagar in 1924, and secured a Masters in Physics from the Royal Institute of Science in Mumbai. Later he taught Nuclear Physics at the Siddharth College of Arts and Sciences,Mumbai,becoming its Vice Principal. Having participated in the "Quit India" struggle, from 1948 onwards, he was a member of the Praja Socialist Party, then plunged into the Goa Liberation Struggle in 1955. Newspaper headlines of those days were full of the ebullient Dandavate and his 80 followers who entered Goa at sunset through Netarda and marched into Portuguese territory unchallenged to a delirious reception.

After being at the forefront of the Samyukta Maharashtra struggle, he was elected to the Maharashtra Legislative Council and in 1971 to parliament from the Raipur seat in Maharashtra which had also been represented by that legendary parliamentarian barrister Nath Pai. Thus began an illustrious parliamentary career which spanned about two decades. After being in jail in Bangalore during the period of emergency, Professor Dandavate was selected to be Minister of Railways in the Cabinet of the late Morarji Desai when the Janata Party assumed power at the Centre. He will long be remembered for making second class railway travel more comfortable and for laying the foundation for the Konkan rail line. His ministerial style was earthy and he was easily accessible. His integrity was beyond question and was one of the first ministers to talk of introducing computerization in the railways to check corruption.

When he demitted office in 1979, he sent a list of his assets and liabilities to the President, Prime Minister, leader of the opposition, Jayaprakash Narayan and Acharya Kripalani. A leading national daily *The Statesman* wrote an appreciative editorial about his action entitled “Nothing to Hide”. As Minister of Finance he gave emphasis to his socialist principles by bringing more of the richer sections into the tax net while reducing the burden on the poorer classes as well as giving impetus to agriculture and rural development. The last public office he held was Deputy Chairman of the Planning Commission during the United Front regime from 1996 to 1998. His late wife Pramilla Dandavate was also a member of parliament from Mumbai.

Dandavate could be seen at bookshops and other public places moving around like a common elderly gentleman, so unlike a politician. One could drop in at his residence and he would answer the door bell himself, entertaining you to a cup of hot tea and stimulating intellectual conversation. I doubt if any kind of arrogance ever entered his head, he was humility personified.

His last act was also one of service. He donated his body for medical research.

(Published in The Himachal Times Dehradun, November 22, 2005)

□

11

Morarji Desai: The Pilgrim of Eternity

The last day of February is usually the day when the Government of India makes its annual financial statement in the shape of the Union Budget. It is also the birthday of one of modern India's most illustrious sons, Morarji Ranchodji Desai, who was the fourth Prime Minister of independent India and the first non-Congress Prime Minister who attained this high office from March 1977 to

The Author shares a lighter moment with former Prime Minister Morarji Desai, Bombay, 1987

July 1979.

An able administrator, a person of the highest integrity, truthful in word and deed,a staunch prohibitionist,and a man of high principles are some of the 'clichés' often used for him. But above all, he was a fine human being both human and humane. He combined within himself a rare mixture of stoical discipline and feeling for the humble toiling masses of Indian people. He maintained this throughout his long career in the service of the nation.

In him, one found the rare combination of true spiritualism in public life, the combination of *karma* and *dharma.* In a political career spanning more than five decades, he played many parts with great distinction and ran through a whole spectrum of high public office including the highest political office, that of the chief executive of the country. He was undoubtedly a man of destiny, in whose life destiny had played a major role.

A graduate of Wilson College Bombay, Morarji picked up his basic knowledge as administrator as an officer of the Provincial Civil Service of the Government of Bombay Presidency during the years 1918 to 1930. This stood him in good stead in the years ahead as he will be remembered as one of the finest political administrators this country has produced. He joined the Congress in 1930, and was designated revenue minister in the Bombay Cabinet under the leadership of the late Balasaheb Kher in 1937. He played an admirable role in overcoming the opposition from the British bureaucracy and restored the land to the Bardoli peasants who had lost it to the government during the *satyagraha.*

As chief minister of Bombay from 1952 to 1956, his government was successful in giving a good deal to the masses of the province which consisted of the present states of Maharashtra and Gujarat. He believed in prohibition and implemented it with rare single mindedness. His concern was genuinely for the poor masses that ruined their lives on liquor. He took tough and stern administrative action against the agitation for Samyukta Maharashtra and Maha Gujarat, for it was an article of faith for him that the government must act with impartiality in certain situations and have the capacity to take unpopular decisions in the long term interest of the country. Morarji was of the firm view that a leader must mould public opinion and not pander to it. He felt it was his duty to improve the moral outlook of the nation so that our society could rise to lofty heights. He was in that sense a singular man in the field of public life.

In the early 1960s he was seen as Nehru's logical heir, as after the death of Pandit Pant in 1961, he was ranked second only to Nehru in the cabinet hierarchy holding the Ministry of Finance since 1958. In 1963, under the Kamaraj Plan he had to quit office in order to work for the party with several other ministers. Had this not happened, he in all probability would have come to occupy the prime ministerial chair on the death of Nehru in May 1964. As it turned out,the prime ministership came to him a full thirteen years later in circumstances of great national euphoria. When he became finance minister he had already been treasurer of the Congress Party for some years, but he laid down the office on assuming the finance ministership as he believed that "the treasurer of the nation should not be the treasurer of a political party." Such were the sublime ideals Morarji subscribed to. As deputy prime minister to Mrs. Gandhi, he was again given charge of the finance department which he held with distinction even though his preference was for the Ministry of Home Affairs, which he thought would make him more effective in the cabinet. His resignation on the issue of nationalization of banks was principled as he was of the opinion that it was harmful in the long run. Such populist gimmicks have indeed done colossal harm to our country. The JP Movement and the Emergency was to follow. For nineteen months Morarji was in detention without trial, like countless others but a great irony was attached to it, as he was interned by the very government of which he was once the deputy prime minister.

Quite often he was called an obstinate person, but this was not true, as being a person of strong convictions cannot be called obstinate. He had in him characteristics of a true democrat in every sense of the term. The late Madhu Limaye, who was for many years a leading socialist parliamentarian, once commented that it was Morarji who would often come to his rescue in Parliament when Congressmen barracked him, 'meet logic and argument with logic and argument, not with shouting,' he chided them. This was when he was a leading light of the Congress. It was an example of his sense of fairplay. Morarji opposed the creation of linguistic states, the use of the army for liberation of Goa and the merger of

Sikkim with the Indian Union. He never hesitated in calling a spade a spade.

In March 1977, after a historic election, the Janata Party stormed to power and the dictatorial emergency regime was ousted, Morarji at the age of 81 was elected Prime Minister, but his mind and body had been trained with remarkable equipoise and he did justice to the high office he occupied. Whether in office or out of it he showed remarkable equanimity.

Neither did success inflate his ego nor did failure drown him in sorrow. Those who were with him during the fateful air crash at Jorhat in November 1977, record that he showed a rare control over his emotions. As Pime Mnister his government will be remembered for taking economically sound decisions which elevated the lot of the common man. Essential commodities were freely available and prices fell. Government during that period was truly austere. It was known that the head of the government viewed wasteful expenditure with displeasure. On the international field he made rapid strides in improving relations with both America and the Soviets. However his real achievement was in mending fences with India's neighbours. Had he continued a full term he could probably have solved the Kashmir imbroglio in our favour. President Ziaul-Haq was planning to visit India and an accord could have been reached. It is a known fact that Zia could not enjoy the same rapport with Morarji's successors. Morarji was the only public figure to have been awarded both the Nishan-e-Pakistan and the Bharat Ratna.

In retirement many noble aspects of his character came to light, he gave the impression of a satisfied man whose life's work was done. He was accessible to the high and mighty as well as the humble masses. On his last birthday, February 28, 1995, he addressed all those who had gathered at his residence, with feeling and expressed his gratitude. It was as if he was taking leave of the nation. He was a great personality who left his indelible mark on the sands of time.

(Published in Bhavan's Journal April 2004)

□

12

Nani had a Magnetic Personality

When one thinks of Nani Palkhivala, one thinks beauty and dignity. He was undoubtedly a colossus of his time who strode tall and erect on the wide canvas of India's public life. Many of his achievements as a lawyer have been widely chronicled, most prominent among them being the famous Keshvananda Bharati case. But I feel his tallest act was to return Mrs. Gandh's brief in June 1975 in protest against the Emergency when she was at the height of her power and naked dictatorship stalked the land. It required rare courage which is difficult to describe. Only those who have lived through that period can really understand the meaning of this act. The country's topmost lawyer had told the all powerful Prime Minister that she was unfit to be his client. Future generations owe him a debt which can never be repaid.

Nani was a human being who can be described only in superlative terms. He was an "*ajatshatru*" and did not have a single enemy in the world. This is something very rare in life. As an orator he had hardly any equals. From humble beginnings he rose to dizzy heights in the legal fraternity. He never hesitated to express his honest opinion without caring for the consequences. He could be biting in his comments, like for example, his saying "that nothing except the river Ganges moves in the state of Bihar" but he always succeeded in driving his point home to his audience. He could equate himself with equal ease to the commoner on the street as well as highbrow society. He led a hectic and active life and used every minute positively. He believed in the dictum "*time is precious, work and save; Idleness is robbery*". The Annamalai University was apt in saying while conferring the degree of Doctor of Laws on him in December 1986: "In Dr Palkhivala`s life we see a man whose overreaching life purpose is to provide a dynamic motivation for the people to be open-minded and open-hearted and pursue a line of valid direction."

His humility, as is well known, was legendary. During his last years when he was not in good health, the Chief Justice of the Bombay High Court expressed a desire to call on him to pay his respects. Palkhivala went to the High Court in a wheel chair to call on the Chief Justice instead. He felt that as an advocate it was his duty to go and see the Chief Justice rather than the latter coming to his residence, notwithstanding the physical difficulty involved.

He could reel out facts and figures from memory and continue to speak extempore for hours together. He once said that he learnt the value of memory from a story about the great lawyer Bhulabhai Desai who was taking notes in the library when a senior walked in and tore up his notes telling Bhulabhai, "Lawyers make notes in their memory, not on paper." Palkhivala followed the adage in letter and spirit.

I think it was in 1980, or thereabouts that the late Mrs Indira Gandhi sent him a feeler as to whether he would serve as Law Minister in her cabinet. Palkhivala politely declined the offer as he felt that since he had ideologically consistently opposed Congress policies, it would not be correct to do a volte-face and join the Congress government. He was not after the loaves and fishes of high office.

However, it must be said that had he joined a party he was ideologically close to, or even contested as an independent for parliament he would have made an impact on the political map of the country. There are times in history when a single man can change the course of events and improve the quality of public life. His being in politics would have undoubtedly motivated people of better calibre to come forward into the political arena for the benefit of the country. When he returned from the USA, he should have taken this step. This is one opportunity I felt he missed.

I would now like to turn to some personal reminiscences of this great individual whom I had the honour to know fairly well.

I first met him on May 29, 1980 when, after lecturing at the Defence Services Staff College, he had come to dinner at our residence. He spoke with great feeling for the armed forces and mingled with the guests of the evening with great ease and informality. When the evening drew to a close one felt intellectually on a higher plane. The memory of that evening is alive even today.

I was to meet him on numerous occasions and heard him speak at various venues in the years that followed. Whenever I was in Bombay and he knew of it, he would insist that I have a meal at his residence. He and his wife Nargesh were perfect hosts and made sure one was comfortable and had more than one's share of their delicious cuisine. The conversation was always interesting, lively and stimulating. I remember once in the mid-1990s, I broached the subject during a dinner with him about India changing over to the Presidential form of government to avoid the uncertainty of coalition politics under the Westminster system. I still remember his immediate response, "For God`s sake, we should never do that, with the level of casteism prevalent in present-day politics, you may get a President elected on the basis of caste which would be disastrous for the country." It was a very relevant point which had not occurred to me.

In March 1996, Palkhivala visited my hometown Dehradun as he had been invited for a few public functions. He took time off from his hectic schedule to visit my residence, to the great joy of our entire family. Ours was the only private residence he visited during his brief stay at Dehradun.

After his wife Nargesh died on June 4, 2000, I specially went to Mumbai to see Nani the following month. It was painful to see him so weak and in bed, but he was able to talk even though it was in a very soft voice. I saw him again at his office at Bombay House before I left. He seemed to have lost interest in life.

I last met Nani Palkhivala in December 2000 when I visited Mumbai. He could not speak even though he nodded his head vigorously when his nurse asked him if he recognized me, indicating that he did. It was painful to see him in that condition and after speaking to him, I left with the premonition that I would never see him again.

Nani Palkhivala left this mortal world on December 11, 2002.

It can be rightly said that passion for justice and fair play, tolerance and consideration for others were the most prominent features of his life. I think the greatest tribute to him would be to live by the ideals he preached. "He did not fail us, let us not fail him", said Dr S. Radhakrishanan of Jawaharlal Nehru, after his death. The same words apply to Palkhivala in equal measure.

(Pubished in Bhavan's Journal March 2005)

□

13

Narain Dutt Tiwari Mulls over the Past and Future

In the scenic and tranquil surroundings of the Forest Research Institute where his new dwelling is located I was able to catch veteran Congressman and former Uttarakhand Chief Minister Narain Dutt Tiwari in an expressive mood on a late winter morning.

I began by asking him about the freedom movement and his role in the weaponless war for independence.

"Well, I started off as a teenage boy activist in the Congress Seva Dal in 1939–40," he says, referring to the starting point of his career,then in 1942 following the failure of the Cripps Mission the Quit India movement was launched. On Gandhiji's call 'satyagraha dictators' were appointed in each district and each bloc of the states. In Tiwari's village Padampuri in Kumaon, a person called Keshav Dutt Maurya was appointed dictator. Tiwari wrote a letter to the British Deputy Commissioner of Nainital asking him and his government to quit India! Suddenly one night while reading in his house by the light of a kerosene oil lamp, a six foot tall strapping Sikh Inspector called Natha Singh and a British Superintendent called Galon arrested Tiwari and his father (who was also in the movement, though an agriculturist by profession) and made them walk handcuffed fourteen miles in the dead of night to Bhowali. Later he was sentenced to two months imprisonment and twenty lashes. The lashes were later condoned at the protest of the Nainital bar association.

After another eleven months in Bareilly Central Jail, Tiwari, was released in March 1944. It was during this stint that he contracted typhoid and lost the hearing in his left ear. He was also put in solitary confinement for singing patriotic songs. There was even a "bandariyawala" or monkey man who unleashed a monkey on prisoners who misbehaved!

Events were moving fast and the advent of the Labour Party in Britain in 1945, heralded independence for India in 1947. Tiwari continued his education through assistance from the Political Sufferers Relief Committee founded by Feroze Gandhi and some acadamic support from Dr Amar Nath Jha of Allahabad University. He also earned some money from working as a professional pandit or priest. Tiwari was President of the Allahabad University Students Union which in fact was banned by the Governor Sir Maurice Halett, which according to Tiwari led the students to hum a ditty, "Halett ka janaaza jara dhoom se nikalae, Allahabad ke sadkon par jara ghoom ke nikalae" (let Halett's funeral procession proceed on the streets of Allahabad with pomp and glamour)!

He began his career in the UP legislature as a member of the Praja Socialist Party of Dr. Ram Manohar Lohia. During his four tenures as UP Chief Minister, Tiwari says he concentrated on development and has a record of presenting 9 budgets. He points out that he began his ministerial career in the Department of Finance & Planning in the cabinet of the late C.B. Gupta. During the Janata Party rule of 1977–79, he remained steadfast and loyal to the late Mrs Indira Gandhi and was looking after the fateful by-election of Chikmagalur which the late Prime Minister won by a staggering margin of 77,000 votes. Tiwari has held the portfolios of Planning, Industry, Finance and External Affairs at the Centre.

I quizzed him about the relevance of Gandhian philosophy today, to which he quoted the slogan at the Dandi March re-enactment in 2005 that "Gandhi is not only a part of India's history, but India's present and future as well." He recalls his interaction with the Mahatma as President of Allahabad University Students Union when the Mahatma emphasized the use of *khadi* by all young people. He recalls meeting Gandhi later in Valmiki Colony and Birla House, at Delhi. He feels that Gandhian principles should be put into practice in the future as that is the chosen destiny for our country.

Tiwari cites Jawaharlal Nehru as the leader who made the utmost impact on him as he was a captivating personality, along with being an intellectual, articulate in both English and Hindustani. He recalls the book *Glimpses of World History* which was written in Dehradun jail. About the future, he mentions the need to have a healthy mix of our ancient ethos and modern technology including IT. He refers to the IT Park at Sahastradhara which will be the pride of Uttarakhand. India can compete with the Chinese model favourably. Regarding his five years in Uttarakhand he is satisfied that he has laid the foundation for the administrative and industrial infrastructure for the new state which will become apparent in days to come.

As I take leave of one of our senior most stalwarts of our national life, one cannot but get a feeling which is both fulfilling and rewarding.

(Published in The Himachal Times, Dehradun, March 28, 2007)

□

14

Remembering a Politician of Substance

I often felt that Ramakrishna Hegde was in the wrong profession. He seemed too sophisticated to be a politician, and was perhaps more cut out to be a writer. Whenever one had an occasion to meet him one could not help coming back with an indelible impression etched in one's mind that there was a tinge of the philosophical about him. In the early and mid 1980s Hegde was the knight in shining armour for the non-Congress opposition. It seemed only a matter of time before he donned the Prime Ministerial mantle for more than anything else "RK", as he was known to his large circle of friends and admirers was a man with his heart in the right place. But alas! It was not to be.

The man from Sirsi in Uttara Kannada had an education which was varied; being a product of the Banares and Allahabad Universities and soon made his mark in politics when he was included in the government of Mysore State in 1957. He was to make many moves and counter-moves on the chessboard of politics in the years that followed. He stood steadfast (with Veerandra Patil) in support of the Congress Organization of the old guard led by Nijlingappa and Morarji Desai. It was not a popular thing to do, but undoubtedly he and his colleagues did it out of deep conviction. He was then Finance Minister in the Veerandra Patil government. During the Emergency, he like many other opposition leaders from the great and the eminent to the humble and the nameless, chose to court arrest under the dreaded MISA. At Bangalore Central jail, he was in the august company of messrs A.B. Vajpayee, L.K. Advani, Madhu

Dandavate and H.D. Deve Gowda among others.

Though the Janata Party was victorious in the historic 1977 elections, Hegde was defeated in the contest to the Lok Sabha as Karnataka remained loyal to the Congress. He was the Janata Party General Secretary in Delhi throughout the period of the Morarji Desai regime. In the 1983 elections, history was made in Karnataka State, with the first opposition Janata Party government taking office with Hegde as the helmsman. The first 24 months of this government were crucial, and brought out the best in Hegde. At that time there was no anti-defection law, and he had a Herculean task maintaining his wafer thin majority. In the 1985 mid-term poll he came back with a thumping majority defying many political pundits. From now on it seemed as though his political graph could only go up. His government did make pioneering efforts in Panchayati Raj and socio-economic fields and he showed the grip of an able administrator, but somewhere along the line, Hegde failed to maintain the brightness of his earlier incarnation. He fell prey to certain weaknesses which flesh is heir to, and his final months as Chief Minister were rather dismal.

Although he held various posts such as Deputy Chairman of the Planning Commission and Minister for Commerce at the Centre, the old fire was missing. In his passing, India has lost a stalwart of a bygone era when convictions and principles were interlinked deeply with public life. Above all, Hegde was no hypocrite; he openly lived a life on his own terms and was not apologetic about it. When you visited his house he was always courteous and saw you off to the door when you left. Such grace is rare among public men.

(Written on the Death of Ramakrishna Hegde in 2004)

□

15

Field Marshal S.H.F.J. Manekshaw, MC

Introduction and Early Life

In the military history of the subcontinent of the post-independence period, India's first Field Marshal Sam Manekshaw occupies a pivotal position. On the stage of military matters he strode tall and erect undeterred by any force which may have challenged the professionalism of this soldier's soldier. The object of the article is to give a fair pen picture of the legendary soldier with necessary objectivity.

Sam Manekshaw's crowning glory was undoubtedly 1971. A victorious nation was at its pinnacle of ecstasy. At one stroke, the humiliation of 1962, and the self-doubts of 1965 were removed by the lightning campaign both in Bangladesh and the Western Front. If Indira Gandhi could be hailed as 'Durga' in the hour of glory, her Army Chief could undoubtedly be hailed in Napoleonic terms. What kind of a person, therefore, is Manekshaw who was born on April 13, 1914? He was born at Amritsar, the holy town of the Sikh community where his father was a doctor. He studied at Sherwood College Nainital with his two brothers. The Sherwood magazine of those days mentions him in a poetic vein:

Now Manekshaw we are to add,
Who no doubt is a jolly lad,
He's keen on Mathematics too,
Our Trig Sums for us he does do.

Sam joined the very first batch of cadets to be commissioned from the Indian Military Academy (IMA) at Dehradun in December 1934 aptly called the 'Pioneers'. In a letter to a friend published in the June 1933 issue of the *IMA Journal*, Manekshaw describes the Adjutant of the IMA as "a big man with funny trousers from a barbarous English sect called the Scots who are regarded as untouchables in England." A word of advice follows, "make a friend of the mess sergeant, he is worth cultivating." Manekshaw was pretty irrepressible even at the age of 19. Of the first batch, it is significant to note Smith Dun, Mohmmad Musa, and Sam Manekshaw rose to be Chiefs of Burma, Pakistan and India respectively. He was given an appointment of Corporal, but was de-tabbed due to overstaying his day off in Mussoorie for a night without permission.

The Author with Field Marshal Sam Manekshaw,MC at a Dinner Night, Indian Military Academy, Dehradun, 2002

In 1969, he visited Amritsar after assuming office as Chief of Army Staff. He got a tumultuous welcome from the people over there and was literally mobbed wherever he went and crowds seemed to gather around him everywhere. After finishing most engagements on an afternoon without displaying the stars or flag and dressed in civilian clothes he and his military assistant set out to visit the house where he was born. He posed for a photograph in front of the eucalyptus tree which was planted on the day of his birth. He went around the house till the young lady who had opened the door for him recognized him and the entire family gathered around him and offered much hospitality.

On the Burma Front

On joining the Army in 1934, after an attachment with the 2nd Battalion of the Royal Scots he joined his parent battalion 4/12 Frontier Force Regiment, usually referred to as the 54th Sikhs. He was to see action on the Burma Front as part of the 17th Division of the 14th Army. His first annual confidential report had the rather caustic comment 'this officer, I beg his pardon, may some day become an officer.' During the retreat, he was wounded at Sittang Bridge on February 22, 1942, when as a result of a machine gun blast seven bullets riddled the stomach of Captain Manekshaw while engaged in hand-to-hand combat. The Divisional Commander Major General Sir Richard Cowens who reached the scene pinned his Military Cross Medal on Sam's chest as he was not expected to live very much more than a few hours and the Military Cross is not awarded posthumously. His orderly, a soldier of his unit called Sher Singh evacuated him to the nearest Regimental Aid Post where the Medical Officer of 4/12 Frontier Force, Captain G.M. Diwan treated and had him speedily evacuated to Pegu, from where he was subsequently transferred to the larger Military Hospital at Rangoon. He sailed back to India in one of the last ships just before the Japanese overran Burma. The scars of this wound are still carried by the Field Marshal.

As a Staff Officer in Military Operations

Manekshaw came to serve as GSO 1(General Staff Officer Grade 1) in the Military Operations Directorate at the rank of Lt Col after the second World War. In one of those strange games that fate plays in the affairs of men, Major Yahya Khan served as GSO 2(General Staff Officer Grade 2) in the same Directorate under him. About twenty-five years later the GSO 1 and the GSO2 went to war with each other as Chiefs of Staff of the respective armies of their respective countries. Officers of this particular era remember Sam as a jaunty looking Lt Col moving about Delhi on a black motorcycle. Due to the quick pace of promotions following the departure of the British from India, Sam could not hold the assignment which is pre-eminent in the career of every infantry officer, which is the command of an infantry battalion, even though his orders had been issued to assume command of the 3rd Battalion of the 5th Gorkha Rifles(Frontier Force) these could not be implemented as Lt General P.N. Thapar Chief of General Staff at Army Headquarters wanted Sam to remain with the Operations Directorate. However, it must be noted that he was not alone in this predicament as some of his contemporaries also were not able to fulfil this criteria.

He had a ringside view of events when the Instrument of Accession of Jammu and Kashmir was signed on October 25, 1947. General Sir Roy Bucher C-in-C of the Indian Army walked into his room and told him to be ready in one and a half hours time to fly to Srinagar with Mr. V.P. Menon as the military situation was worrying them. An Air Force Dakota flew them in. Sam was to recall later on, that the tribesmen who had entered Kahsmir with the overt support of the Pakistanis indulged in rape and plunder on the way thus taking longer than normal time to reach the city of Srinagar by which time the Army had already got there. The Maharaja's forces, he mentions were 50 per cent Muslim and 50 per cent Dogra. The Muslim elements had revolted and joined the Pakistani forces. At that time the tribesmen were about 7–9 kilometres away from Srinagar. The soldiers were prepared to be flown in. The situation, Sam and V.P. Menon found on arrival at Srinagar, was chaotic. Maharaja Hari Singh was running from room to room with all his jewellery and gold items. A convoy of vehicles was ready for departure. Hari Singh was saying, "All right if India doesn't help, I will go and join my troops and fight it out". Sam could not help butting in and saying, 'That will raise their morale, Sir'. As Sam was discussing the military situation, V.P. Menon finished his discussions with the Maharaja and triumphantly told Manekshaw, 'Sam we've got accession'. Srinagar airfield had to be lit with pine torches and Sam and Menon got back only at about 4 in the morning. General Sir Roy Bucher took Sam to the cabinet meeting called at 9 am Sardar Vallabhbhai Patel who was Deputy Prime Minister asked Manekshaw, whom he addressed as Manekji, 'What is the military situation?' Manekshaw gave the cabinet a resume of the situation and said that unless troops were flown in immediately the airfield would be lost, and if that happened, Srinagar would also be lost. Pandit Nehru beat around the bush, and according to Manekshaw talked about the United Nations, Russia, Africa and everybody untill the Sardar lost his temper and said, 'Jawaharlal, do you want Kashmir, or do you want to give it away?' Nehru said, 'Of course, I want Kashmir'. Then Patel said, 'Please give your orders' and before Nehru could say any more, he turned to Manekshaw and said, 'You have your orders'. During this period he was quite often called by Sardar Patel for consultations with H.M. Patel ICS, who was Defence Secretary at that time.

The first sortie of Dakotas flying the troops of the 1st Sikh Battalion left the same afternoon of the cabinet meeting referred to above. Throughout the Kashmir Operations Sam Manekshaw continued to be in the Military Operations Directorate. The Signal ordering the cease-fire was also signed by him. He was later promoted to the rank of Brigadier.

Even during this period when there was stiff adherence to the British traditions of decorum, Sam practised great informality with his subordinates. There was a young lady called Daisy Chandra, an Auxiliary Corps Officer working in the Staff Duties Directorate. He one day called three young bachelor officers to his room (he was staying alone at this time) and said in the presence of Miss Chandra "Listen boys, I do not know why this young lady is wasting her time on me. I'm married and have two daughters and she has made some socks for me. So young lady, here are three young bachelors from whom you can take your pick".

Along with Brigadier (later General) Thimayya and Major S.K. Sinha (later Lt General and currently Governor of Assam) Manekshaw participated in the delineation talks which were held in the UN at Paris. Vishnu Sahay, ICS represented the civilian administration.

On completing his tenure as DMO, Sam had a stint as Director Military Training and then commanded a Brigade at Ferozepur in the Punjab. Subsequently he moved to the Infantry School, Mhow as Commandant, where he conducted the affairs of the School in a totally unorthodox manner, doing away with the completely outdated British Army pamphlets which held sway at this institution. He introduced 'state-of-the-art' pamphlets which were much more professionally oriented.

A Controversy at Wellington

During the late 1950s Manekshaw commanded the 26 Infantry Division at Jammu. Here began the genesis of acrimonious relations with Lt General B.M. Kaul who at that time commanded the 4th Infantry Division at Ambala. During a joint exercise, a caricature of Kaul was made out in 26 Infantary Division much to the discomfiture of Kaul. Manekshaw is also credited to have termed Kaul's supporters in the Army as 'Kaul boys' which, phonetically understood, can be quite a term! However, Kaul was unnecessarily sensitive and mainly wanted to get rid of his rival Manekshaw whom he feared would be a threat to his becoming the Chief. Krishna Menon at that time, being the Defence Minister, was only too willing to assist Kaul, his 'Favourite General' in getting rid of this up and coming colleague of his. He instituted an inquiry to go into the 'anti-national activities' of Manekshaw who was by now Commandant of the Defence Services Staff College at Wellington. According to the inquiry, Sam had commented while inspecting a sand-model on Shivaji's tactics that there were really no horses in Maharashtra, and if anything. Shivaji must have ridden a 'tattu' (country pony) and words to the effect that history must be given its due. It later transpired that it was Commodore Mehta, Chief Instructor (Navy) who had made the comments and not Manekshaw. Also he was alleged to have displayed Warren Hastings's and Clive's portraits in the Staff College. Another rather outlandish charge was that he was known to cultivate undue friendship towards European students at various social functions not caring much for Indian students present. It speaks volumes for the kind of sycophancy and intrigue that Krishna Menon had allowed to prevail in the Ministry of Defence that a non-combatant officer, Lt General B.M. Kaul, was allowed to call the shots in the army. Kaul was exposed at the time of the Sino–Indian conflict and his career ended in disgrace.

Lt General Daulat Singh and Lt Gen Bikram Singh who were part of the Court of Inquiry exonerated Manekshaw and recommended that action be taken against the officers who gave evidence on such baseless and frivolous accusations. Had the Chinese aggression not intervened, Manekshaw would not have continued in the army, and would have been weeded out in all probability. Apart from the above episode, it may also be mentioned here that Manekshaw was once asked by Defence Minister Krishna Menon about his opinion of the then Army Chief General K.S. Thimayya. Sam told Menon that since Thimayya was his C-in-C he could not comment on him. Menon then said that he could get rid of Thimayya anytime. To which Sam said in his breezy way, "Good. Today you are asking me, a Major General about my Chief, tomorrow you will be asking Brigadiers and Colonels about their opinion of me. It is the surest way of ruining discipline. Don't do it Minister."

Approaching the Top

On November 28, 1962, he took over as General Officer Commanding the ill-fated 4th Corps in Tezpur which had borne the brunt of the Chinese attack. His first words to his staff, "Gentlemen, I have arrived, there will be no more withdrawals, thank you" was enough to instill confidence in the badly shaken officer cadre. Manekshaw was GOC-in-C of the Western Command from December 4, 1963 to November 16, 1964. Interestingly it was quite by chance that he was given the charge of the Eastern Army from November 1964. The Defence Minister Yashwantrao Chavan solicited his views on the most difficult operational area of the army's deployment and Manekshaw assessed that the Eastern theatre was by far the most formidable area of operation given the border with China, East Pakistan and Burma, armed insurgency of a serious nature in Nagaland and the Mizo Hills as well as the politically volatile State of West Bengal.

Chavan, therefore, asked Sam to take on this challenging assignment to which he immediately agreed. In the East he moved around like a human dynamo going to the highest peaks where the army was deployed and took a great interest in the activities on the ground. A battalion not performing too well in counter insurgency operations in Mizoram would, for example, receive a packet of bangles from Sam with the cryptic comment, "if you are avoiding contact with the hostiles give these to your men to wear". After the performance showed marked improvement, he would send another significant message, “send the bangles back”. Once on the way to catch a flight from Kolkata, he was held up by a politician, blocking the road with a public meeting. Taking the bull by the horns, he walked to the tall stout fellow and got him to vacate the road by simply saying, “I’m Sam Manekshaw, and I’ll miss my flight”. Needless to say the man soon cleared the road.

He was able to get several ex-servicemen jobs in the various industrial undertakings in Kolkata. He later commented that he could do more for ex-servicemen in Kolkata then as Chief of Staff. It is a tribute to the industrialists of Kolkata.

Heading the Army in Peace and War

Sam Manekshaw was named full general to succeed General P.P. Kumaramangalam in April 1969. He was to assume his office on June 8, 1969. It was a touch and go thing as rumours were afloat that Defence Minister Swaran Singh had indicated his preference for Lt General Harbaksh Singh who was also another battle scarred veteran and whose combat experience was of a high order. In the ultimate analysis of course combat experience cannot be overriding criteria for the office of Chief of Staff as his job is more administrative in content. Sam was to prove the aptness of this dictum in the 1971 operations.

On assuming command of one the finest fighting forces of the world, Sam’s first order of the day was remarkable in its brevity. “I have taken over as Chief of Army Staff. I expect everyone to do his duty”. The period following his assuming office in South Block was of political uncertainty. The split in the Congress Party had reduced the Indira Gandhi government at the centre to a minority being propped up by Communist support. Delhi was rife with rumours of a possible coup by Sam Manekshaw. The Prime Minister bluntly asked him what his intentions were. “You do your job and I’ll do mine” was his reply.

At the end of March came the crucial meeting between Sam and the Cabinet regarding intervention in East Pakistan after the crack-down by General Tikka Khan’s forces on the fateful night of March 25, 1971. Mrs. Indira Gandhi virtually ordered Sam to move the Army into East Pakistan and said that she and her government were prepared for war if required. To which Sam said,

'Have you read the Bible?' and the Minister for External Affairs Sardar Swaran Singh asked, "What has the Bible got to do with this?" and Sam told him that in the Bible in the first chapter the Lord said, "Let there be light and there was light" and the Cabinet was today wanting to go to war without going into the vital aspect of the preparedness of the army. According to him, the Army was not prepared for war. The Himalayan passes would open up causing a threat from China which could not be taken lightly. The Chief went on to point out that his Armoured Division was in Jhansi/Babina and one of his Infantry Divisions was in Sambha in Jammu and Kashmir and the other in Andhra Pradesh/Tamil Nadu, they were so far apart. Only eleven of his eighty-nine tanks were operational as the Finance Ministry was not sanctioning adequate funds. The rains in the East would begin in April/May. The Prime Minister was then asked by Sam to give her orders, on which she adjourned the Cabinet till the evening. She asked Sam to stay back and asked him whether the picture drawn by him was authentic and she got an answer in the affirmative. He asked for six months to prepare for the battle.

Manekshaw gave ample illustrations of his professional honesty in the above mentioned episode. He brought home to the political leadership the pitfalls of launching an offensive in the summer of 1971. He also highlighted the lack of equipment and problem of logistics. Apart from all this,he brought to bear on the leadership the danger of Chinese intervention with the snows on the passes having melted. It required moral courage of a high order to do all this,a basic ingredient of good leadership. Once the decision was taken, Sam Manekshaw gave a solemn assurance to the Prime Minister that he would conduct a lightning campaign to overrun East Pakistan in a matter of two weeks. This proved accurate as the Bangladesh War concluded in 14 days. On being asked by Madam Gandhi as to how much of a period would be required for preparation to launch the offensive, he replied that late November would be the right time as this would also bring to naught the chance of a Chinese attack with the onset of winter. In the intervening six months he would busy himself preparing the army for war, working in tandem with the other two services. Very shortly, however, certain rumours, which had some rather unfortunate intent, began to abound in the political and bureaucratic circles of New Delhi, it was mentioned that the army had developed 'cold feet' to take on the enemy. It was rather an absurd suggestion and was obviously motivated. At the Independence Parade, Sam was sitting next to a Minister who was known to be one of the rumour mongers. The Minister remarked that the army guns were firing at the time of the unfurling of the national flag with greater vigour than usual. To which Sam could only comment that he was a somewhat taken aback to hear this, as he was under the impression that some people were saying that the army had 'cold feet'. Needless to say the Minister looked a bit shame-faced, and Sam had asserted his 'no-nonsense' attitude once again.

In the actual run up to the battle, Sam was able to prepare the army well. He selected an engineer officer, Major General Kini to step up tank production at the Heavy Vehicles Factory at Avadi near Chennai. He was able to give a major boost to tank production which resulted in the production of Vijayanta tanks ahead of schedule as well as brace up other affairs connected with tanks in Avadi.

On August 9,1971 India inked the Treaty of Peace,Friendship and Cooperation with the USSR. It was indeed a turning point in the preparation effort for war as all our military needs in terms of hardware were speedily taken care of. Sam had obtained a sanction from the Prime Minister in the early days of the crisis to raise guerilla groups to work in tandem with the 'Mukti Bahini' or freedom fighters army of East Pakistan. Code named 'Operation Jackpot', Major General Onkar Singh Kalkat was the officer deputed by Manekshaw to oversee these operations. He belonged to Manekshaw's regiment of the 8th Gorkha Rifles. Kalkat however could not keep pace with the daily updates required by Sam as he was a conventional soldier of the old school. He was replaced by Major General B.N. Sarkar. Training of 8000 guerrillas in border areas was to be taken care of in three months. About 400 naval commandos and frogmen were trained to bring about an effective offensive against enemy port facilities which proved accurate to a large extent. The Mukti Bahini was to prove successful with one gunboat armed with a 40 mm Bofors against 15 Pakistani ships,11 Coasters,7 Gunboats,11 Barges, 2 Tankers and 19 River craft. These were the most prominent achievements of the Mukti Bahini.

On the western border India was required to face a well equipped and strong army. Therefore Manekshaw was able,during the intervening months after the March episode, to build up strong defences so that the army was ready for the onslaught on this front. The deployment which took place by the time of the onset of winter left little scope for strategic surprise in this area.

In the Eastern Sector during the run up to the battle, some brigades had been moved down from the Indo-China border in the mountainous terrain. This was done by Major General Jacob, Chief of Staff of the Eastern Army, who had taken into confidence the Director of Military Operations, Major General I.S. Gill. As soon as Manekshaw came to know of this he sent back a rather rude message to the Army Commander General Aurora. 'I have nursed you better than any woman. Who told you to move these brigades down? You will move them back at once'. Later these brigades could not be moved back as this incident occurred in November when it was already too late to re-deploy them. However Jacob and Gill by mutual agreement did not deploy these brigades in East Pakistan. Later on Manekshaw realizing that a Chinese threat did not exist re-deployed the brigades elsewhere showing a fair amount of flexibility, which is an important ingredient of a good commander.

Both in the run up to the war as in the actual operations, Sam functioned as an exceedingly good Chairman of the Chiefs of Staff Committee. He took along with him the other Chiefs of Staff, Air Chief Marshal P.C. Lal, DFC and Admiral S.M. Nanda. It was not of little consequence that Sam had a very close one-to-one relationship with the then Prime Minister Indira Gandhi. Also the top echelons of the bureaucracy which included Mr D.P. Dhar, Mr P.N. Haksar, Mr T.N. Kaul, Mr P.N. Dhar and Mr L.P. Singh to name a few,had an excellent working relationship with the Army Chief.

The Chairman of the Chiefs of Staff Committee, like in the European countries before and during the Second World War, has a secretariat consisting of the other two Chiefs of Staff and intelligence staff. In the post Second World War era however, in Europe a system of the office of Chief of Defence Staff had evolved, particularly in America and in the United Kingdom. The Chief of Defence

Staff deals directly with the political leaders of the Defence forces like the Defence Secretary of the United States. Sam Manekshaw was like any good soldier, a votary of the Chief of Defence System or CDS System as it is more popularly known. Unfortunately successive governments since 1947 have fought shy of a CDS System in the rather mistaken belief that it could throw up a soldier who may develop political ambitions and may become too powerful to control by the national leadership of the country.

In a press interview published after laying down office as Chief of Staff in 1973, Manekshaw said, "At the outset, the Prime Minister had left me free to conduct my affairs as I chose. In consequence there was never any interference by or conflict of views with the government. What more can a soldier ask for?" This gives a clear impression how professionally oriented the entire campaign in Bangladesh was. The relations of Sam Manekshaw and Air Chief Marshal P.C. Lal were at one time, discreetly cold, but it stands to the credit of both that they did not allow this to interfere in the conduct of operations. Only on one occasion did Lal protest strongly when certain direct orders were issued to the Eastern Air Command but this was not repeated as the intention was not to score any points.

Sam was resolute on the issue that no cross movement of troops should take place in the run up to or during the outbreak of hostilities. He was openly against what he described as 'horse-trading'. Therefore, each commander knew his troop strength and made his plans accordingly and this led to the proper utilization of troops. Sam was to go on whirlwind tours to troops on the western and eastern front in the intervening months. His words in these 'pep' talks usually covered three aspects, he would say, "There will be no scavenging during the battle. My army has soldiers in it, not thieves". Another point he stressed was the importance of no womanizing. With a twinkle in his eye, he would continue, "I have been all over the world and I can say on authority that we have the most beautiful women in the world, why go for lesser women? Furthermore our fight is not with their women, it is with their army. So, when you feel tempted you may put your hands in your pockets and think of Sam Manekshaw". Inevitably people had a good laugh but understood his seriousness. His third and last point pertained to valour and aggressiveness as well as letting the troops know about the various up-to-date equipment procured to meet the shortfalls in these fields.

It must be borne in mind that he had an excellent memory and was in a position to talk spontaneously on the various figures of imports of equipment,date of delivery and so on. This made his talks motivating to the troops down the line. While speaking to officers he did so in a sterner vein, bringing home the need for mutual trust and camaraderie so that they could live up to their obligations in a fair manner. He also felt that unlike in 1965, no officer would be removed for any failure in command, as it played havoc with the discipline of the army and led to officers putting in various representations. He, therefore, made it clear to senior commanders that no removal from command would be resorted to, and if any such demand was made he would cross question them on the help they had rendered to their subordinates and there would be a problem if their answers were unsatisfactory.

Lt General K.P. Candeth suggested the removal of two Commanders whom he believed might not fit the bill in battle. A process of screening the dossiers of the two was undertaken and an exhaustive study on them was taken up by checking out with their previous Commanders. On this basis the two were kept in their position, though Candeth was later vindicated in these two cases. It is to Sam's credit, however, that he followed the system and did not resort to a knee-jerk response as another overall commander may have. His direct access to the Prime Minister also proved a boon in getting the pressing requirements for arms and equipment approved directly by Mrs. Gandhi and then being sent to the government bureaucratic channels for action. Needless to say they were taken care of with express speed as no bureaucrat would have it in him to take on the Prime Minister's diktat.

Once the intensive visits were over and the Army's operation plans were fully worked out and undertaken after taking care of the shortfall of material and equipment,Sam set forth into going into the Air Force and Naval Operational plans with the respective Chiefs of these two wings. Threadbare discussions ensued which resulted in plans being changed, the changes being subtly suggested in order not to ruffle any feathers.

It so happened that Manekshaw had an interesting exchange with the Pakistani High Commissioner in the run-up to the war. The Higher Commissioner wanted to know why the Army Chief was indulging in so much war-mongering to which he received a rather sharp retort, 'Mr High Commissioner, be realistic, do you really believe all the propaganda your country is putting out? If war comes this time it will be entirely your doing. I can assure you it won't be ours. Furthermore, you might be able to gain here and there but I guarantee that you will lose East Pakistan. Tell your politicians that'.

It may be pointed out that Sam took pains in going through intelligence with great care and posing many of questions on the Intelligence reports thus perused. He would ask for reports and replies by a specified deadline thus taking care of this aspect also. As part of the preparation aspect courses being run at the Defence Services Staff College, Wellington, the College of Combat in Mhow and the National Defence College, New Delhi were terminated ahead of schedule so that these senior officers could be available for being utilized in the war.

Sam Manekshaw and Lt General J.F.R. Jacob former Governor of the Punjab, and then Chief of Staff of Eastern Command had a rather heated discussion when he visited the Eastern Command operations room in August along with the then Director of Military Operations, Major General K.K. Singh who highlighted that Khulna and Chittagong should be the main thrust of the attack as then Dhaka would automatically fall An acrimonious discussion ensued with Jacob taking the view that Dhaka being the geopolitical capital and centre of power, it should be the focus of the planned attack and would thus hasten the course of the operations. This will be discussed subsequently while recounting the course of the battle.

Shri D.P. Dhar who was incharge of the Policy Planning Cell in the Foreign Ministry had a meeting with the Army Chief almost every day so that Manekshaw was in the picture of what was going on in the civilian government circles. It was a welcome development and thus both the policy makers and military leadership were on the same grid. It is a good example to be followed by military planners of the future. It may not be out of place here to mention that Manekshaw's relationship with the Defence Minister of the day Jagjivan Ram was not cordial. Jagjivan Ram resented Manekshaw having such a good working relationship with the Prime Minister. It is also possible that some people at the bureaucratic level may have poisoned his ears.

November 1971 had come and gone. Manekshaw's stipulated six months were over. By November 30, the armed forces were ready. The Prime Minister sanctioned the attack for daybreak on December 4, 1971. The army had wanted a dusk attack so that the night could be used for penetration by the columns. The Air Force preferred the first light in order that the whole day should be available to carry out sorties. Thus ultimately day-break was the time agreed upon. Orders were accordingly issued to all concerned. But Jagjivan Ram was still in the dark, and an officer was to leave for Bangalore, where he was on tour, to convey to him the momentous news, and to inform him that the decision had been taken since the Minister was not in Delhi.

Manekshaw was being briefed by the DMO, Major General Inderjit Singh Gill, in the Operations Room when the news came at 5 pm that Pakistan had launched a pre-emptive attack in the western sector. General Candeth, unable to get through to the Chief on the telephone (as the Operations Room did not have one), had conveyed the news to the Defence Secretary Mr K.B. Lal, ICS who came rushing in. Manekshaw's immediate reaction was that the date everyone was waiting for had arrived and now action to get the enemy was on. He immediately told his staff officer to get hold of the officer who was carrying the letter for Jagjivan Ram and ensure that the letter was burnt as Pakistan had launched the attack.

Since neither Mrs. Gandhi nor Mr. Jagjivan Ram was in Delhi, (the Prime Minister was in Kolkatta and the Defence Minister as stated above in Bangalore) it fell upon Sam's lot to issue the orders to enforce the operational plans with immediate effect. Since it was known that he had the absolute confidence of the Prime Minister there was no problem in obtaining concurrence down the line. It is indeed a remarkable level of co-ordination which prevailed in the Ministry of Defence on the fateful evening of December 3, 1971. One of his first instructions to his staff was to get a telephone line installed in the Operations Room. By 6 pm. Sam spoke to

Jacob in Kolkata and asked him to convey the news of war, General Aurora, immediately left for the maidan where Mrs Gandhi was addressing a rally and gave her the news. She immediately returned to Delhi to take charge of affairs of a nation at war.

The progress of operations in the Eastern Sector proceeded on schedule with the help of 50 Para Brigade. Nine Infantry Divisions pushed into Jessore by afternoon of December 7. Comilla town fell on December 9. On December 9, Manekshaw rang up Jacob in the Eastern Command and ordered him to send a force by sea to Cox Bazar to forestall any Pakistani troops escaping to Burma. Unfortunately the operation ended in a fiasco as no enemy troops were found in this area, and only a Mukthi Bahini camp was found in the vicinity of the beaches. Two of our troops drowned while disembarking. General Jacob, in his book, *Surrender at Dacca* refers to this episode and feels that it was a rather 'cavalier' order on behalf of Manekshaw and the other two chiefs as equipment,planning and training to launch amphibious operations of this nature were not adequate. No written orders were issued for the operation.

At Khulna the army got bogged down in the marshy terrain of this area. On December 13, Manekshaw issued a signal to the Eastern Army instructing them to, without any loss of time, capture all towns which had so far not fallen to our troops. These included Dinajpur, Rangpur, Sylhet, Maynmati Cantonment, Khulna and Chittagong. Significantly Dacca did not find mention even at this stage and by this time the Army was on the outskirts of Dacca. Manekshaw wanted to take as many towns as possible because at this point of time (December 13) a resolution sponsored by Poland and backed by USSR was pending in the UN Security Council calling for an immediate cease-fire. The unpredictable and mercurial Zulfikar Ali Bhutto, Foreign Minister in Yahya Khan's administration unwittingly came to the rescue of the Indian Forces. By walking out of the Security Council in a mighty huff after tearing the resolution he assisted India in the speedy creation of Bangladesh giving the armed forces sufficient time to plan for the air strike on the Governor's house at Dacca which clinched the battle.

In answering Jacob's criticism of not outlining Dacca as the objective in the run-up to the battle and during the operations Manekshaw's viewpoint was that the inhabited area is usually not looked upon by a professional military man as a worthwhile objective, given many lives which can be lost and the time taken to conclude an operation of this nature. Therefore, a city of the size of Dacca should seldom be made an objective in an operation plan. Apart from both these viewpoints it is fairly probable that there was some political direction from the government or from D.P. Dhar on this matter. These are nuances which are sometimes left unsaid.

Jacob has criticized Manekshaw's 'school-masterish' approach while dealing with his formation commanders and said that this had a demoralising effect as it was akin to a headmaster scolding his senior staff. Manekshaw believes that he was only being blunt and forthright which was needed at certain junctures. He had otherwise fine relations with all his commanders. Jacob also does not fail to make mention of the fact in his book that Manekshaw was a highly successful chief who restored the esteem of the Army after the humiliation of 1962 and the 'self-doubts' of 1965.

It was Manekshaw who called up Jacob at 9.15 am on December 16, asking him to proceed to Dacca immediately so as to organize the surrender at Dacca. Jacob raised some queries about the draft surrender document which he had prepared sometime back. Sam said it would be dispatched with Lt General J.S. Aurora in the afternoon. Sam showed considerable propriety by not going himself to take the surrender, according to some sources he was even told to do so by the Prime Minister. He rightly felt that this was the prerogative of the Chief of the Eastern Army, Lt General Jagjit Singh Aurora.

On the Western Front there were reverses at Chhamb in Jammu and Kashmir, Husainiwala in Punjab and Longewala in Rajasthan. Chhamb was undoubtedly a debacle of some magnitude. One of the participants of this battle mentioned that it was a mess akin to 1962 on a micro scale. It was first decided that a defensive operation would be carried out in this sector which was at the last minute altered to an offensive operation. The divisional commander Major General Jaswant Singh and Lt Genenral Sartaj Singh were in favour of an offensive or 'forward' policy which meant crossing the Manawar Tawi River and attacking Pakistani territory. As a result the Division was not adequately prepared either for offensive or defensive operations.

On one of his visits to the sector, probably in November 1971, the Corps Commander Lt General Sartaj Singh went up to Sam just before he was getting into his jeep and said, "Sam would you re-consider the defensive posture as we have had quite a lot of discussion on this issue", to which Sam said, "All right, but only on the condition that Chhamb does not fall", Therefore, Sam was in the picture of this plan. Lt General K.P. Candeth GOC-in-C of the Western Army did,according to this senior partici pant,convey to Sam the inadvisability of making an offensive plan in this sector but was over-ruled by Manekshaw. The worst casualties were suffered in Chhamb apart from the loss of territory.

After the operations, Sam visited the Division responsible for the Chhamb action –10 Infantry Division. A Sanik Sammelan (gathering of troops at one single ground, in this case about 5000 troops) had been organized. According to a person present it was expected that Sam would commiserate with the troops down the line to boost their morale, keeping in view the large number of officers and men who fell on the battlefield. However, Sam said the following, leaving the audience quite shocked. "I had said that I would talk to this Division in Pakistan territory on an earlier visit, therefore, I am in no mood to talk to you. Does anybody have any doubts or questions?" At this a Junior Commissioned Officer raised his hand and said he had a doubt. To which Manekshaw said your officers will answer your queries and left the meeting leaving the audience rather stunned. The person who had got up was later asked by his officer what his question was. He said that while the officers and troops were fighting valiantly against heavy odds, the order for withdrawal was given by the higher command and the troops on the ground could hardly be blamed for this. The point was undoubtedly valid. This incident according to this senior commander in Chhamb throws light on Sam`s impulsiveness and the tendency to only hear of success and being unable to take failure in his stride. The senior commander also mentions an incident which took place in the 5/8 Gorkha Rifles battalion where Sam was presented a 'khukri' which was supposed to have enemy blood on it. Sam told the Commanding Officer to recommend the soldier presenting the 'khukri' for an MVC which according to the senior officer present was not deserved. This was a case of

Sam playing to the gallery a bit. On the whole, however, he does comment that Manekshaw was a very popular commander whose visits were looked forward to by the rank and file with enthusiasm. He doubts if anybody else would have been able to win a victory at that time on that scale. The object of mentioning this is to point out his warts also, as everyone has these.

Our army, however, offset the losses in Chhamb in the Western Sector with gains at Chicken's Neck, the territory lying between the two branches of the river Chenab as well as gains in the Kargil Sector. Likewise the losses in Husainiwala and Fazilka were offset by gains at Dera Baba Nanak, Sejhra Bulge and Basantar River. We lost 55 villages and 52 sq. miles to Pakistan but were able to gain 630 villages and 419 sq. miles of their territory. During the period of the fourteen-day war, Sam would usually come to office at 7.30 am and after a quick update from his staff, who were in touch with the senior hierarchy of the various commands from the early hours; he would nip across to the Operations Room. He would proceed, thereafter, to brief the Prime Minister at her house and be back at South Block, at his office by 8.30 am.

It was usual during the period of hostilities that the Chiefs of Staff Committee would meet at 9.30 am. The Director in charge of Operations of each arm of the services was also present. These officers would present a summary of events of the last 24 hours giving an account of the gains and setbacks. This was then followed by a discussion of the proposed moves for the next 24 hours. A tie up for projected naval and air support would also take place as part of the co-coordinated effort for the following day. Then the Chiefs of Staff would assess the proceedings so that formal approval for naval and air support could take place as per norms. Only authenticated versions of advances and setbacks were discussed during these meetings so as to avoid embarrassment. Mr Jagjivan Ram, Minister for Defence, would be briefed on the conclusion of the Chiefs of Staff meeting. He used to often come over to the Army Chief's Office showing that no strict protocol was followed and a 'hands on' approach was adhered too during the crisis.

This provided a very high degree of synchronized effort which produced excellent results. On one occasion when the situation in Chhamb was critical the Western Army Commander General

Candeth was able to obtain air support virtually within minutes due to the presence of the Chief of Air Staff in the Operations Room. Later in the day, Manekshaw was to have detailed discussions with the Command GOC-in -C's of Southern, Western and Eastern Commands which were involved in the war. Also a comprehensive discussion with the Corps Commanders was not an uncommon feature. Post lunch he would have some meetings at the bureaucratic level followed by an extensive briefing to the Defence Minister in the Operations Room before calling it a day at about 8 pm.

It would be only fair to mention the extremely effective role played by the Minister for Defence Mr. Jagjivan Ram throughout. Despite his differences with Sam Manekshaw he had a firstclass grasp on the strategic aspect of military planning, was a seasoned administrator and took adequate steps to ensure that nothing was lacking in the run-up to the battle on various fronts so that a well prepared army was ready for action. Lt General J.F.R. Jacob in his book *Surrender at Dacca* describes him as the "best Defence Minister we have had". Some years later when he had a second tenure as Defence Minister in the Desai ministry he again showed remarkable administrative acumen and worked for the betterment of the services in a remarkable manner.

Sam Manekshaw's staff was reduced to only one Lt. Col Military Assistant and one ADC even though the authorization was for two more officers of the rank of major and captain (a second ADC). Sam had very little personal security and used to say "my Gorkhas and dogs are more then adequate to look after me". It must be pointed out that terrorist attacks of the level of the present day were hardly prevalent in 1971, but a fatal attack could also not be discounted and therefore, it was a matter of great personal bravery.

Leadership Qualities of Sam Manekshaw and Certain Other Aspects

'Sam Bahadur' as he was popularly known showed remarkable qualities of leadership throughout his career and had the courage to stand by his convictions. As recounted earlier, he was instrumental in the government postponing offensive action in the spring of '71 which may have resulted in a disaster, as we were not at all prepared. His words to the Prime Minister, "Are you prepared? I am certainly not" have been often quoted as an example of professional integrity and rare guts.

Once a list of cadets passing out of the Indian Military Academy at Dehradun for commissioning into the army, was sent up to the Ministry of Defence and in due course reached the minister's desk. Mr Jagjivan Ram being a member of the Scheduled Castes was prone to looking for their welfare, which was understandable. Surprisingly, however, he sent down this routine file with the query as to how many of the officers being commissioned belonged to the Scheduled Castes/Tribes. The figure was worked out by the Adjutant General's Branch and sent to the Ministry. It was a figure of 0.5%. Jagjivan Ram was livid with rage and wrote on the file that since the accepted policy of the Government of India was that 15 per cent of all government jobs were reserved for Scheduled Castes and 7.5 per cent for Scheduled Tribes, an omission of a grave nature had been committed. He desired that responsibility should be fixed and severe action be taken against the person/persons guilty.

Manekshaw called for the Deputy Adjutant General and asked him to prepare a response which said, "The Chief of the Army Staff, General Manekshaw was responsible for this grave ommission and whatever action desired should be taken against him." Sinha, therefore, prepared the response saying in the last 30 years the army had been either preparing for a war or participating in a war. Therefore keeping in mind the high degree of professionalism required in this vital sphere merit had to be the prime consideration at the time of inducting officers. It was also pointed out that members of Scheduled Castes/Tribes had been accommodated in the lower ranks of the army in certain infantry regiments. Then came the clause in the report that Manekshaw should be charged with the omission if any. Jagjivan Ram maintained a predictable silence on this issue as this happened in 1972, when Sam's popularity was at its peak in the aftermath of the war. Therefore, the armed forces remain the only organization without any caste-based reservation quota.

As he had imbibed and practised the true qualities of leadership he could create an impression on any type of crowd and had a unique and magnetic personality. Thus, after the war culminated in the spring of 1972 he, in order to raise funds for the Defence Fund, was presiding over the Filmfare function at Mumbai. A huge crowd of people awaited him for his autograph at the cinema hall where the function was to be held. Scores of stars and starlets lined up for his autograph and to have a word with him. David, one of the stars of the Bombay Film Industry was the master of ceremonies and a memorable evening ensued. In the introduction of the chief guest, it was said, "General Manekshaw is the architect of our great victory and while Pakistan is sacking its soldiers we our honouring ours." In his typical style, Sam responded, "I was not aware that I would be seeing so much beauty and so much talent, if I had known this, I too would have put on my war paint. It is perhaps, because I lack this that the knocking sounds you hear are my knees. The film industry deserves my thanks for all they have done for my soldiers by providing them with so much happiness and joy in forward areas by going to those inhospitable areas and putting up shows. Next time the income tax chaps raid your houses and catch you, remember the sympathy of all the soldiers is with you." At that particular time a number of Income Tax raids were being conducted on film stars. While the awards were being presented, David said, "I would like to give the 'best comedian' award to General Manekshaw who has brought so much humour and fun to us this evening". He presented the award causing much merriment all around.

Again Sam had proved his prowess to break the ice with any kind of gathering. Some of his speeches, which were well prepared and rehearsed, are worth recounting. While reviewing the Passing Out Parade at the Indian Military, Dehradun on June 14, 1969 and March 30, 1972, he emphasized the changes which had come about since he joined the army in 1934. But he also reminded the cadets on the verge of receiving their commission that the main task of winning wars and defeating the enemy remained the same. He said that at the Academy they had been taught to become leaders who were resourceful, deliberate, unyielding, determined and above all completely honest. In the second speech made after the 1971 victory he told his audience that they were indeed fortunate to be officers leading a victorious army. He mentioned further that given a fair share of luck, some of the young officers could rise to dizzy heights, keep their head above the water or fall by the wayside. He told them that the future beckoned to them with a life of hardship and adventure and they could make the most of it.

Sam, as has been earlier pointed out, had throughout his career laid stress on a single commander who could coordinate the affairs of the three services not only in peace time but more significantly during battle. It was this he rightly feels was the main cause for his success in the 1971 war as he had a one-to-one relationship with the Prime Minister of the day and was able to get on the spot decisions without going through the rather cumbersome bureaucratic channels where one could often get delayed in getting decisions and get frustrated in the mountains of red-tape.

It must be said to his credit that Manekshaw had the decorum and dignity of the service uppermost in his mind and protected its independence and autonomy to the best of his ability. His press statement at Ootacummund on July 20,2001,regarding the Tipnis controversy (the Chief of the Air Staff at the time Air Chief Marshal A.Y. Tipnis had failed to salute the visiting Pakistan President Parvez Musharraf at the Rashtrapati Bhavan reception) was also in the same spirit of upholding the dignity of the services. Sam said, "It was indeed a mistake and against military ethics. If I were in uniform, I would have saluted President Parvez Musharraf". I have earlier referred to his having the guts to stand up to Mrs. Gandhi and have the war plans postponed for 6–7 months in March 1971 ensuring a fully prepared army confronted the Pakistani forces. In 1984, a pliable Army Chief agreed to take on a non-military operation Bluestar in the Punjab with disastrous results. Had Sam Manekshaw been at the helm of affairs in 1984, he may have had the courage to call a spade, a spade and tell the truth to the political leadership,and much blood-shed could have been saved. The above mentioned example amply demonstrates the value and importance of a professionally sound and independent viewpoint being put across to the leadership of the country.

During Manekshaw's tenure an Additional Secretary by the name of Mukherjee was posted in the Ministry of Defence. One morning the Chief of Army Staff strode into Mukherjee's office, file in hand. He opened a certain page of the file and pointedly asked the aghast Mukherjee,"Mukherjee Babu, are you responsible for this villainy?" Mukherjee, collecting his wits replied that he had not intended anything offensive, which was probably the implication of the noting. He received a sharp rebuke from Sam, "You better be careful about not repeating this in the future or else I will personally throw you out of the window". The impact of his boldness was felt by everyone around and the incident speaks for itself. The Army Chief could not be pushed around on any matter. He once mentioned emphatically, "Nation building is not purely the preserve of politicians, bureaucrats or defence personnel but that of the entire community – even the common man has a role to play. While leadership must bloom and a National Security Organization must take shape and function effectively, it is the awareness and feeling in the common man that would compel the people in the corridors of power to discharge their functions effectively, efficiently and remain accountable to the nation".

The issue of national security and higher defence planning in the interest of the country were not just of academic interest to Manekshaw, and it must also be pointed out that he did not mince his words on the issue. At an address at the National Defence College titled "The Army in the Eighties" a probably loaded question was asked on the issue of the Chief of Defence Staff and integrated functioning of the three services. To which Manekshaw replied that, since the army was an older wing of the three services as also numerically superior, if at the present juncture such a system was introduced the overall commander would have to be of the army for a considerable period. As the two other services were still developing, it might put a brake on the two services and cause a loss of great proportion to the nation as a whole, even though it could be inadvertently done. He held the view however, that in the ultimate analysis the country would have to go in for such a system keeping in view the economic factor, integration and the needs of up-to-date military action in the post Second World War era. It was a clear exposition of the vital issue.

Another issue which he referred to in his talk was bringing the Border Security Force for all practical purposes under the Army and calling it the 'Border Command.' This way he felt, exhaustive training could be given to the army which would be relieved from manning the international border. Thus the army would be much more ,prepared for actual battle proving the aptness of the well known cliché 'the more you sweat in peace, the less you bleed in war.' In the 1971 Operations the Border Security Force was deployed under the overall command of the army and was to achieve excellent results.

Sam also took care to see that retired officers were well looked after, At the Army Horse Show he discovered that some retired generals were given seats in the second and third rows, he was soon with them exclaiming to them, "Good God, Sir who has given you a seat there? You won't be able to see a thing, please come up here". He took the Principal Staff Officer to task the next day saying, "If you respect them today, others will respect you when you retire. While they were in service you and I used to vie with each other to bum suck them. Why this sudden change now?"

His sense of humour used to erupt all of a sudden. Once Lt General SPP Thorat organized an Ex-Serviceman's rally at Kolhapur. Sam made mention of the fact that General Thorat had made a bit of an incorrect statement to call him (Sam) warlike in his behaviour. The only warlike person in his family, he went on to say is this lady, pointing to his wife. She fights with me day and night, he said! Everyone was bowled over with laughter. He was a stickler for politeness also. Once his car emerged from the gate of his house at a rather fast speed causing the car of the Scientific Adviser to the Minister of Defence to swerve to avoid a collision. Upon reaching the office, he dictated a rather charming note to the official who was too enamoured to mind!

Before the Simla Summit which brought about the Simla Agreement of 1972, it was decided that General Manekshaw meet with his opposite number in Pakistan General Tikka Khan to sort out the issue of Thakochak, a small enclave of which the claims of both nations seemed accurate. The Prime Minister was of the view that it would be appropriate if both the Chiefs sorted the issue out amicably. Sam accordingly had to fly down to Lahore where he had a meeting with Tikka Khan. The Pakistanis had made rather lavish arrangements for this meeting. It went fairly well but the issue of Thakochak seemed to elude both parties. Therefore, the deadlock had to be reported to the government.

The Prime Minister Mrs. Gandhi wanted Sam to have another

'go' on the issue so he found himself in Lahore again. He asked the Prime Minister why she did not send the Foreign Minister to which Mrs. Gandhi said that such a decision would be accepted coming from a soldier not a politician! Manekshaw's comment to his staff was, "She's making a monkey of me, but it's for the country". During the second parley with Tikka Khan, Sam made two things clear, one that it would look ridiculous and be embarrassing in the extreme for both the parties if a solution regarding such a small area, involving a few kilometres could not be decided upon. Bigger issues would confront them in the future and a starting point had to be made somewhere. Two, since the issue had been publicized and gained political importance a kind of 'give and take' should be worked out with Pakistan taking some part of Indian territory of the same dimensions as Thakochak. Some of play-acting also took place in the talks when Manekshaw suddenly got up when Tikka Khan was getting bogged down, to say that he was walking out and felt that it was rather absurd that he got called to Pakistan if Tikka was going to beat about the bush.

After lunch, the ice broke quite suddenly during coffee on the lawns of the Mess. Both Tikka Khan and Manekshaw had some interest on the building and designing of housing for the officer cadre. Manekshaw spoke about high rise buildings and flats being the best alternative to house officers. Tikka Khan, on the contrary, was of the view that single units with lawn space and area around it were more desirable for an officer's needs. Pat came the clincher from Sam, "If you desire single units, its obvious that you have large tracts of land and, therefore, don't have a problem on that score. This being the case, why don't you part with Thakochak?"

The accord reached between the Chiefs of the Indian and Pakistani armies had Thakochak go to India and Kayian, a place north of Srinagar, which was enveloped by Pakistani territory being given to our neighbour. A joint communiqué was issued and the talks concluded on a happy note. Undoubtedly it was a diplomatic triumph par excellence. One of the rather interesting incidents of this trip was when Manekshaw wanted to present an Indian made high quality watch of the Hindustan Machine Tools to General Tikka Khan's driver, who refused to accept it till General Tikka Khan persuaded him to do so!

During one of the visits he was entertained quite lavishly by the Governor of West Punjab. At lunch the governor asked him if he could do him a favour. On Sam's agreeing to do so, the governor took him to meet his personal staff lined up outside his room. The 10th or 11th person in the line removed his turban when Sam passed him and placed it at his feet, at which Sam returned the turban to the man asking why he did so. The man said, "It is because of you that we were saved". After this the man explained that his 5 sons were in the Prisoner of War camps in India and he was receiving letters from them to the effect that they were being well treated in the POW camps and Manekshaw's visits added a personal touch as he shook their hand, gave them copies of the Koran Sharif, and went to the kitchen to personally check on the cooking. The old staff member then went on to say, "Now I will never say that Hindus are bad people". It was a touching scene full of emotion.

Manekshaw was given an extension by the Government of India on the pleasure of the President 'till further orders' on April 1, 1972. Interestingly he went shortly thereafter to inaugurate the Military Hospital of the Eastern Command Kolkata, which had been planned and authorized during his command of the Eastern Army. In a witty speech he remarked, "There has been a race between my retirement and completion of this building. The former almost won, then the President was pleased to order me to continue in service, so I stand here today and perform this most pleasant task. Having done this, I now await the President's displeasure! Thereafter I can retire a happy man". A member of his staff had to go around requesting all members of the press corps present not to carry the "displeasure" bit! Fortunately, none did. On the minus side it must be mentioned that Manekshaw did have a habit of talking at times out of place and inappropriately. A relevant instance is quoted here.

On October 12, 1966, while still Commander of the Eastern Army, Manekshaw was on board an Indian Airlines flight to Delhi, and had a rather free-wheeling conversation with William K. Hitchcock, American Consul General, a co-passenger. Hitchcock reported, "He seemed less guarded than during any of the many talks we have had in the last two years. He was quite critical of the conduct of

General J.N. Chaudhari, Chief of the Indian Army during the 1965 conflict. It was ridiculous he said, that the Indians allowed the Chinese who made a few menacing sounds to pin down 30,000 troops he had in his command (this is the first time he had mentioned the figure to me). On being asked whether he had any further thoughts of going to the United States, he interestingly replied that he would be delighted to go if selected as Chief. He said that he was deeply concerned over the degree to which India was becoming militarily dependent on Soviet equipment. This dependence had developed out of arrangements made during discussions Chaudhari, and more recently Kumaramangalam had held with the Soviets in Moscow. Discussions, which he adds, have resulted in producing a lot of equipment for India. He believes that if he were to go to the US now it could be interpreted as follows: (a) That he would identify with a Western bias (which he most definitely has). (b) That such identification might thwart his promotion to Chief of Staff. (c) That not being Chief of Staff he would not be able to effect action to redirect Indian military thinking away from the Soviet Union". To put it mildly, one can only be somewhat aghast at Manekshaw's indiscretion of talking in this vein, to a Counsel General at that.

It would be pertinent to point out here that Sam as Chief was very meticulous about certain things. In the secretariat he would be extremely annoyed if anything was out of place or out of order. He once enquired why the other side of South Block which houses the Ministry of Foreign Affairs was cleaner than the Defence Ministry side. Since the reply he got was not satisfactory in nature he put up a proposal for the creation of a post named Welfare Officer, Ministry of Defence, who was instructed to take steps to ensure the proper upkeep of the rooms and offices in the Defence Ministry. Once he lined up all the peons who had been given new uniforms and growled at a member of his staff, "Do you call this fitting?" The cleanliness and well groomed staff in the office had an impact on visitors. He added a personal touch to all letters and made sure that almost each letter was unique to the person and not a duplicated format. The pace was so fast that a new electric typewriter had to be purchased for the office as a single one would not suffice. He would be at his staff officers to prepare drafts speedily and ensured efficiency of his clerical staff and stenographers.

As a Chief he was conscious of his looks and was invariably seen with a black side cap (usually used by officers as mess dress). Once when asked why he wore this particular cap, he said, "I like it, my nose shows up". He blew his top, however, if he saw any officer wearing it during working hours, saying, "You wear this with your mess dress, only Sam Manekshaw can wear this during office hours". On once being asked by a lady whether he liked dancing, he quipped,"No,I am afraid I am not a very good dancer",and then came a one liner with all the naughtiness at his command, "but I make up for that as I hold extremely well".

Sam was of the opinion that senior officers should be correct in their conduct and never demean the uniform by unbecoming conduct. He issued instructions at the very outset of his tenure as Chief of Staff, that officers should only address the President and Supreme Commander as 'Sir'. A secretary to the government or a minister should be addressed as 'Mr. Secretary' or 'Mr. Minister' as the case may be. This was of course very much in line with his right thinking to maintain the dignity of the uniformed service which was always high on his list of priorities

Once the Defence Secretary strode into the conference room and said rather abruptly to a Colonel sitting among the officers, "You there, will you open the window" (as it was a hot day). Sam angrily told the officer to sit down, and gave the Secretary a piece of his mind, saying, "Mr. Secretary, don't you ever again address my officers in that tone of voice. You may say, Sam, would you please open that window and I shall do it for you. The officer is a Colonel and not 'you there'." The Defence Secretary replied that offence was not meant. To which Sam was to remark angrily, "I don't care what you meant, I heard what you said and don't like it".

It was on his visit to a Gorkha Unit that he acquired the nickname "Sam Bahadur." He asked the smart Gorkha stick orderly if he knew who the Chief was. The soldier replied that he did. He asked him then to name the Chief and pat came the reply "Sam Bahadur." The nickname stuck. It is also the title of a military tune played by the Indian Army. The first occasion that it was played being 'Beating Retreat' at Rajpath on January 29, 1973. He also organized proper training for the army cooks so that at least a proper variety of dishes Indian and Continental dishes were available at the officers messes as well as for the soldiers. He even told the Quarter Master General to have them trained at a five star hotel chain if necessary. Soon both quality and variety of food improved. After K.B. Lal, ICS was appointed Defence Secretary he and Sam went into great detail in preparing the annual report for the Ministry of Defence for the year 1971–72. The result was that a very comprehensive document for the year was presented to Parliament, something hitherto unprecedented. It won the accolades of most Parliamentarians.

Once on a visit to a military unit he enquired from the office commanding the unit,as to what was the disciplinary action called for if a soldier was found to be suffering from Venereal Disease (AIDs was an unknown phenomenon those days). The CO replied that due action would be taken and the hair of the offender would be shaved off. Bringing the retort from Sam, "shave his hair off? Dammit, he didn't do it with his head". In 1972 Manekshaw paid a visit to Nepal and had an audience with the late King Birendra of Nepal. He had been advised by the ambassador not to speak much unless spoken to. He brought the house down by asking the queen during a break in the conversation, "Does his majesty help you in the kitchen?" He also attempted going around Kathmandu alone with Mrs Manekshaw in civilian clothes; but was recognized and had to be rescued from a crowd.

While visiting a Military Hospital he would have a cup of tea with the nursing staff and ask them if they had any sort of problems. The nursing staff would invariably ask for radios, carpets and curtains. Sam would then ask one of the nurses if he could see her room, which could be embarrassing for the nurse as many of her private items would be found in the room. Subsequently it came to be known that his object in visiting the rooms was to find out whether the living accommodation was really comfortable and if anything else could be provided. The word soon spread that he was keen to improve things, so the nurses were better prepared about the upkeep of the room, as well as the items required by them. The local commander would be taken aback and give vent to his annoyance by glaring at the nurses, only to be put at ease by Sam who would say, "They like me so, they talk".

Once a parade commander gave a report ending with the word Shriman. He replied saying, "Same to you". A perplexed commander asked him after the parade what he actually meant. Sam said I thought you said 'be-sharam' (shameless) and, therefore, answered back in the same coin! Once again an officer at the 58 Gorkha Training Centre before beginning a demonstration sought permission by asking "Parade arambh karne ki anumati chahta hun Shriman". To which Sam replied with a smart salute, "I don't know what you said, but you may start"!

The composition of his travel party included usually Mrs. Manekshaw, an ADC, sometimes his Military Assistant and an attendant (which usually meant an orderly attached to him). Once having emplaned he would remove his shoes and shirt, put on his slippers and relax with a novel or peruse files while Mrs Manekshaw used to do crosswords among other things. Of the on flight snacks, Manekshaw's favourites were chicken patties from the Oberoi or the Ashoka Hotel. He was a good host even on the plane and saw to it that everyone on board got enough. Once due to delay even whisky was available for the flight guests, much to the delight of certain bureaucrats on board. Before landing he would give Mrs. Manekshaw some information of relevance to the visit. For instance, that a certain person meeting them was a widower and therefore she should not ask him where his wife was or that he was with them at a certain station and his wife's name was so and so.

After attending the official reception at the airport he would proceed to his place of stay during the visit. He would take the compliments of the guard on duty and meet the guard commander. He would personally meet the guard commander and instruct his staff not to pass the message that the guard was not expected to turn out daily which is the usaul practise in the army.

After a rather speedy wash and cup of tea, Sam would be off on the programme previously decided, meeting the various officers and JCOs of the unit or formation and addressing a Sainik Sammelan or being introduced to troops in their barracks. His famous 'one liners' would be in evidence. If he came across a man who had a longer moustache than his, he would comment, "How dare you have a moustache longer than your Chief". Or on being the number of children, if the reply was more that two, he would retort thinking of his two daughters, "You've beaten your Chief" or "I am junior to you". At the kitchen he would ask the cook, "Who is the better cook, you or your wife?" To Sikh troops it was always "Sat Sri Akaal", "Pind Kera Hai?" (which is your village?) and "Singhni Kite Hai?" (where is your family?).

Earlier reference has been made to Sam's somewhat strained relations with the then Defence Minister Mr Jagjivan Ram. During a talk at the National Defence College after the war, Manekshaw took great delight in emphasizing the close rapport he had with Mrs. Gandhi throughout the war implying rather explicitly, that the Minister for Defence and the bureaucracy had little or no role to play in the execution of operations much to the chagrin of bureaucrats. Later the word went up to Jagjivan Ram who issued instructions to the National Defence College and the Defence Services Staff College, Wellington not to invite Manekshaw to lecture for future courses. But it must be pointed out that Sam once put Mr. Jagjivan Ram in the shadow. At a victory celebration at Bareilly, Jagjivan Ram waxed eloquent about the great contribution he had made towards the victory in the 1971 war. At the end of the talk he was requested to unveil a portrait of the 'Hero of Bangladesh'. It turned out to be a portrait of Sam Manekshaw! Needless to say, Jagjivan Ram left the meeting fuming.

Military historians will undoubtedly be tempted to compare Manekshaw with one of the other great Generals the Indian Army has produced, the legendary General K.S. Thimayya who was described as a soldier's general. He was the only Indian to command a brigade during the second World War and had led the first tank across Zojila during the Kashmir operations thus having an excellent field record. But somehow as Chief he seemed somewhat at sea. He unnecessarily got into a scrap with the political leadership and resigned in 1959 and then withdrew it. Sam, on the other hand, had not had any war experience except in Burma where he received the MC. He had missed the wars of 1947–48, 1962, and 1965. His war record was nothing to compare with Thimayya or Lt General Harbaksh Singh for that matter. But as a Chief of Staff he compares favourably because he more than made up for lack of war experience with brilliance as a staff officer. He handled the political leadership admirably well and the net result was the historic victory where 93,000 POW were taken by the Indian forces.

Manekshaw also took great care and monitored the issue of new cantonments being constructed in various parts of the country. He went into great deliberation to see that every such cantonment was planned as an independent unit with amenity centres, sports grounds, institutes, gardens/parks, movie halls and the like. On his prodding, Army Headquarters insisted on concealed wiring for the new cantonments. The government however preferred overhead wiring on that plea the concealed wiring was very cost-intensive. Ultimately a kind of compromise was reached with some cantonments having concealed wiring and some having overhead wiring. Manekshaw was rather shocked to learn that officers had not received medals awarded to them 5–7 years earlier. He got two cases put up which recommended increasing the capacity of the existing mint or raising a new one by the Ordinance Corps.

Ready wit has always been his forte, once while being interviewed by a lady journalist he kept referring to her as 'sweetheart' constantly, the lady was blushing rather a bit too much, thinking the Army Chief was being fresh with her. At the end of the interview he told his Staff Officer in his usual style, "Sweetheart please see the lady off". At which the journalist said, "Oh you call everyone 'sweetheart'. I thought you were being fresh with me". His Staff Officer felt that he had a ready answer coming given the twinkle in his eye, but probably knowing the ways of the press corps decided not to air it. He could be witty with his staff as well, once in a biographical sketch put up for approval; his date of birth was erroneously shown as April 4, 1969 he sent it back with the comment, "I must have been an absolutely fantastic genius to have been appointed Chief at the tender age of three months". Once the Prime Minister's secretariat sent an anonymous letter for Manekshaw's comments bewailing rampant misuse of authority and nepotism in the army and quoting as a case in question the appointment of a certain major general as Director,Weapons and Equipment. Though a response was not called for, Sam replied on the following lines: "The Oxford Dictionary defines 'nepotism' as 'undue favouritism to relations.' The major general referred to is a caste Hindu and I am an equally high born Parsi. Therefore, there is no religious relationship. The officer is fifty years old and I am fifty-eight,therefore, although I was a precocious child, best medical opinion would rule out paternity in this case. Unfortunately, I have not much scope for nepotism, it is almost too frustrating. The only compotent officer from my community is already the professional head of the Army." The issue was closed thereafter and there was no comeback.

While appearing before the Pay Commission he presented the situation in his typical style. He asked one of the civilian members to get up and stand by his side, when the kit allowance question came up. He now went on to draw a comparison to the man's crumpled shirt, crease in his trousers and shoeless feet with chappals on, he then pointed out to his own polished belt and shoes, ironed shirt and trouser with starch on it, his haircut and asked them to feel his chin for the perfect shave. Manekshaw continued, "At lunch time I will go home, take off my uniform for my batman to straighten out, have a wash and then after lunch relax by reading a book or listening to music, after this I will put on my uniform, brush my hair and come here for the afternoon session. Now take this gentleman, he will sit on one of these sofas and eat from a tiffin box he is carrying. After we finish for the day I will go home have a bath, have a whisky, put on a lounge suit and go to a party. This gentleman will be at the same party having gone to it straight from here, wearing the same clothes as he is here." Thus the officer's kit allowance became quite safe and was not questioned for a long time to come! Even after relinquishing the Chief's office he could make the best of a situation. Once he was dining at an army formation where a meal was being hosted in honour of the President of the day, N. Sanjeeva Reddy. On being served a non-alcoholic drink he accosted the Corps Commander and asked him whether he was supposed to drink only this! The General Officer with all the diplomacy at his command indicated that since the President was present, in accordance with the government policy, no alcoholic beverage was supposed to be served to the guests. Sam would have none of this. He asked one of the waiters with a tray of soft drinks to accompany him and marched up to the President. "Mr. President am I supposed to be drinking this?" he asked, to which the President of course said that the Field Marshal could have a drink of his choice. He now triumphantly told the host that he had it on the authority of the President of India to have a hard drink, and he did so.

He would often tell his staff that he got all the information he required because of his long nose! He was also not hankering after any post retirement sops or sinecures and was not in need of any such jobs. His popularity in the services was high and he could interact to the advantage of the service with the government. He also initiated the process of academic qualifications for service institutions, a Bachelor's Degree for those who qualified from the National Defence Academy, a Master's Degree for those who qualified from the Defence Services Staff College and a PhD for those who qualified from the National Defence College, except in the PhD proposal. All these proposals saw fructification in later years. Whenever a discussion took place on the issue of India developing nuclear capability, Manekshaw, was of the view that any army man worth his salt should be in favour of the most state-of-the-art weapons being made available to the armed forces, and he was no exception to this rule. The only rider he would add was that huge sums of money and talent would be used for the purpose and would only add to the development of a carrier. With all this expense he wondered as to what real use the weapon would be to us. After India exploded its first nuclear device in the summer of 1974, Manekshaw, in a press interview stated that one could not automatically conclude after a single explosion that we had nuclear capability; the most glowing aspect of the explosion was its low cost and the level of secrecy. He added that we had enhanced our strength as a nation, "as we are apt to be kicked around if we are weak".

In the area of the Eastern Sino-Indian Border, he was a votary of the 'Forward Policy' because of its obvious strategic plus points since we now had the infrastructure unlike in 1962, to sustain it. One of these aspects was his decision to locate a brigade at Tangkar La in North Sikkim. We could now assume an offensive position against the Chinese lines of communication in the Chumbi Valley and defend it from a firm position, South Sikkim and the Siliguri corridor. Unfortunately after he demitted office, the policy changed due to the feeling that provocative steps should be avoided. However later it was reverted to, showing Manekshaw`s foresight on the issue.

The post of military secretary to the president was vacant due to the posting out of the incumbent and rumours had started to float that the post, which was by an unwritten rule an army post, would become a rotatory one between the three services. As no major general was available, Sam moved one of his area commanders to the post immediately rather then let it be surrendered. A similar issue pertained to the Inspector General of Assam Rifles (now known as Director General of Assam Rifles) for which the police had put up a case through the ministry of home affairs, for it to be allotted to them as the role of the Assam Rifles covers a spectrum of law and order related affairs. Manekshaw was determined not to let it go and said that all military officers would have to be withdrawn from the Assam Rifles as under military law no police can enjoy the right to issue orders to military officers. The Home Minister had to withdraw the proposal ultimately. Sam did not compromise on the army's traditional rights no matter how great the pressure.

It would not be out of place here to make a mention of Mrs. Manekshaw, a very dignified and straightforward lady, who was a great asset to her husband in tune with the old saying "behind every successful man there is a woman". She worked extensively after the war in raising funds for the Army Wives Welfare Organization and moved about to various places in the country to raise funds for the noble cause. She organized fetes, premieres, sales and the like, making a vast contribution of Rs 2.5 crores in cash and Rs 5 crores in gifts to the Army Wives Welfare Organization by the time she demitted office as chairperson in 1973. Mr. Yashwantrao Chavan who at that point of time was Minister for Finance in the Government of India was approached by Sam to exempt income tax on donations made to the Army Welfare Fund. Mr. Chavan was unable to do so given the rules on the matter, but suggested that the rules could be circumvented if a donation was made to the Prime Minister's relief fund which was exempt from income-tax and the donor had simply to mention in the covering letter that the amount was to be used for the welfare of the armed forces. Chavan himself had been Minister for Defence (1962–66) and was well disposed towards the armed forces. A particular industrialist made the donation of Rs 15 lakhs (which was the cost of one battle tank), in the presence of the President, Prime Minister and three Service Chiefs. Manekshaw aptly said on that occasion "My wife and I go around with a begging bowl to collect money so that none of my wounded soldiers or any of my war widows ever has to beg."

During the battle for Bangladesh, when the decisive stages were being reached, Manekshaw in his appeals to the Pakistan Army had given an assurance that troops who laid down their arms would be treated with dignity and their security would be guaranteed. The Instrument of Surrender also made mention of it. Immediately after the surrender, therefore, people of West Pakistan origin were provided full security by the Indian forces. The setting up of Prisoner of War Camps was a fairly huge task, given the fact that 93,000 personnel laid down arms. Camps were set up literally overnight as the troops had to be brought out of Dhaka with no loss of time. Barracks were arranged for the POWs who stayed in India for nearly two years. When our troops returned from the front they were made to live in tents, whereas the POWs were kept in the barracks. It was a rather ironic scenario that the victors were roasting in tents outdoors but the vanquished army was in barracks enjoying all the comforts of fans, water and coolers. Manekshaw took a great deal of interest in the welfare of the captured troops and saw to it that they had adequate provisions like mosquito nets in summer and warm clothing in winter. During festivals such as Id and the like, he would send greetings to all the inmates of each individual camp. He moved about in the camps with a minimum level of security freely intermingling with them. He would take only his ADC with him and say, "I am in my own country I don't need any protection." He would make enquiries about their welfare and see their bunks, washrooms and kitchen. He was able to communicate well in Urdu, the result of which the Pakistanis felt quite at home with him. Once when he shook hands with a Subedar Major, the latter said to him, "We now see why you have such an excellent fighting force. I have been for 25 years in the Pakistani Army and no general has ever shaken my hand."

Some attempts to escape took place and some were successful as a prisoner of war as per military tradition is duty bound to make an attempt to escape. Since the soldier of the Indian Army has been taught to "shoot to kill" it is well near impossible to expect him to shoot to maim after all his training. Therefore some

POWs were killed in attempts to escape from captivity. At a press conference at the Ashoka Hotel in New Delhi in January 1973, Sam was asked by an American correspondent, "Why have such a large number of prisoners been killed?" to which he replied, "More prisoners die in the US prisons in one year than have died in all my improvised camps. Secondly, so far as a POW of war is duty bound to try and escape, so too, is the sentry duty bound to prevent it. The sentry sees a prisoner running away, he picks up his rifle, aims at the biggest target he can see, the man's back and fires. He has only one simple intention which is to hand over the same number of prisoners to his relief as he took over and not be accused by his superior of permitting a prisoner to escape during his tour of duty."

He had during his tenure as head of the Army an eagle eye for detail. Once while motoring past the officers' flats on Sardar Patel Marg, he noticed seepage in some parts of the housing blocks and immediately ordered the Quarter Master General and the Engineer-in-Chief to take stock of the situation and report back in an hour's time. He proposed multi-storey construction for new accommodation being constructed for the army. He felt that scarcity of land, security, maintenance and economy were overriding factors in favour of high rise buildings.

While travelling to various army stations during his stewardship of the army, he would not use his time in going through the usual routine of witnessing various training demonstrations, mentioning that he had seen enough of it during his career, and that he preferred to see how his troops and officers lived. While visiting the accommodation he would have an array of detailed questions for people accompanying him like, for example, "Why is the light switch so far away from the bed?" "Is it not possible that the lettering on the houses be done more neatly?" "Why is a wardrobe not made in the wall of this bedroom?" Then he would intone, "Who is the clot who designed this house?" This would result in the accompanying Engineer Officer going red in the face as he was the most likely culprit! He summed up his interest in construction works fittingly in the following words, "When the government has accepted the commitment of providing housing for my officers and men, my engineers must ensure they get the best possible."

Earlier mention has been made of the trumped up case against Sam Manekshaw which the then Defence Minister V.K. Krishna Menon had instituted against Manekshaw at the bidding of the late Lt General B.M. Kaul. Once as Chief, Sam found himself walking with Menon at a reception in the President's house. After wishing Mr. Menon, he enquired after his health, and turned to Mrs. Manekshaw and said. "Darling don't you remember Mr. Menon?" Mrs Manekshaw who never hesitated calling a spade, a spade said, "No, I don't" to their former tormentor.

It must be said to his credit that Manekshaw did not indulge in any witch hunt against the officers who gave evidence against him in this trumped up case. Only in one case did he recommend suppression for a particular officer who he felt was lacking in moral character, a trait which showed up during this infamous period of 1961–62, when Sam was Commandant of the Defence Services Staff College, but accepted the ministry's suggestion that the officer be cleared for promotion as the board was of this view. Had Sam put down his views in writing, the officer would have not been able to attain the next rank.

A year after the Indo-Pak war, General Manekshaw was appropriate in his comments while addressing a Rotary conference at Kottayam, Kerala, "There is much joy on this day but there is also much sorrow. In 1943, a beaten and shaken Captain Manekshaw first spoke to the Rotarians. Today I command an excellent army. I have many nightmares. My army fought a gallant and tenacious armed force. Although the war lasted only fourteen days, 3000 of my men were killed and 8500 wounded. I am glad that 50 per cent of the wounded are cured and have rejoined duty. But the remainder are maimed for life. Some will never walk, some will never see, some will be bedridden for life". He then appealed for the retrenched soldiers and officers to be helped to find avenues of employment.

Another anecdote throws light on his rather colourful demeanour. On a visit to an infantry unit, he walked up as per the usual practice while visiting the officers' mess, to sign the visitors' book. A young lady handed him a silver pen from the ink stand, (silver pens in the officers' mess usually do not work) and therefore, Sam told the young lady, "I bet it won't write", to which the lady responded, "I bet it will" and surprisingly enough the pen did. Sam did not fail to send the lady a box of chocolates on his return. He had given instructions to his staff at the headquarters that all visitors' must sign on a single line in the visitors' book irrespective of the rank or status of the visitor and not on one whole page as some VIP visitors' did. Sam also had a great fascination for music which he used to constantly play while in the army house. His collection of records and cassettes was considerable. Visitors to "White Gates" (4, Rajaji Marg) the residence of the Army Chief, would invariably be greeted by a wonderful selection of music if Sam was in the house.

He initiated the practice of sending regimental contingents rather than those selected by battalions for the Republic Day Parades so that the regiment had a wider scope to choose from for this national event. The turnout of the contingents did show a marked improvement. He was also the first Chief of Army Staff to visit the Soviet Union in the spring of 1972.

Earlier in this work, one finds the name of Sher Singh, the brave soldier who saved Manekshaw's life during the Burma campaign. During Manekshaw's tour as Chief, Sher Singh and a few other soldiers of yore belonging to the 54 Sikhs used to call at the Army House with various requests. Manekshaw's instructions were that if any soldier from the 54 Sikhs came to his residence or office he should be allowed to meet them at any time of the day. These venerable gentlemen would then bombard his staff with various requests which were as different as arranging a bag of sugar for a daughter's wedding or securing an immediate out-of-turn promotion for a relative. This was rather impossible at times and his staff had to explain with all the tact at their command that these things were impossible nowadays, only to be told "That in the British time the 'Jangi Lat' (officer in charge of the war office), could issue an order on which immediate action would be taken without question". Even though the Staff Officer to the Chief would then explain that nowadays such unilateral orders would open a Pandora's box of protests, these old veterans would remain unconvinced and make a complaint to Manekshaw about the uncooperative staff officer he had from the 8 Gorkhas, feeling that a Sikh regiment officer would produce better results!

After the 1971 war was over, it became a pressing need to

reorganize the Army with a view to operational experience gained as well as to take care of the needs of the army of the future. The Western Command of the Army which stretched from New Delhi to Jammu & Kashmir was split up and a new command called the Northern Command was established to deal with the operational efforts of the vital territory of Jammu and Kashmir. Sam selected Lt General P.S. Bhagat,a gallant soldier and recipient of the Victoria Cross to head this new command. Incidentally, on the eve of his laying down office as Chief, Sam recommended to the government that this immensely popular and capable officer succeed him as Chief of Staff, but it was shot down, as the then Finance Minister, Y.B. Chavan, lobbied hard for General G.G. Bewoor (who belonged to Maharashtra) A new corps headquarters was also raised at Bhatinda, 10 Corps to reduce the pressure on 11 Corps at Jalandhar which had the task of manning the Punjab border.

After the Shimla Accord between Indira Gandhi and Z.A. Bhutto a team headed by Lt General P.S. Bhagat, VC and Lt General Hamid Khan of Pakistan was formed. Sam had great confidence in Lt Gen Bhagat. During the talks an interesting sidelight was that Generals Bhagat and Hamid Khan, when wanting to consult a lower member of the staff used to give the excuse of "going around the corner". How contact was made from the washroom was not exactly known!

Once the Director of Military Intelligence, Major General D.K. Chandorkar raised the issue of junior officers being with foreign nationals and diplomats. Sam felt that too much snooping in these matters was counter-productive and yielded little or no results. To illustrate the case he mentioned to the Chief of Military Intelligence that if an ADC of his got drunk at the house of a US diplomat and blurted out some kind of information the diplomat tried to get from him in his drunken state, the diplomat would be hard pressed to decipher what the young officer had come out with. The best security he felt was to function at various levels on 'a need to know basis'.

He believed that everyone in the army must give his optimum performance, and felt that decisive leaders who got the job done were needed in the Army, not mere onlookers who could not contribute much. He also laid stress on the ability of the Commander to delegate authority which is an essential ingredient of a competent leader as it allows the junior lot to come to their own conclusions, think for themselves and become leaders of the future. He also laid stress on humility, which was of vital importance.

India's First Field Marshal

Manekshaw was to be appointed a Field Marshal for life and designated Chief of Defence Staff on the eve of Republic Day 1972. As Manekshaw and the other two Chiefs were to be awarded the Padma Vibhushan on that day it was felt that the announcement could be concurrently made. However this was not to be. Particularly due to bureaucratic designs to the contrary. It was decided to refer the matter to the other two Chiefs and the Air Force objected on the ground that it would belittle the Air Force achievements in the war if the Army Chief was appointed Chief of Defence Staff! Since the Defence Minister Jagjivan Ram was also not well disposed towards Sam, it is probable that he had a hand in it.

By the end of 1972, however, the proposal was to arise again and Manekshaw was appointed Field Marshal for life in December 1972. The appointment was to take effect from January 31, 1973. It was proposed that Manekshaw should be given half pay of the retiring Chief and certain perks in tune with the status of the rank, like a small staff and secretariat, residence in Delhi, a car and flag. This was in tune with the practice in the United Kingdom where a Field Marshal is also a government assignee which takes care of his perks. However, these proposals were turned down by the government for no reason, but personal prejudice. Probably, many feel that this was at the instance of the late Mr Jagjivan Ram. In fact, Mr Jagjivan Ram had also made a statement in Chennai in November 1972, that the army was not going to have a five star General or a Field Marshal, but obviously Mrs Gandhi overruled him on this issue. Manekshaw was ultimately given a General's pension of Rs 1200/–and Rs 400/– as extra allowance for the rank of Field Marshal. This was certainly no way to treat a person who occupied the highest rank a soldier can reach. Much later it was rectified towards the end of his days.

In the immediate months following his retirement he remained in Delhi where he availed six months accumulated leave. The government was said to be considering creating a new post called Member Planning Commission (defence) and appointing Field Marshal Manekshaw to it. This was conveyed to him by Prime Minister Indira Gandhi. However, the proposal fell through mainly on account of a press interview Manekshaw gave to a weekly entitled *Dateline Delhi.* He was quoted to have said that had Jinnah asked him to opt for the Pakistani Army and had he risen to the post of the Chief, Pakistan would have won the 1971 war. Also it had him saying words to the effect that London was his favourite city and that he felt at home with the people there. This led to a furore in the parliament in April 1973, on the eve of the defence debate of parliament even though the interview was published in January 1973. It could therefore be justifiably concluded that it was a deliberately motivated report due to the fact that the news agencies carried it a full three months after it first appeared in print. This caused a fairly big hue and cry.

When examined in detail the question about London being his favourite city was absolutely in order. The interview had gone like this:

Q: Field Marshal which is your favourite city?
A: In India or abroad?

Q: The whole world.
A: My favourite city abroad is London, as I feel at home there. I know the language and the people and they know me.

When put in the right perspective one could well understand the context in which the comments were made, but both statements were blown out of proportion by certain vested interests to deny an appointment with honour to the Field Marshal. The first statement regarding the Pakistani Army was given in a lighter vein but this is something his enemies cashed in on. During the six months grace period of his accumulated leave he was staying at the Military Engineering Service Inspection Bungalow at Delhi Cantonment, Manekshaw was provided with a rather old Dodge car for his personal use. It may be pointed out that no appropriate house was provided for the Field Marshal even though he was entitled to the same. When he was asked by an interviewer while inaugurating the Statesman

Vintage Car Rally if he had interest in vintage cars and had any intention of acquiring one, Sam gave the following reply: "Oh yes indeed, I am most interested in vintage cars. As far as acquiring one is concerned I don't have to go very far as the Defence Ministry have been kind enough to give me a vintage car for my use which I am running these days!"

In the spring of 1973, the Field Marshal and Mrs. Manekshaw had been invited to tour the United Kingdom and this visit took place in May 1973. His only request to the British Government was that he should be able to visit the 2 Battalion the Royal Scots, the Battalion to which he had been attached when commissioned into the army. When the visit took place in May 1973, Manekshaw presented the battalion Officers' Mess, a silver khukri, sometime later he received the following letter from Major General W.T. Campbell CBE, Colonel of the Regiment:

> *I have just returned home from a visit to Edinburgh and our Regimental Headquarters where I was so delighted to see the beautiful khukri which you have so kindly presented to us as a reminder of your association with the Regiment. It is now proudly displayed in one of our show cases with an appropriate description.*
>
> *My attention has also been drawn to an important 'double' which you have achieved for the Regiment through your promotion. We have already the distinction of having had the first Field Marshal from the British Army when it was bestowed in 1736 by King George II upon George Hamilton the First Earl of Orhnay who was then Colonel of the Regiment and I now hope that you will permit us to claim this 'double.' I thought you might be interested in this remarkable coincidence.*

The late Prime Minister Morarji Desai called upon the Field Marshal in 1978 to head the Sports Authority of India but nothing effective which was recommended by him was implemented by the government during this period. He, however, has taken on several directorships and chairmanships of various private sector companies. During the time that Sam was Commandant of the Defence Services Staff College in Wellington, he bought a piece of a hill top (about 3.5 acres) in upper Coonoor,the township adjoining the Wellington Cantonment. Here he built 'Stavaka', his residence since 1973. 'Stavaka' is the name of the headquarters of the senior most military authority in Russia and was the name of the headquarters of Field Marshal Stalin. It finds mention in Leo Tolstoy's novel *War and Peace*. The Field Marshal spent 5–10 days at Coonoor in a month as he was out of town in connection with the various companies he was associated with. His wife, Mrs. Siloo Manekshaw died in 2001.

His statement at New Delhi on November 3, 2002, regarding Ayub Khan's conversation with Jawaharlal Nehru regarding his (Ayub's) intention to solve the Kashmir problem once and for all is a true fact but Nehru rather arrogantly spurred Ayub's offer away. One finds mention of it in Ayub Khan's *Friends Not Masters*, an autobiography. Sam was also right in recounting that Bhutto had given an assurance of a similar nature to Indira Gandhi at Shimla in 1972 on the issue of converting the Line of Control as the International border.

At a recent function while reviewing the Indian Military Academy Passing Out Parade on the occasion of its 70th Anniversary on December 10, 2002 he addressed the cadets from the saluting base at the hallowed drill square of the Academy, his own alma mater. Looking sprightly and erect at 88 years of age, he impressed upon his audience that changes had taken place in the army down the seven decades since he had joined it. As a young Lieutenant, he recalled he used to be sent across to the enemy lines at night to find their positions, now the satellites took care of all that, he also mentioned vast changes in the mode of transportation from the mule to the motor vehicle and from the .303 rifle to the finest gun in the world. He went on to point out to the young officers that the nation had no room for losers and if they were defeated they should not come back as they would be a disgrace to the nation. "Even your gharwali (wife) will despise you". The audience roared its approval.

S.H.F.J. Manekshaw: A Life in Retrospect

The narration of the life of Sam Manekshaw is also the narration of the story of the life of the modern Indian Army. He had been witness to both failures and success of the Indian Army. All his life has been dedicated to soldiering and it must be said that true leadership has been his greatest asset. He showed rare personal courage during the Battle of Sittang in Burma for which he won the well deserved Military Cross. He later proved his mettle as a staff officer in the Operations Directorate during the Kashmir Operations of 1947–48. As Commandant of the Infantry School he gave new orientation to military strategy and planning. As Commandant of the Defence Services Staff College, he had to face the worst crisis of his career which was almost wrecked by the ambitious Lt General B.M. Kaul. He kept his cool and maintained equanimity during this crisis which lasted about eighteen months, not allowing the working of this premier institution to suffer. The army called upon him during its darkest hour to take charge of the ill-fated 4 Corps which had been mauled by the Chinese. As Western and Eastern Army Commander his leadership was of a high order. History called upon him as head of the Indian Army to play a role which will undoubtedly be remembered in golden letters for years to come. He thus deservedly was conferred the highest rank any soldier can aspire to reach. Above all these factors it must also be noted that he was humane and had a great sense of humour. All these are great attributes of a decent human being and a good leader. Sam Manekshaw fulfilled both these qualifications.

(Published by United Services Institution of India, 2003)

□

16

Jacob's Revelations on Manekshaw

Former Governor of Goa and Punjab Lt General J.F.R. Jacob or 'Jake' to his friends, is in the news for his views on Field Marshal Manekshaw's role in the 1971 conflict. In an interview to well known TV journalist Karan Thapar on CNBC TV 18, Jacob claims that early in April 1971, Sam had asked Jacob as Chief of Staff of the Eastern Command to be ready to attack East Pakistan at short notice which Jacob opposed on grounds of lack of required amount of transport in the given terrain, the monsoon being around the corner which could lead to the advancing army getting bogged down, and more significantly international opinion could be hostile to India at that juncture (in April 1971). Thus Jacob has contradicted the claim which Sam Manekshaw has made on several occasions that he had given a spontaneous rejoinder to Mrs Gandhi and the cabinet in late April 1971 opposing intervention in East Pakistan, asking for time to prepare the army for war, and going on to say that defeat was "guaranteed 100 per cent" in case of immediate intervention. In other words, Jacob has categorically tried to prove that Manekshaw was being economical with the truth by making tall claims that he single-handedly overturned the cabinet decision which could have brought a Waterloo on the nation.

The truth probably lies somewhere in between. Unfortunately, neither Mrs Indira Gandhi nor Mr Jagjivan Ram, the then Defence Minister are alive to testify on Manekshaw's behalf regarding the Cabinet meeting he talks about. Some members of that cabinet like Dr Karan Singh are still alive, but he has not expressed his views. It is also possible that he may have for some reason been absent at the meeting. Manekshaw did probably speak out, but not after first sounding out Jacob who opposed the move. Jacob has also debunked Manekshaw's pronouncement that he never sought any office of profit from the government upon his relinquishing office as Chief of the Army Staff on Jan 15, 1973. In an interview to Karan Thapar on July 28, 1999, Manekshaw said that he had offers of the High Commissionership of UK and Governorship of Maharashtra from the government but had turned them down as he had taken "an oath" not to accept any office from the government upon completing his tenure as Chief of Staff. Jacob says that on the contrary, Mankeshaw was "dejected and lonely" and upon being asked by him (Jacob) what the matter was, said he had just returned from a meeting with Mrs Gandhi, wherein he had requested that he be appointed as Deputy Chairman of the Planning Commission which Mrs Gandhi turned down and offered him a High Commissionership of a Commonwealth country (Jacob does not specify which one.) In substance Jacob once again accused Sam Manekshaw of misrepresenting the facts of the matter.

Jacob does mention during the course of the dialogue that his not testifying against Manekshaw during the course of the inquiry held against him when he was Commandant of the Defence Services Staff College Wellington and Jacob was a member of the faculty led to Manekshaw being absolved by the inquiry which was based on the charges of Sam's supposed "anti-national" activities. He was supposed to have referred to Indians publicly as natives and being too close to certain foreign officers who were under training. By saying this, Jacob means obliquely that there was some substance in the accusations. Some other people who were posted at the DSSC at the time have also confirmed this.

About the actual 1971 conflict, Jacob says that contrary to his advice, Manekshaw did not want Dhaka listed in the war plans as an objective and kept on harping on Chittagong and Khulna as objectives, whereas Jacob kept insisting Dhaka and taking the then Director of Military Operations General Gill into confidence shuffled troops (3 Brigades) in such a manner that the objective of Dhaka was not compromised and has even quoted the late Air Chief Marshal P.C. Lal from his memoirs to the effect that the

Army plans did not anticipate any fall of Dhaka. (P.C. Lal: *My Years in the IAF*). During the course of the battle as Jacob claims, he ignored Manekshaw's instructions to the contrary and kept the thrust on Dhaka. Jacob goes on to add that had Manekshaw been more emphatic about Dhaka as an objective the war would have ended much earlier and had he (Jacob) not ignored his instructions (of not mentioning Dhaka) the army could have got bogged down resulting in many more casualties and not so glorious an outcome. It must, however, be borne in mind that Jacob certainly functioned with more powers than normal as Chief of Staff at the Eastern Command as Manekshaw for reasons best known to him preferred to deal with Jacob rather than the late Lt General J.S. Arora who was Army Commander of the Eastern Command. J.F.R. Jacob has mentioned these facts in his book *Surrender at Dhaka* published in 1997. The non listing of Dhaka as an objective by Sam and Jacob shuffling troops with Gill's connivance is also mentioned in the book. Gill and Arora were alive at that time and to the best of my knowledge did not contradict Jacob.

Close on the heels of Jacob's interview, Gohar Ayub Khan (former Foreign Minister of Pakistan and son of the late Pakistan President Field Marshal Ayub Khan) has come out (also in an interview with Karan Thapar) with the shocking accusation of coming close to naming Sam Manekshaw as the officer who leaked out Army plans of the 1965 war for a paltry sum of Rs 20000 as his wife wanted to start a canning unit for fruits and vegetables. Given Gohar Ayub's well known record as an India basher, his own less than credible record of alleged graft when his father was in power, and the vague nature of his charges no one will probably consider them worth the paper they are written on. It should be added that he first mentioned these vaguely two years ago, he has now published his father's diaries and promises another book later.

However, Jacob's interview must be given some credence as Manekshaw did have the tendency of speaking with a bit of bluff and bluster bringing his own role to fore. It must also be added that he made up for his shortcomings by ample leadership qualities which deservedly won him the honour of being India's first Field Marshal. It may have been in the fitness of things if Jacob had put down all his experiences in his book in 1997.

□

17

Surjit Singh Barnala: The Man for all Seasons

A constitutional statesman is in general a man of common opinion and uncommon abilities....
Walter Bagehot, 1826–1877

Surjit Singh Barnala presently occupies the prominent office of Governor of the State of Tamil Nadu. He is however an unconventional governor in more ways than one, practising what he preaches and has a rare humility that is seldom seen in occupants of high office. His fondness for the fine arts is well known and is himself an artist of some repute, having held art exhibitions at Patiala, Hyderabad, Chennai and Puducherry. The Hyderabad exhibition was held exclusively to help pay for the dwellings for landless, roadside labourers of Hyderabad, to be provided to them by the government of Andhra Pradesh. The proceeds of those in Chennai and Puduchherry have been donated for the relief of the October 8, 2005 earthquake victims.

In 1996, Barnala wrote his autobiography titled, *The Story of an Escape*, which was republished in 2002. In 2005, its Braille edition was published and released at Dehradun, the capital of Uttarakhand state, which he had served during his term as the first governor after its formation. The book is available in Urdu, Hindi, Punjabi, Tamil and Telugu. At present he is working on a sequel to those memoirs. His autobiographical musings are written in the racy style of a travelogue. He was so irked by living in a high security zone that he often chose to travel incognito in a truck passing off as a humble Sikh farmer. Often he was mistaken for a militant on the run, and on one occasion this landed him in police custody at Lucknow. That account gives a vivid picture of the trauma experienced by the Sikh community in the years when terrorism stalked the Punjab.

Barnala had his university education in Lucknow, a city which retains a special place in his heart. He worked as a volunteer when the exodus of refugees from Burma took place in 1941. It was during this period he learnt that helping others makes one more fulfilled and gives one greater joy in life. He passed his LLB examination in April 1946.

Emerging from the background of a flourishing district lawyer, Surjit Singh ventured into the mired and treacherous field of politics. (He had been an activist of the Akali Dal since the 1950s) during the assembly elections of 1967 that. Soon the man from Barnala was rubbing shoulders with the greats of the political arena on equal terms. Two years after he entered the Punjab assembly, he was designated Education Minister of the Punjab. Among his handiwork was the establishment of the Guru Nanak Dev University at Amritsar and making Punjabi the medium of instruction in schools and colleges. Then came the years of struggle, which culminated in the declaration of internal emergency on the fateful midnight of 25 June, 1975. Barnala was among those apprehended under MISA. It is true that he was kept under sub-human conditions at Jalandhar jail along with many inmates like Jagdev Singh Talwandi. The depressing atmosphere of the draconian emergency convinced many of them that they would spend the rest of their lives behind prison bars. Later he was moved to the Patiala gaol where he was kept in circumstances which were much improved and it was here that he began to develop skills as an artist. He gained proficiency as an amateur painter of portraits and improved his skills in the art of landscape painting during his tenure in Dehradun as governor of Uttarakhand (2000–2003). He used to say that the Uttarankhand countryside offered a new landscape, after every kilometre. Thus one understands the many parts a consummate player on the stage of the world can in his time play.

The author in the company of Sardar Surjit Singh Barnala, Governor of Tamil Nadu, at the Morarji Desai Memorial function organised by Bharatiya Vidya Bhavan Dehradun. Mr Barnala had just been presented the author's book on the late Prime Minister

In the historic year 1977, parliamentary elections were called by Mrs. Gandhi when no one expected it, least of all the gentlemen of the opposition. Victory at the hustings beckoned, high office lay ahead. After hectic electioneering during which the public unstintedly supported him with funds to the extent of throwing full purses at him, Barnala won the Sangrur seat by a record margin of 1.70 lakh votes. This support was required because the opposition candidates, having been in detention for 19 months, had a meager financial pool at their disposal. He records in his memoirs a scene of the campaign, *We went from shop to shop in Sangrur asking for votes. Our party symbol, the scales could be seen everywhere. A roadside cobbler fished through his day's earnings and produced a soiled one rupee note and handed it to me. I did not refuse as it would have hurt him and made him unhappy. Tears welled up in his eyes as I hugged him and accepted his token offering. That one rupee note is still with me.*

Barnala was selected to join the cabinet of the late Morarji Desai, as Minister in charge of Food, Agriculture, Rural Development and Irrigation, an omnibus ministry which is now split up into many departments. His tenure in the Janata cabinet was marked by the decontrol of sugar which allowed people to jettison the Public Distribution System and opt for the commodity in the open market. He was also able to remove restrictions on the movement of food grains throughout the country. He held hectic negotiations which led to the conclusion of the Farrakka Accord with Bangladesh and he once had an interesting conversation with President Jimmy Carter of the United States during his visit to Delhi. President Carter flooded him with a volley of questions on agricultural output and much else. Barnala saw the able administrator Morarji Desai in his element, and also got a glimpse of his well known fads. However, it was all over too soon and when the Charan Singh ministry demitted office in August of 1979 and Barnala was within striking distance of becoming the Prime Minister but fate willed otherwise.

Then followed the bloody years of terrorism in Punjab, when all hope seemed to be lost as folly mounted upon folly. Operation Blue Star was launched, with dire consequences. In those crucial times Barnala underwent detention in a government rest house at Panchmari (MP) in central India. He was released in April 1985, and was one of the chief architects of the Rajiv-Longowal Accord. It fell upon Barnala to administer the healing touch when the Akalis stormed to power in the elections of September 1985, and he was named Chief Minister. We see through his eyes in his memoirs the tight-rope walking he performed with Akali rebels on one side and the hostile centre on the other. On a number of occasions he had a narrow escape as the spectre of terrorism overshadowed the land of five rivers from dawn to dusk and dusk to dawn. Abruptly in the spring of 1987, Barnala's government was dismissed by the Congress government at the centre under Article 356. It is felt with some justification that had he continued for a full term, militancy could have been curbed much earlier.

On December 5, 1988, Barnala appeared before the Akal Takht to accept the order of excommunication which had been passed against him in 1986. Barnala appealed for forgiveness as no man was above committing mistakes. The Akal Takht under the leadership of Darshan Singh Ragi pronounced its judgment, a wooden placard was to be hung around his neck for twenty-one days with the words,

'We sinners ever falter, you are the forgiver.' He was then tied to a pole and directed to recite the *mool mantra* (the intial three lines of the Granth Sahib) five times. Thereafter he was ordered to clean the *sangat's* shoes and wash utensils at the *langar* for seven days, recite Japji Sahib five times extra for twenty-one days, organize five Akhand Paths (non-stop recitation of the Granth Sahib) and make an offering of Rs 1100/– to the Akal Takht on completion. On the twenty-second day he was readmitted to the Sikh Panth.

In 1990, the National Front ministry sent Barnala to Tamil Nadu as governor where, though he held office only for 8 months he created a precedent unparalleled in the working of the constitution and became possibly the only governor who has refused to send an indictment against his ministry at the bidding of the centre. This was regarding the alleged activities of the LTTE as suggested by the Chandra Shekhar government. Because of this the people of Tamil Nadu have a special regard for him. During this period he had a chance meeting with an astrologer who made shocking predictions all of which came true. He was also responsible for the establishment of a gurudwara at Rameswaram.

Barnala was included in the Vajpayee Ministry of 1998 as Minister for Chemicals and Fertilizers. It was his shock defeat from Sangrur in the Lok Sabha polls of 1999 which led to his being excluded from the NDA government. Thus it came to pass that he came to Uttarakhand as head of that state when the province was formed. During the two years that he was in Dehradun he functioned as a 'people's governor' with his finger on the pulse of the people's problems and aspirations. He toured the state extensively, reaching every nook and corner and will be long remembered for his genuine approach to men and matters. In January 2003, he was transferred to Andhra Pradesh as Governor. In November 2004 he began his second innings in Tamil Nadu. Without doubt here also he has proved to be a true head of a state for whom service to the people of the state is paramount. He is at present catching up on learning the Tamil language which he began during his first tenure in 1990–91. It is interesting to recall that writing in *The Harijan* on August 17, 1947, Gandhiji had noted that a provincial Governor must acquire the knowledge of the language of the state he heads, in this respect Barnala is fulfilling an ideal laid down by the Mahatma. In June 2006 he was re-appointed Governor of Tamil Nadu for a fresh five-year term.

It can be justifiably hoped that this sprightly political leader who has entered the eighth decade of his life will play a valuable role in the political life of the Indian republic for a considerable number of years to come.

(Based on an article published in The Himachal Times, Dehradun, December 2003 and duly updated later on)

□

18

Veer Savarkar: A Historical Review

The recent controversy regarding the unveiling of the portrait of Barrister V.D. Savarkar in the Central Hall of Parliament the Mecca of the world's largest democracy by President Abdul Kalam is of consequential importance for the Sangh Parivaar and its allies.

The main opposition party, the Congress boycotted the function and according to press reports the Congress President pulled up Mr. Pranab Mukherjee and former Speaker Shivraj Patil who were members representing the Congress in the all party committee which unanimously decided that Savarkar's vignette should adorn the Central Hall.

In the twentieth century among the revolutionary leaders of India, no doubt Savarkar has a place of eminence; his copy book was however blotted by his role in the Gandhi murder conspiracy.

Born in May 1883, Vinayak Damodar Savarkar hailed from Bhagur in Nasik district of present day Maharashtra. While graduating from Fergusson College, Pune, he organized the first revolutionary outfit in Bombay Presidency called "Abhinav Bharat". His writings had a patriotic flavour which brought him eminence in this field. He also produced novels and plays from his versatile pen. In 1906 he set forth by ship to England and qualified as a barrister and was called to Gray's Inn but enrolment to the bar eluded him.

On the occasion of the 50th Anniversary of the Great Mutiny, in 1907 he organized a function in London. Around this time he had his first contact with Gandhi who was also in England from

South Africa. The "Abvhinav Bharat" was becoming more active in its functioning in Maharashtra. Madan Lal Dhingra went to the gallows for assassinating Sir Curzon Wyllie. Three youths from Maharashtra were hanged for killing the collector of Nasik. In the Nasik conspiracy case Savarkar was deported to India. The rugged barrister however jumped overboard through the shi p's port-hole of the water closet as it neared Marseilles but was re-arrested on French soil. He appealed for sanctuary in the form of political asylum from France and ultimately the case went to the International Court of Justice at The Hague whose judgement went in favour of the British government. Savarkar was sentenced to 50 years imprisonment and spent 14 years in the Andamans toiling in the swamps. It is during this period that he supposed to have pleaded for mercy. He was later shifted and detained at Ratnagiri from 1924 onwards. After the Congress ministry came to power in Bombay Presidency in 1937 "Tatyarao" as he was popularly known, was released from captivity.

Savarkar joined the Hindu Mahasabha and it is a tribute to his popularity that he was elected for six consecutive terms as President. He was however in close touch with the Mahatma's assassin Nathuram Godse and his accomplice Narayan Apte.

On January 21, 1948 after the bomb blast at Gandhi's prayer meeting, Prof J.C. Jain of Mumbai's Ram Narain Ruia College passed a bit of vital information to Morarji Desai, Home Minister of Bombay Presidency (later Prime Minister of India 1977-79). It was based on this information from Jain who knew Madan Lal Pahwa(who had thrown the bomb) that Desai ordered on the same day, J.D. Nagarwala Deputy Commmissinor of Police (CID) to apprehend Vishnu R. Karkare,a former Munci pal Councillor of Ahmednagar and place Savarkar under unobtrusive surveillance. Jain had told Morarji that Savarkar according to Madan Lal was encouraging the militants like Godse in their activities and a conspiracy was afoot to eliminate the Mahatama.

Two independent witnesses saw Godse and Apte at Savarkar's residence in the first two weeks of January and they were conferring with him. According to Digamber Badge who turned approver, Apte told him that "Tatyarao (Savarkar) says that Gandhi's 100 years are up" but this could not be corroborated. Also Savarkar is supposed to have said to Godse and Apte on the last occasion they met "return successful" ominous words indeed. Savarkar was arrested on February 2, 1948.

Even though Savarkar was acquitted for lack of evidence on February 10, 1949 a shadow of doubt remained and Sardar Patel felt that he was undoubtedly a part of the conspiracy. Morarji Desai's testimony in the trial also pointed to it.

Fifty-five years after the sacrilege at Birla House when the Mahatma fell to Godse's bullets a debate regarding his assassins and the conspiracy has returned to haunt the nation.

(Published in The Himachal Times, Dehradun)

□

MISCELLANY

19

Review of "Missed Opportunities: Indo-Pak War 1965"

This book authored by Major General Lachman Singh Lehal, a veteran of the Indian Artillery who has had considerable experience of battle has been re-published after a gap of several years. He has won the VRC in the 1947 Kashmir Operations. Although primarily on the 1965 Indo-Pak combat, which broke out after a series of hostilities the volume covers the genesis starting with the partition of the subcontinent in 1947. Of the partition the author quotes a contemporary source: "The killings were pre-medieval in ferocity. Neither age nor sex was spared; mothers with their babies in their arms were cut down...Both sides were equally merciless."

In the run up to the battle, Lehal has wisely gone into the military geography of both nations. India had to its advantage geographical unity. Pakistan however had a good network of roads and the cantonments of Sialkot, Kharian and Jhelum are well located for an offensive warfare. The bulk of our army was built up from the concept of "martial races" devised by the British which covered certain races from Punjab, NWFP, UP, Rajasthan and Maharashtra. Field Marshal Wavell had said in March 1947, "I believe that the stability of the Indian Army may perhaps be a deciding factor in the future of India. It has shown how all communities may work together to meet a common danger with comradeship and devotion."

Pakistan was keen to rekindle the Kashmir dispute following

the Chinese invasion of 1962, which resulted in the well known debacle for the Indian Army, Nehru had died in the summer of 1964, and talks of Sheikh Abdullah with General Ayub Khan and his advisers had failed. The hawkish Pakistani Foreign Minister Z.A. Bhutto was also goading his President to begin hostilities.

The Rann of Kutch incident was the starting point in the spring of 1965. The launch of the Gibraltar force began in early August and this heralded the first infiltration of the Kashmir Area. The offensive in the Haji pir Kishangana bulges began in late August. On 28 August Haji pir fell to the Indian Paratroopers led by Major Ranjit Singh Dayal who won the coveted MVC. The battles at Chhamb, Khem Karan and Sialkot are vividly described. The victories at Assal Uttar and Dograi were indeed historic wherein our troops of the Jat Regiment reached the outskirts of Lahore after crossing the Ichhogil Canal (Battle of Dograi). The author in his narration does not give much credit to the IAF, a claim disputed by the Air Force commanders of the day who talk of the massive air strike at Sargodha, and other strikes at Kohat and Rawalpindi as well as attacking many supply trains.

On the whole the author is of the view that the 1965 operations were a "draw". His analysis is undoubtedly one of great detail.

(Review published in Defence Watch)

□

20

The Mecca of Military Learning: Under a Coffee Table Scanner

The armed forces in Post Independence India had a fairly equitable deal as far as the assets division due to the partition of the country was concerned. However one set back, in no manner trivial, was the loss of the Staff College, a vital institution for any army, to Pakistan, as it was located at Quetta. The story of the Indian Staff College, to be located at Wellington in the Nilgiris is well described in the elegant 242-page coffee table book recently brought out by this famed institute aptly described as the 'Mecca of military learning'. The Wellington Cantonment nestled in the Nilgiri hills of Tamil Nadu is situated in environs which have a touch of being both quaint and romantic.

The heritage of Quetta was formidable, and the Staff College which was established there in 1907 had Field Marshals Auchinleck and Montgomery on its faculty in the 1930s. Field Marshal K.M. Carriappa was the first Indian alumnus and Lt Gen Kulwant Singh the second. Brig S.D. Verma from Quetta was given the duty of setting up the Indian Staff College and after visiting various military stations zeroed in on the scenic place called Wellington on November 3, 1947. Thus began the saga of the Defence Services Staff College. The credit for laying the foundations of this unique military college must go to a doughty British General 'Joe' Lentaigne who was its Commandant for seven long years from 1948 to 1955. Lentaigne was a soldier's soldier, and saw to it that the College had its permanent home at Wellington. The ambience of the DSSC and the major portion of its layout and buildings as they stand today, are a tribute to Lentaigne's far-sightedness and sound judgment. Described in minute detail in this glossy edition, is the absorbing story of how the College became more Indianized in its training, getting rid of the 'Camberly hangover', going in for a broad-based training approach, how the system of competitive examination was introduced, how the Sino-Indian conflict of 1962 brought about a definite shift in studying tactics and problems related to India and Indian conditions, how a chance visit by the Vice Chancellor of Madras University resulted in the College acquiring postgraduate status, how the emblem of wisdom 'the owl' changed its motto from Latin to Sanskrit and how guest speakers from prime ministers and presidents have held forth with words of wisdom when addressing the officers who were doing the course.

One gets a ringside and technicolour view of the intensive training of the three service wings of the army, navy and air force as well as civilian officers of the bureaucracy and foreign officers from a diverse range of countries. The Forward Area Tours which cover Ladakh as well as the eastern frontier, the all India Industrial and Demonstration Tour, the joint services war games, the institutionalized training of officers' wives and adept use of Information Technology is also covered.

It is pertinent to point out that the two students who passed through the portals of the DSSC, Obsanjo of Nigeria and Rabuka of Fiji became Presidents of their respective countries. Three of its Commandants became Chiefs of the Indian Army. The book also features a pictorial write up on the British style bungalows of Wellington which still retain their British names like Cedars, West Grove, Cyclesmere, etc. the main buildings of the DSSC, the flora and fauna of the Nilgiris, the Staff College Amateur Dramatics Society, and the Ooty Hunt, the only hunt that survives in the Southern Hemisphere East of Suez and much else capturing the spirit of much of the Wellington lore.

Edited by Brig R.K. Arora this volume will occupy pride of place in the list of books on defence matters. The last word must belong to the foreword by Field Marshal Sam Manekshaw himself a former Commandant of the DSSC who says, "The requirement of 'Jointmanshi p' amongst the various services for effecting suitable military responses, is becoming increasingly evident to armies the world over. Our countrymen should be rest assured that this College is imparting requisite training to the future Commanders and Staff of the three Services to face these challenges."

(The Defence Services Staff College: A Coffee Table Book; Published by Defence Services Staff College, Wellington)

□

21

Defence Budgeting X-rayed

Wing Commander Srinivas is eminently qualified to write about India's Defence Budgeting system. An officer of the accounts department of the Air Force, he is a Postgraduate in Business Administration and an alumni of the prestigious Defence Services Staff College.

This volume deals with a background of defence budgeting system, trends of defence expenditure, the national budgeting vis-à-vis defence budgeting, planning of mordernization through budgeting in the armed forces, need for reforms in this sector, the debate on arms imports vs indigenization, cost of military manpower, defence procurement policy, expenditure in defence and pointers related to China and Pakistan and affordability of defence expenditure, to mention some of the topics covered.

The veteran defence analyst Air Cmde (Retd) Jasjit Singh in his introduction emphasizes that defence and development cannot, by any stretch of the imagination be taken as mutually exclusive entities, and that human development cannot have much chance of success under an atmosphere of violence, and insecurity. He also laments that the Finance Commission's recommendation of increase in defence expenditure by 3 per cent by 2004 was ignored without any plausible reason.

The manpower intensive standing army demands a lion's share in pay and allowances. A certain amount has also to be reserved for disaster management. These are pertinent issues which every defence economist must be well aware of. Also the term 'value for money' highlights not only the appropriateness of the best of modernization but also the optimum use of the state of the art equipment.

On the whole a comprehensive study of our Defence Budgeting.

(Review of 'Budgeting for Indian Defence: Issues of Contemporary Relevance' published in Defence Watch October 2008)

□

22

The Reflections of a Thinking Man's General

Lt Gen S.K. Sinha is a genuine intellectual in every sense of the word. His career in the army was distinguished and he finished his innings in olive green as Vice Chief of Staff in 1983. Unfortunately his claim for the top job of Chief of the Army was overlooked in favour of a junior officer in the same year leading to Sinha seeking premature retirement. However in later years he excelled himself as ambassador to Nepal. In 1997, the Gujral government sent him as governor of Assam and he was given a second term in 2002 (a rare occurrence). In 2003 he was transferred as governor of Jammu & Kashmir, in which capacity he continues to serve the border province with distinction. It is doubtful if Jammu & Kashmir could have a better head of state at this crucial juncture when terrorism is raising its ugly head.

This book consists of Sinha's speeches at various universities, military institutions and other functions. He is fairly candid in his views and deals with his subject objectively with the incisiveness of a bibliophile. The first section of this volume deals with the secessionist threats to India. He describes the Naga problem, throws light on Indo-Nepal relations, the Assam imbroglio of foreign migrants, the Punjab terrorist menace in which thirty thousand innocents lost their lives, and the continuing internal war in Jammu & Kashmir with the grasp of an insider with an eye for detail highlighting the crucial phases of these tragic events.

While in Assam, Sinha was able to identify with the local populace to a large degree. He was described by a leading daily as "our man in Raj Bhavan". He had a portrait of Sankardev, the patron saint of Assam installed at the Governor's residence, he had the Bharat Ratna awarded to former Chief Minister Bordoloi and much else which is chronicled in this writing. Turning to Jammu and Kashmir, Sinha is fairly emphatic that the worst is over in the troubled state.

Sinha's writings on military matters are well researched and have the touch of a veteran with a sprinkling of humour in the right places. He touches upon the ups and downs that the uniformed personnel have been through both in pre and post independence India. Apart from our Thimayyas and Manekshaws, he dwells on personalities as diverse as Field Marshal Sir William Robertson who rose from Private to Field Marshal and Gen Douglas Macarthur who was one of the most celebrated Generals of the second World War.

This book is a 'must read' for a diverse audience.

(Review of 'Governor's Musings' published in Defence Watch May 2006)

□

23

Sam – Who is India's Bahadur

Military legends are difficult subjects for biographies. For there will always be two or more opinions to the historic role they have played. Be it Montgomery, Patton, or Slim the story is similar. Our very own Sam Bahadur is somewhat apart no doubt; the entire nation went euphoric about him in the heady days of 1971-72 when he was a sort of a 'cult hero'. Even his worst detractors would admit he was a commander to whom leadership came naturally. But controversy he has courted; or controversy has courted him. Depinder Singh`s book fulfils a long standing wait for an authentic work on India's First Field Marshal written by the officer who was his Military Assistant and who himself has had a chequered career in the Army which ended as head of the IPKF in Sri Lanka. "No man is a hero to his valet" goes the oft-repeated saying, but for Depinder Singh Sam obviously has no warts. This is not without justification. If any Chief after Thimayya upheld the dignity of the man in uniform with a pinnacle it was Sam and Sam alone. The book throws light on many interesting hitherto unknown facets. His interaction with the political leadership in the run up to the Bangladesh war, his fiercely independent presentations to the higher echelons of bureaucracy, some political tales of the late L.N. Mishra, how he received the nickname "Sam Bahadur" from a humble Gurkha soldier called Harka Bahadur, his cool calm throughout the war, his meticulous choice of detail in welfare matters, his heroic efforts along with Mrs Manekshaw to care of the maimed veterans and widows, his strained relations with Defence Minister Jagjivan

Ram and his almost being appointed Chief of Defence Staff are highlighted for the first time.

Manekshaw's ready wit and sparkling humour gets the place it deserves in the volume. He once asked a Commanding Officer what punishment was given to a soldier who had venereal disease, the latter replied that his head was shaved off. Only to invite Sam's rather biting answer, "Dammit, he didn't do it with his head!" Such anecdotes are Sam's forte. No narration on him can be complete without these and the author does not disappoint his readers on this score. The book is full of these encounters.

However a full and critical account of the legend is still to come. For example, the book does not go into much detail of the controversy with the late Lt General B.M. Kaul which almost led to Sam's exit from the army when he was the Commandant of the Defence Services Staff College. Researchers of the period know that it was a caricature of Kaul which was done by Sam at an army exercise while Sam was commanding a division at Jammu and Kaul at Ambala that led to the caustic relationship. It took a nasty turn when Kaul began targeting Manekshaw for being too Western in his approach and citing the putting up portraits of Clive and Warren Hastings in the Staff College as evidence. The enquiry headed by the late Lt General Daulat Singh exonerated Manekshaw and desired that his detractors be censured. The episode would deserve at least a chapter worth mentioning; but the author does not go into much enumeration. Another notable omission is Sam's well known obsession of being unable to take defeat in his stride. A senior participant of the battle of Chhamb once mentioned to this writer how the entire division was left stunned when Sam virtually walked out on them after the war. It is imperative in army life to take success and failure in one's stride. Also he had a tendency to play to the gallery which is a prominent failing.

One aspect the author deals with appropriately is Sam's independence in his functioning and warning the Cabinet of the disastrous pitfalls of launching an offensive in East Pakistan in the spring of 1971 in the wake of Tikka Khan's crack-down. The nation will be forever indebted to him for upholding its prestige during that crucial hour. Some of Sam's successors could not live up to that degree of independence with dire consequences as in the launching of Operation Bluestar in 1984.

The book rightly bemoans the fact that Sam was not given a fair deal as the senior most serving officer when he was conferred the rank of Field Marshal. Indeed to give him Rs 400/- as honorarium in addition to the Chief's pension was a bit too thick. No secretarial assistance was given to him during the first few years. Following his demitting the Chief's office, Sam was in the news for a rather astounding statement that had he opted for Pakistan in 1947 and risen to be the Chief of Pakistan's army, India would have been the defeated country in 1971. Not many people feel that he had a right to talk in this vein even in jest. Another noteworthy mention is Manekshaw's engaging parleys with Tikka Khan after the operations at Lahore.

Sam Manekshaw undoubtedly functioned as a true leader who unleashed the full power of the organization and released the potential and energy in the rank and file of the army by means of personal impact. This book will be an important addition to the writings of post-independence military history of the subcontinent.

Review of "Field Marshal Sam Manekshaw Soldiering with Dignity"
By Lt General Depinder Singh
(Published in Defence Watch February 2003)

□

24

A Field Marshal in War and Peace

(A Film Review)

This film was released on the occasion of Field Marshal Sam Manekshaw's 90th birthday in Delhi recently. The veteran soldier stands out, as usual as a class by himself. Defence Minister George Fernandes aptly commented at the release function, "Sam Manekshaw's life is his message."

The documentary gives a panoramic view of the life of Manekshaw, who was named India's first Field Marshal on December 31, 1972. Set in the picturesque atmosphere of his beautiful home in Coonoor, in the Nilgiri Hills, where he has lived since relinquishing the post of the Army Chief in 1973, the Field Marshal is interviewed by none other than his grandson Jahan.

Manekshaw talks about the starting point in his life as a child in Amritsar where his father was a doctor. He joined Sherwood College Nainital, as a young boy, and there is a twinkle in his eye as he talks of his first girlfriend in the neighbouring girls' school of "All Saints". But he will not tell you her name! Manekshaw wanted to be a doctor; but the medical profession's loss was the army's gain. When attached to the Royal Scots as a subaltern, Manekshaw was called "Mackintosh."

The film covers the historic battle event when the Field Marshal was shot in the stomach in Burma. The doctor asked him what happened'. "A bloody mule kicked me," said Sam. Humour was in evidence even when he suffered near fatal wounds. Also important facts mentioned are his role in Kashmir's accession as Director of

Military Operations and quelling the communal violence in Kolkata.

An important episode which Manekshaw and his contemporaries give due weightage to is the fraudulent inquiry ordered by V.K. Krishna Menon and Lt General B.M. Kaul on his being too Western in his approach as Commandant of the Defence Services Staff College. It is indeed sad that the higher echelons of the army indulged in such petty chicanery at that time.

The interviews with people who served with and knew Manekshaw could have been enlarged upon. Lt General J.F.R. Jacob would have much more insights than has been shown. One glaring omission is Lt General J.S. Aurora the man who took the surrender at Dhaka. One wonders why he was not interviewed.

Manekshaw gives ample evidence of his considerable magnanimity in dealing with junior officers and discipline cases. His comment on Bhutto's Simla Accord "making a monkey" of Mrs Gandhi is also prophetic. The documentary gives you a taste of vintage Manekshaw. Mrs Manekshaw is remembered as an unassuming and fine person, missed by the Indian Army family.

However, one cannot help feeling that "Conversations with Sam Bahadur" would have been a more appropriate title for the film.

"In War and Peace: A Film on the Life of Field Marshal Sam Manekshaw, Mc". A Unesco Parzor Presentation, Directed By Jessica Gupta.

□

25

The Timmy Legend Chronicled

The late General K.S. Thimayya, popularly known as "Timmy" was a military luminary in more ways than one. His charismatic hold on those who had the good fortune of meeting him, service personnel and civilians alike was legendary as has been referred to by Dr Karan Singh in the foreword. General Thimayya, the only Indian to command a brigade in the Second World War, had led the attack on Zojila during the Kashmir aggression as commander of the Sri Division which won him a place of honour undoubtedly. In the latter part of his career he was chairman of the Neutral Nations` Repatriation Commission (NNRC) in Korea as well as Commander-in-Chief Western, Southern and Eastern Commands of the Indian Army (in fact all the commands of the army during this period) before being designated Chief of Army Staff (C-in-C) and full general in the spring of 1957.

His tenure as chief of staff began with much expectation and excitement in the army circles only to end in deep disappointment in 1961. This was mainly due to his stand-off with the Defence Minister V.K. Krishna Menon as well as his disillusionment with Prime Minister Nehru on his condemnatory statement about him in parliament following his controversial resignation, which he withdrew in the autumn of 1959. Yet Timmy the man could be quite different to Timmy the General. As a C-in-C he would think nothing of donating Rs10000/-(a princely amount in those days) to a charitable dispensary or Rs 500/- each to needy widows from his personal funds. This was Timmy at his best offering a bar of chocolate to a boy he met by chance while passing a road and so on. The book is full of such glimpses apart from giving a detailed profile in conventional form. Brig. Chandra Khanduri has proved his penchant for detail as he did in his previous work on that other great Coorgi warrior of yore Field Marshal Carriappa.

A word may not be out of place here about the resignation in September 1959. Undoubtedly the issue of briefing Nehru on Chinese intrusions and capturing our personnel over Menon's head may have provided the spark; the haystack had been lying for quite sometime. Primarily the differences were on the out-of-turn promotion of the inexperienced Lt General B.M. Kaul who as is well known was the blue-eyed boy of Nehru and Krishna Menon and was later to play a crucial role in India's debacle against China in 1962. After the resignation episode, Timmy was a broken man. Those who knew him said they were two Thimayyas. The one after the resignation was a pale shadow of his former self. The volume also gives interesting details of Timmy's last assignment as commander of the UN Force in Cyprus in 1964–65, where he had an untimely death in harness on December 18, 1965. The biography contains some avoidable errors like describing M.O. Mathai as Nehru's Secretary in September 1959 when Mathai had in fact quit the office in January of the same year. Morarji Desai is described as Deputy Prime Minister in Nehru's cabinet, Desai held the designation much later in the cabinet of Mrs. Indira Gandhi. Also one would have looked forward to a more critical appraisal with a human element, like Thimayya's fondness for the good things of life. But one is a trifle disappointed on that score. **On the whole a well researched memoir.**

Review of Thimayya: An Amazing Life by Brig. C.B. Kandhuri
(published in Defence Watch January 2007)

□

26

Memoirs of a Controversial Figure

Gohar Ayub Khan has been a controversial person. He tried to make his memoirs no less controversial by floating an allegation that Field Marshal Sam Manekshaw had supplied operational plans of the Indian Army to Pakistan in the early 1950s for a consideration. The absurd charge has been denied by all contemporary sources.

His narrative begins with his childhood days spent in many of the cantonments of undivided India and shows the glimpses of life in a military family. Gohar seems to have an attachment to the city of Dehradun where his parents lived in the Dalanwala area and he studied along with his siblings at the St Joseph's Academy. Bangalore is another station he remembers.

Gohar Ayub Khan was commissioned into the Pakistan army and had his training at Sandhurst. He gives us a taste of the usual cadet anecdotes here like a cadet putting up the Russian flag on the mast, and himself getting lost during a map reading exercise only to come out to be the first cadet to reach the base. On commissioning he joined the Sher-dils, his father's old battalion. He had a ringside view of the coup of 1958 which brought Ayub Khan to power as he was then serving as ADC to his father who was Commander-in-Chief. It is however true that the President Iskander Mirza brought it on to himself by asking Ayub to declare martial law and within a few weeks was woken up by the army and told to sign his resignation letter!

The author gives his version of the Gandhara Industries he was associated with but despite this it is a fact that tongues wagged in Pakistan about his accumulation of sudden wealth. Gohar Ayub had a rough time during Bhutto's regime and had to face arrest. He mentions that when his father died in 1974, his death was first announced by All India Radio, whereas the Pakistan radio and TV later merely announced that a former President had died without even mentioning his name. This was the extent of Bhutto's vindictive attitude. Needless to say, he did not have the grace to attend the funeral of the President in whose cabinet he served as Foreign Minister among other posts.

Gohar Ayub also deals with the period when he was Speaker of the National Assembly and was Foreign Minister during Nawaz Sharif's regime before being transferred to the less important Ministry of Water and Power, giving a glimpse of the twists and turns of the internal politics of Pakistan. He has since parted company with Nawaz Sharif and is a member of the pro-Musharaf PML-Q.

On the whole the work is interesting but cannot be described as a book of lasting value.

(Review of Glimpses into the Corridors of Power by Gohar Ayub Khan published in Defence Watch September 2008)

□

27

Remembering Pakistan's Field Marshal

This is without doubt an engrossing volume for a serious researcher of the sub-continent. For good measure it is edited and annotated by Craig Baxter who is an eminent defence analyst and has reliable knowledge of the Indo-Pak region, having worked in both countries. The annotations give the discerning reader a good insight into the intricacies of the personalities and some other aspects of the Pakistan in the 1960s and early 70s.

Field Marshal Mohammad Ayub Khan (1907-1974) ceased power in a bloodless coup in October 1958 and reigned supreme as President of Pakistan till the spring of 1969, when the anti-government agitation led by Zulfiqar Ali Bhutto and discreetly supported by his loyal Chief of the Army, A.M. Yayha Khan forced him to hand over power to the latter.

This work in some ways could be considered a sequeal to Ayub's autobiography *Friends Not Masters* published in 1967. Pakistan's first Field Marshal began to pen his diaries in September 1966 and continued to do so in November 1972, when ill health prevented him from continuing the exercise. He died on April 20, 1974. He mentions that he undertook the task to have material ready for a second book or to leave behind his diaries for the historians of the future. The book deals with the tumultuous period of the late 1960s and early 70s where Ayub gives expression to his various views. His dislike for "Hindu twisters" appears fairly often as also the term "Brahamanical arrogance". One has to give him allowance for the kind of brain-washing which must have resulted in his having a natural inclination to use some phrases, although one would have expected a little more sophistication from a President of Pakistan who according to contemporary sources was one of the more sincere rulers as far as Indo-Pak ties go. Many believe that his meeting with Sheikh Abdullah in May 1964 could have paved the way to a permanent solution for Kashmir had Pandit Nehru not died on the 27th of that fateful month. The reflections which emerge in the diary show a man genuinely concerned about the economic plight of his people and the population explosion, which is a matter of deep concern this side of the subcontinent as well.

Ayub's targets in the book are mainly Zulfiqar Ali Bhutto and Yahya Khan, both of whom were antagonistic to him. Of Bhutto he says, "demagogy became his stock in trade, he started drinking himself into a stupor and led a very loose life" (referring to his tenure as Foreign Minister under Ayub). In another context Bhutto is referred to as "a man with all froth and no substance." He compares Bhutto and Mujib as both unreliable, though one is sophisticated and the other uncouth. Where Yahya is concerned, he dwells in ample measure on the drinking and merry-making the late General was known for. It seems that he spent far more time on these activities than on affairs of state and the result was there for all to see. The "butcher of Baluchistan and Bangladesh", General Tikka Khan, is described as a "big goof".

Also in evidence is a West Pakistani's contempt for "the Bengali shudras" and disdain of Bengali pride in Tagore. Ayub is all in favour of his system of "Basic Democracy" and makes no effort to conceal his scorn for the "one man one vote" Westminster form of government. Another conspicuously jaundiced statement is his feeling that his rather controversial son, Gauhar Ayub "would lead Pakistan one day". It can only be hoped that this prediction is averted for the sake of cordial relations in the region!

Entertaining asides of his encounters with Lyndon Johnson, de Gaulle, Kosygin and Queen Elizabeth among others, along with some takes of foreign junkets are of interest. Pakistan also received a huge dollop of foreign aid and one can make out that the Field Marshal and LBJ got on like a house on fire.

Ayub also comes across as a man with liberal views on matters of religion; in an entry dated April 1, 1969, he states, "Islam as propounded by the theologians has ceased to be a living philosophy. It does not offer socio-economic satisfaction in an institutionalized form." Imagine Zia u-Haq even thinking in these terms! On a statement by Pope Paul VI rejecting artificial birth control methods he says, "Nothing could be more absurd and baseless as these arguments...only a priest obsessed with dogma and hide bound with tradition could have such an impractical approach. That is why any form of rule by the priest[hood] is so reprehensible and irrational in any educated society."

It is quite apparent that Mohmmad Ayub Khan apart from having an imposing personality was a man of substance.

(Review of the Diaries of Field Marshal Mohammad Ayub Khan published in Defence Watch August 2007)

□

28

A Holistic Analysis of Indo-Pak Relations

Apart from being a seasoned journalist, Mr Rajinder Puri is adept at the various aspects of the Indo-Pak affairs having written on the subject for many years and having witnessed from close quarters the various ups and downs both the countries have gone through diplomatically or militarily for well nearly six decades.

In this volume he has reproduced his columns in various sections of the press, chiefly in *Outlook* and *The Statesman* on the subject. Divided in three parts on "The Foreign Hand", "The Common Enemy: Terrorism" and "The New Order", the writings cover the period from the end of 2003 to late 2007, that is to say from some months before the advent of the Manmohan Singh administration on the Indian side to some months prior to the final exit of Parvez Musharaf as President in August 2008 on the Pakistani side. (It is to Puri`s credit, that he foresaw that Musharraf's days were numbered as far back as March 2007, when Iftikhar Chaudhary was dismissed as Chief Justice of Pakistan.)

Puri has propounded a theory which runs as a common thread through most of his writing in this work that China is the king-pin in what he calls the "axis of evil" which includes Israel and the United States. Pakistan and its army are minor players in this "great game". On the Indian side also there are some quislings of this axis according to him.

His ultimate solution is a South Asian Confederation on the lines of the European Union. He noted on November 7, 2007, "The tide of history renders change inevitable. If governments do not anticipate change events take over and lead....One day the nations of South Asia will have to coalesce. Diplomacy might very gainfully be employed for this. It is the destiny of South Asia, the tide of its history."

The author has also expressed given his view on the partition of the subcontinent in 1947. He believes that Britain wanted to create an "Islamic crescent" encircling the Soviet Union and Red China to put a check on the spread of communism with the approval of the United States. Even the riots and the transfer of population was part of this "great game".

Puri also refers in fairly intricate detail to the "anatomy of terror" and the powerful "milbus" or military-business nexus which has influenced many policy decisions in the ISI-dominated administration of Pakistan. It is these events which culminated in 26/11.

One hopes that a newshound of Puri's calibre will have more to write in the same engrossing manner on this crucial subject in the days to come. This book is a must read for all those who want to learn about the tempestuous relations of the two nations.

(Review of 'A Tale of Two Countries: Chronicles of a Columnist' by Rajinder Puri published in Defence Watch February 2009)

□

29

A Book of an IAF Veteran

Group Captin Arjun Subramaniam has held a number of vital posts in the Indian Air Force and has intimate knowledge of the works of the men who guard the Indian skies. He was commissioned into the IAF's fighter stream more than twenty five years ago. At the time of writing his book he was an instructor at the Defence Services Staff College Wellington. He is also a qualified Flying Instructor.

Subramaniam's book is a compilation of his writings in various defence journals as well as some research material used by him at seminars over the years. In his foreword, Air Chief Marshal F.H. Major remarks,"Awareness of aerospace power,leadership skills and operational-cum-safety orientation are vital areas for development. Each of these areas is deeply impacted by the spread and dissemination of organizational wisdom, personal and collective experiences." The Commandant of the Defence Services Staff College, Lt General BJ Gupta notes in his introduction, "What is unique about the book is its direct personal style, emanating from firsthand experiences of command,training and peacetime leadership."

The author deals in his writing with the leadership style in the Air Force and notes that the personality-oriented style often made units sway to the samba beat of the Commanding Officer. He rightly points out that handing over and taking over command is a vital aspect and the new 'skipper' must be thoroughly briefed.

Subramaniam has laid sufficient stress on management skills and flight safety based on his own experience as squadron commander and in other appointments as a flyer.

Another weighty aspect to be mentioned about this volume is its emphasis on the need for Joint Operations of the three services as the combat of the future. He gives examples of the past like the Burma Campaign, Kashmir war of 1947–48 and the Bangladesh action of 1971 as classic cases of the great benefits of joint action. He stresses revising the DSSC syllabus to make it 'truly joint' in all aspects and the need of a joint High Command Course.

Arjun Subramaniam can be described without doubt as a 'scholar warrior'.

(Review of Reflections of an Air Warrior published in Defence Watch)

□

30

"Landscapes of the Jihad: Militancy, Morality, Modernity"

The word "Jihad" or holy war is of significant relevance in the times we live in. The events of September 11, 2001 have unleashed a string of happenings which has brought about a conflict between Western powers and the extreme practitioners of Islam, represented by the Al-Qaeda and the Iraqi regime of Saddam Hussein as an illustrative example. Will these military offensives be much more lethal than the post-war period of Cold War? Only the passage of time and posterity will deliver the final verdict.

This book written by Prof Faisal Devji of the New School University, New York encompasses various features of Jihad from its origin to the present day. He begins his narration with the 1998 bombing of Dar-es-Salaam and the American embassies in Nairobi., which proved to be a prelude for a final showdown on that fateful September morning. He gives sizeable space in the writing to the forms of Jihad prevalent in the Islamic world of today. He quotes the recently slain Zawahiri who was seen invoking the Palestinian struggle as an exclusively Pan-Islamic movement, "The fact that must be acknowledged is that the issue of Palestine is the cause that has been firing up the feelings of the Muslim nations from Morocco to Indonesia for the past 50 years. In addition, it is a rallying point for all Arabs, be they believers or non-believers, good or evil." According to this fanatical fringe the collapse of the Soviet occupation of Afghanistan and the break-up of the USSR is all because of Jihad and the Jihadis! Such is the lethal portion of fanaticism.

Politics in the post-Cold War phase is no longer defined in any collective needs and thus fragmentary issues have emerged at the forefront. State and citizenship is not so prominent in the geo-political world of today, which is the crux of the matter in the context of the main topic of this work of scholarship.

This slim volume however cannot by any stretch of the imagination be called anti-Muslim or Islamic. It gives a fair picture of the failures of Western civilization as we understand it. The same Saddam or Bin Laden who were once show-boys of America are now its arch enemies.

This writing will whet the appetite of any scholar of the post 9/11 world scenario.

(Review published in Defence Watch July 2006)

□

31

Some Thoughts on Dehradun

The Bachchan Dehradun Connection

Film star Amitabh Bachchan, popularly known as the 'Big B' was in Dehradun sometime ago and naturally made it to the headlines of the local press. Few people know that his father, Harivansh Rai Bachchan, the famous poet, had a rather emotional link with our city. After his first wife's death in 1936, he spent about two months over here. In his immensely readable autobiography *In the Afternoon of Time,* a complete chapter of the book is dedicated to Dehradun wherein Bachchan has recapitulated tales of Dehradun of yore. It is amply clear that the place made a strong impression on him.

Harivansh Rai stayed with Brij Mohan, his friend of college days, in Jhanda Mohalla and in the evenings he would stroll down to the parade ground which we all know so well. Here he would recline against the fountain at Gandhi Park and gaze at the lights of Mussoorie. He musingly commented, 'I would see the lights of Mussoorie in the far distance, a necklace of diamonds on the neck of a dusky lady reclining on a bed of sapphire.' That is the poet in Bachchan taking charge. At that time hawkers of various types used to collect at the Parade Ground to sell their wares.

Bachchan also remembers a stormy night in the city when a tornado like storm raged unabated with winds which lashed the city at 90 miles an hour. There is also mention of a visit to the famous homeopath Dr Om Prakash and the chance meeting with a friend who was also a widower. Then he takes us to Sahasradhara where no road or shops existed at that time and Bachchan had to return back to Dehradun for his evening meal. He laments that when he visited Shasradhara many years later he found it rather polluted and crowded, it is the same story everywhere. Bachchan comments critically, 'Our ordinary citizens have not learnt the abc of aesthetics. Overseas I have seen that whenever man has touched nature he has beautified it, but we always do the opposite.' Somewhat harsh undoubtedly, but the bitter truth always hurts. In his narrative we can see Bachchan going up on foot to Mussoorie via Rajpur. It is here that he meets the legendary Dr Amar Nath Jha, Vice Chancellor of Allahabad University who was to play a crucial role in his career later on. Also he gives a glimpse of the *tonga* ride to Kalsi where he remained near the Ashoka inscription for some hours in a reflective mood. Thus Bachchan left Dehradun in a composed state of mind recovering as he was from the tragedy of his wife's death. I wonder if anybody reminded Amitabh of his father's connection with this city, during his visit.

Simplicity in Life

I remember some years ago, having a conversation in Mumbai with former Prime Minister Morarji Desai, which somehow veered around to discussing modern digital watches that had just appeared in the market and were produced by the HMT Company. I made a comment that India should be proud of such gadgetry. Morarji agreed with this, but pointing to his own watch he said that it was a simple piece which he had used for more than 30 years. 'In life,' he continued, 'simple things have an enduring value.' The veteran Gandhian had made a very telling point to me and this has remained enshrined in my memory. When one sees the current rush for materialism all around us, one can only hope that at some stage some simplicity will return to our public life. One often remembers what Gandhi told the cabinet members of the West Bengal Ministry when they called on him, on the morning of August 15, 1947, to seek his blessings in Calcutta

> "Wear the crown of thorns. Strive ceaselessly to cultivate truth and non-violence. Be humble and forbearing. Be aware of power. Power corrupts. Do not let yourself be entrapped by pomp and pageantry.

Remember you are in office to serve the poor in India's villages."

Continuing on the subject of the idea and essence of simplicity, I would like to clarify that I do not mean simplicity should be observed only by those in public life. People in every walk of life must observe austerity and simplicity to achieve the lofty heights of glory that our founding fathers and great thinkers felt should be the destiny which our nation must fulfil.

(Published In Dehradun Classified December 2001)

□

32

Some Musings Around the City of Dehradun

Dehradun as we know it today is a capital city, a city which is over-crowded, bursting at the seams and prone to traffic jams and VIP convoys blinking through crowds, leaving the hapless onlookers aghast and very often puzzled at what is going on. Undoubtedly, however, one cannot deny that as a result of all this activity which at times appears to be a collage of pollution, over-crowding, pompousness and general chaos lies the undeniable fact that Dehra is now a city on the move. In what direction I am yet to fathom! But I have no doubt that ultimately it will be positive. A city of some opportunities, a city with some hope for the younger generation.

But to take a flashback to the Dehra of yore is also a trip down romantic nostalgia. Those were the days when tongas plied, the odd car went by, but the lush green and the unpolluted environs were a feast for the eyes, and it was indeed a city renowned for its charm in every respect. Somebody remarked the other day at the Raj Bhavan (formerly known as the Circuit House) that Pandit Jawaharlal Nehru often used to sit on the bench on the far end of the lawn facing Mussoorie and watch the lights for an hour at least every evening. In 1932, he wrote in *Glimpses of World History* about Dehradun and Mussoorie from Dehradun jail "Beyond the trees there lie the mountains, and perched on top of them sits Mussoorie. I cannot see the mountains for the trees hide them, but it is good to be near them and to imagine at night the lights of Mussoorie twinkling in the far distance." Poetic words indeed!

To return to the present day, I was recently invited to a function at an institute giving training to young people in the hospitality sector on Rajpur Road named the Air Hostess Academy (AHA). On the occasion of its first anniversary it distributed books and school stationery items among 150 lower-income group school students. The Academy has 8 branches apart from the Dehradun branch, 2 in Mumbai,4 in Delhi,1 in Chandigarh and 1 in Jaipur. The Academy has 150 students under training and will be completing the training of its first batch by the end of the year. The Academy is having a cultural evening at Mussoorie on the 26th of November presided over by Governor Sudarshan Agarwal. The Chief Consultant, Sapna Gupta, mentioned that the Institute was only started in 1997 and has shown remarkable growth in 6 years. Uttarakhand as a growing state does need more such centres for vocational training.

Recently the Governor stated that the encouragement of NGOs will go a long way in providing succour for the common man as their attitude is fairly humane in various matters. One cannot but mention in this connection the excellent work done by the "Raphael Ryder Cheshire International Centre" on Mohini Road. The centre has been doing remarkable work among the handicapped and TB patients. Headed by the grand old man of the Doon Valley, Maj Gen Ranbir Bakshi, who at the age of 90-plus is doing yeoman service among both, the mentally and the physically disadvantaged. The National Trust of New Delhi which was formed under the National Trust Act of 1999, has established its local level committee at Dehradun and has its office at "Raphael". The local level committee is taking an initiative in the activities for the welfare of people affected by cerebral palsy, autism and mental retardation. President Franklin Roosevelt of the USA once stated that the *"the test of real progress is not whether we add more to the abundance of those who have much, it is whether we provide enough to those who have little."* It is the kindling of this spirit which inspires the running of such institutions. All this contributes to make Dehra a town of the time ahead as well as the past, a town to be eloquent about.

(Published in The Himachal Times Dehradun, November 2002)

□

33

The Services and Political Leadership: Some Facets of the Relationship

The recent episode concerning Air Marshal Manjit Singh Sekhon seeking a posting from former Punjab Chief Minister P.S. Badal in order to be appropriately placed to take over as the next Chief of Air Staff is but a symptom of a deep malady which has crept into the three services over the years. Sekhon's other reported statement that two other Air Marshals had obtained their postings through political manouevring is also extremely serious in its import. The political role and interference in postings and promotions in the armed forces has assumed greater predominance with every passing day.

In the early years of independence the armed forces had a standing which was nearly completely autonomous as far as the internal administrative policy of every service was concerned. It was V. K. Krishna Menon (Defence Minister 1957-1962) who brought about the rather controversial change in this well-established convention by literally foisting a non-combatant officer, Lt Gen B.M. Kaul, and sponsoring his promotion to the rank of Lt Gen, and ensuring his occupying positions hitherto never held by a non-combatant officer. This was one of the main reasons leading to the resignation of Gen K.S. Thimayya as Chief of Army Staff in August 1959. It was regrettably withdrawn by "Timmy", as the late General was popularly known. Had the Sino-Indian conflict not providentially intervened, Kaul would probably have been thrust on the Army as Chief of Staff. He and Menon had already begun to weed out probable rivals like Sam Manekshaw who was subjected to a wholly fraudulent enquiry as Commandant of the Staff College to prepare the ground for his premature retirement.

In 1975 the Indira Gandhi government gave an unprecedented extension of Service to Gen G.G. Bewoor thus knocking out of consideration the case for appointment as COAS of Lt Gen P.S. Bhagat, one of India's most competent Generals and a recipient of the Victoria Cross. The year 1983 will be remembered however, for the most controversial suppression in the annals of the post-independence era. Lt Gen S.K. Sinha (currently Governor of Assam) then Vice Chief of Army Staff and a former Commander of the Western Army was not promoted to the Chief's post; more controversial was the role of the serving Chief K.V. Krishna Rao in the sordid drama. In his recently published memoirs *In the Service of the Nation*, Krishna Rao has sought to whitewash the whole affair by saying that his role was limited and the government had a prerogative in this matter. It must be borne in mind however, that he was duty-bound to advise the government regarding the dangerous and wholly unwarranted action it was contemplating. His memoirs are also strangely silent about the blatantly political statement given by the late Gen A.S. Vaidya in Tirpura in January 1983, which many feel was the chief reason for his being considered for the top slot.

The dismissal of Admiral Vishnu Bhagwat by the NDA Government in the winter of 1998 was also a ham-handed affair. If the Chief had to be dismissed, there was no need to summon his successor to Delhi in a cloak and dagger style operation when an acting Chief of Staff could have easily been appointed. In an interview with *India Today* magazine dated January 11, 1999 Defence Minister George Fernandes stated that Bhagwat was "indulging in defiance; no government could succumb to the pressure of an individual". Nobody in his senses would doubt a democratic government's right to exercise control over the defence forces and there was little doubt that Bhagwat was flouting many established conventions. However it is also equally important that the government of the day ensures that wrong precedents are not set, and the upshot is not a dent in the morale of the armed forces.

Mulayam Singh Yadav during his tenure as Defence Minister literally forced his way through regarding the promotion of an officer Lt Gen B.S. Malik who was found unfit by the promotion board for further promotion; it was a sad spectacle that the then Chief of Army Staff allowed such an officer to be thrust on him only to please the powers that be. If any Chief is true to his conscience in the wake of an unacceptable government decision, he can exercise the option of putting in his papers. Since 1950, only Thimayya has done so.

However I would like to mention two Chiefs of Army Staff who refused to pander to the whims of the Defence Minister of the day. Field Marshal Sam Manekshaw refused to play ball with Defence Minister Jagjivan Ram's desire to introduce reservations on a caste basis in the army; the late Gen T.N. Raina had refused to accept Mr Bansi Lal's rather shocking proposition that an outstanding officer Brig Sukhjeet Singh be placed under suspension for refusing to meet some unreasonable demands.

Another aspect of the problem needs pondering in the larger context of the morale of the Defence Forces. It pertains to the frequent use of the armed forces in aid to civil authority.

The right to exercise this power originates from a military manual of the British days. Politicians in the first two decades of freedom seldom exercised the power of summoning the army to quell civil disturbance, which was primarily the responsibility of the civil police. Morarji Desai, for example, did not use military support for controlling riots in Bombay State in 1956, even though Prime Minister Nehru felt the need for this had arisen. (Morarji Desai: *The Story of My Life* Vol II; Page 59) Slowly and steadily like in other areas this power has also been misused. The much-criticized Operation Bluestar was also the case of a government taking action on the advice of an army top-brass which was bending over backwards to please the government of the day without deeply going into the disturbing repercussions such a move was undoubtedly fraught with. In November 1984, the army was called out late to quell the anti-Sikh riots in Delhi and many innocent lives were lost. Recently the Modi government also put on the back burner calling out the army in riot-torn Gujarat and ultimately allegedly acted on the goading of the Defence Minister George Fernandes.

All this bears testimony to the fact that things are not very well in certain aspects of the politician-bureaucrat-military man relationship which emanates from South Block. To clear the air in the coming months and years it is of vital importance that discipline of a high order be inculcated in the officer cadre so that they resist from asking for out of turn favours from politicians of all hues; a proper redress of grievances takes place so that officers of the three services have complete faith in the system and do not adopt the course which Malik and Sekhon did; and finally, a proper mechanism is set in place to ensure that the army is called out in aid of civil authority only when necessary and also not delayed when necessary. In this context it may be mentioned that de-politicizing the civil police will go a long way in curbing the use of this power; otherwise it will lead to a serious disciplinary problem in the army in the years to come.

(Published in the Himachal Times, Dehradun)

□

34

Revelations of Service Customs

The Indian Army has had valued customs and traditions from time immemorial something which has in no minor way contributed to its well established record both in battle and in peace. The same goes for the Air Force and Navy. The late Colonel H.R. Roach, a Second World War veteran had authored this book while serving in the Indian Military Academy, Dehradun. It has been updated and improved upon keeping in view developments of the present day traditions by Maj General R.K. Arora, a frontline divisional commander who has had a remarkably high profile service career in India and abroad.

Clausewitz has observed that "tradition is a subtle and indefinable term." The volume in question has a fairly comprehensive first chapter on customs in the services. Saluting for example, can be traced from the times of the caveman when he opened his palm to indicate that he held no offensive weapon. "Present arms" is symbolic of disarming by holding the rifle in such a position to show a mark of trust and friendship. Aircraft also dip in salute over the saluting base,Naval officers are piped aboard the ship to avoid disrespect to a foreigner for non-recognition of his rank. Interestingly toasts in the Navy are drunk seated as an officer was liable to hit his head in the old days due to low beams!

Other snippets which are featured refer to the reverence of colours by a regiment which is a symbol of its spirit, the "beating of retreat" which signalled the end of the day's warfare in times of yore, musical customs and martial songs, wearing of slashes, gorget patches, aiguillettes, funeral customs and erection of war memorials, to mention a few.

The book also deals with the various aspects of military courtesy, social etiquette which underlines the fact that every officer is expected to be a gentleman, salutation to ladies as a matter of both courtesy and respect, correct speech and conversation, the tradition of calling, official calls and calls of courtesy, time and length of calls, appropriate turnout for calls, returning calls and a variety of invitations. A chapter also covers the Officers' Mess and club.

Obviously a great deal of painstaking research has been done by the authors who have also added chapters on "Lady Officers" and "Etiquette on the Golf Course". The book has been fittingly published during the platinum jubilee year of the Indian Military Academy, the alma mater of most army officers and was launched by its Commandant recently.

Review of Customs and Etiquette in the Services
(Published in Defence Watch January 2008)

□

35

Dehradun: A Story of a Valley and a City of History and Hope

When one sits down to write about the city of one's dwelling many thoughts flock to one's mind. Where does one begin and where does one end? In the well nigh twenty-five years that I have lived in Dehradun, or should I say chosen to live here, the city has become an integral part of my being. An English traveller Andrew Wilson who visited the valley of Dehradun in 1873, wrote "*there is no place in India unless perhaps the plateaus of the blue mountains which reminds one so much of England as the little valley of Dehradun.*" Whether the Englishman's nostalgia for his country was just poetic license or based on reality, for the devotee of nature and the admirer of all things beautiful it can be said that the story of the picturesque Doon valley is enchanting being steeped in history, sublime in more ways than one.

"Dhoon" or "Doon" in various Sanskrit and Hindi dialects means a "valley" and it is from this that the area lying between the Shivaliks running to the south and the Garhwal Himalayas to the north in the present State of Uttarakhand derives its name.To its east it is bordered by the hallowed Ganges and to the west the Yamuna flows. It was designated as the temporary capital of the State of Uttarakhand (then known as Uttaranchal) when it was formed on November 9, 2000.

It is the Mahabharata that gives us the first authentic glimpse of the Doon Valley. The rishi Bharadwaj on being seduced by the apsara Ghritachi fathered by Dronacharaya who was born in a bowl or valley said to be the present valley of Doon. During his self-imposed exile, Pandu and his clan are supposed have lived in a place in the vicinity of the Badri-Kedar foothills between the Alakhnanda and Baghrithi watershed. While reaching this place Pandu and his party came to Nagsidh in the Doon after crossing the Ganga at Haridwar. After the death of Pandu, the patriarch of the clan Bhishm is said to have arranged military education to the Pandavas and Kauravas under the guidance of Dronacharaya in his military academy in the Doon Valley. The famous story of Eklavya severing his thumb to show his loyalty to Dronacharaya is said to have taken place in this territory. It is perhaps appropriate that the central entrance gate of Indian Military Academy at Dehradun has been named "Dron Dwar" in memory of the great guru.The episode of Duroyodhan ploting to kill the Pandavas when they were told to go and live in Varanavat with their mother, Kunti also is supposed to have taken place in the Doon Valley. The house made of resinous wood or inflammable conifer timbers which was going to be set ablaze by the Kauravas, so that the Pandavas might perish is located in the Chakrata sub division of the Doon in a place called "Lakhamandal." As is well known, their Uncle Vidur is said to have tipped of the Pandavas resulting in the house being set fire to by the Pandavas themselves, after which they escaped through a tunnel to the bank of a river and the adjoining forest one night. For a long time the Pandavas remained in this area, living incognito. It may be pointed out that Lakh or Lac in Hindi means resin and mandal means region. H.G. Walton, I.C.S. in his "Gazetteer of Garhwal Himalaya" mentions a narrow passage at Lakhamandal leading underground through the rock to the riverside used, by people in time of danger to escape their enemies. During the period when the Pandavas stayed here in secrecy, Bhim is supposed to have killed two local chieftains who were known to be tyrannical. He is also supposed to have married a sister of one of them and fathered a son called Ghatokach. Draupadi was later taken as the common wife of the Pandavas. A form of polyandry still exists in the Jaunsar-Bawar area of the Chrakrata sub-division in the valley. If a mother-in-law dies leaving an infant son, the daughter-in-law brings him up as one of her husbands. Upon growing to manhood, if he desires to co-habit with her, neither she or the family can refuse. Also the practice of the brother leaving his sandals outside his wife`s room when he is entering it, is still in vogue in these parts and is an offshoot of the tradition followed by the Pandava prince`s while entering Draupadi`s chamber.

It is said in ancient lore that the Kulind ruler of Uttarakhand, his three sons with their war elephants and infantry sided with the Pandavas during the Kurukshetra war.

During the rule of Ashoka (274-232 B.C.) the emperor thought it fit to install one of his "rock edicts" in Kalkut (now known as Kalsi)in this valley. The quartz boulder is ten feet high and eight feet wide, has the figure of a white elephant inscribed on it, recalling the descent of the Buddha into that form, gives the names of the contemporary kings of Syria, Macedonia, Syrene, and Epirus. The edict goes on to point out the futility of unnecessary ceremonies and rituals while laying emphasis on necessary ones, goes on to lay emphasis on congenial relations in the society and family, among high and low, rich and poor. Also Ashoka`s denouncing personal fame and glory and striving for uplifting his subjects from bondage and sin is recorded here. The text is more or less a gist of Buddha`s Dhammapada. Also mention might be made of Kings Shiv Bhivani and Sheelverman who ruled over this province in the 2nd and 3rd centuries A.D. These two rulers performed the "Ashvamedha Yagya" or horse sacrifice which was that a horse representing the king would tour the area of his rule for varying periods and be the symbol of the king and on return to the capital would be sacrificed after elaborate ceremonies on a stake or by slaughtering. The amphi-theatre for these sacrificial pits with burnt out bricks exist in village

The amphi-theatre of the Ashvamedha Yagya (Horse Sacrifice) at Kalsi, near Dehradun

Barwala near the township of Vikasnager in western Doon.

In the 7th century A.D. the Chinese pilgrim Hieun Tsang travelled in this area and has given a fairly authentic description in which he says the entire area he covered between the Ganga and Yamuna stretching upto Saharanpur had well populated towns and a good deal of trade and commerce flourished. The populace was generally literate and Sanskrit was the State language. In the time Hieun Tsang's travels this realm of area was under the rule of Harshvardan. After his death his empire split up and the rule of local rajas held sway.

Between the years 1500 to 1548, a ruler called Ajay Pal ruled over this area. After an initial defeat at the hands of the ruler of Champavat he is supposed to have gone into deep meditation and prayed to Lord Shiva standing on one foot, Shiva is said to have appeared before Ajay Pal and asked him to climb on his shoulders and began increasing his (Shiva's) own height making Ajay Pal so tall that the king could see the tips of the Shivalik Ranges of Doon. Shiva is then said to have prophesied while putting him down that his rule would extend as far as his eyes beheld. The prophecy came true. Ajay Pal is credited bringing 52 or 64 fiefs (the figure is disputed by historians) of Garhwal under his flag. His capital was Srinagar (built by him) and he is attributed to introducing several social, economic and religious reforms. It was during Ajay Pal's reign that the rulers of Garhwal became known as the living incarnations of the Badrinath shrine know as "Bolden Badri" which means "Speaking Badri", the appointments, dismissals and various matters of the ritualistic priests known as the "rawals" were to be in the hands of the Garhwal rulers.

Ajay Pal was followed by a number of rulers of which Balbhadra Shah is the most conspicuous and was able in governance. Legend has it that he saved the Mughal Emperor Akbar from being mauled by a tiger during a hunt and was given the title "Shah." The progeny of the ruling family of the Garhwal Maharajas use the title till the present day. Balbhadra`s kingship lasted upto 1591. Incidentally, Akbar had a mint in the neighbouring town of Haridwar where copper coins were minted and the year of minting and name of the mint were embossed on either side of the coins.

Guru Ram Rai immigrated to the Doon Valley in the year

The Mausoleum of Guru Ram Rai, the founder of Dehradun

1675. It might be said that he was the person who can be called the actual founder of the present city of Dehradun. Guru Ram Rai was the son of the seventh Sikh Guru Har Rai and was born at Kiratpur in 1646. The Mughal emperor Aurangzeb who was piqued at Har Rai for his support to Dara Shikoh in the war of succession, summoned the latter to his court, Har Rai instead of going himself sent his son Ram Rai, a lad of fifteen. He instructed him to fix his thoughts on God for the success of his mission. Ram Rai being intelligent and ambitious, instead began to curry favour with Aurangzeb. He is supposed to have performed some miracles before him. Aurangzeb then asked Ram Rai to explain a verse from the Guru Granth wherein Guru Nanak had sought to emphasize that no differences existed between Hinduism and Islam. The verse said "the clay from a Mussalman`s grave is kneaded and finds its way into the potter`s hands, who makes vessels and bricks from it and fires them in the kiln. Burning, it wails-helpless by cinders engulfed. The Creator, sayeth Nanak alone knows what befalls the soul which has departed... whether cremation is better or burial." Ram Rai is said to have shrewdly interpreted the verse to the Emperor by saying that the verse had been corrupted and the word "Mussalmaan" had been inserted instead of the original "Beimaan" (dishonest or faithless). When news of this incident reached Har Rai he disowned him (Ram

Rai) and declared his younger son Har Kishan as the next Sikh Guru. Ram Rai rushed to Kiratpur to make his father change his mind but to no avail. During the Guruship of Har Kishan, Tegh Bahadur and Govind Singh, Ram Rai continued with his machinations laying claim to the Guru`s gaddi(throne.) By now Aurangzeb had also had enough of him, and issued a 'firman' to the Raja of Garhwal to the effect that Ram Rai was to be given refuge in his domain, which he was given thus, first at a place called Kandlee and then a locality called "Khurbura." Khur means hoof and bara means grown. It is said the Ram Rai`s horse`s hoof had grown so much that it dropped at this spot. This however, can be taken as the genre of folklore.

Since Aurangzeb by his firman had enjoined upon the ruler of Garhwal to give Ram Rai enough source of revenue to make him comfortable, he was given the villages of Khurbura, Rajpur and Chamasari as revenue grants followed by the other villages of Dhamanwala. Dharatawala, Mianwala and Panditwari bringing to about Rs 1300-1400 annually.

This amount was supplemented by offerings of his devotees or followers known as Ram Raiyas or Rai Sikhs. They do not follow the tenets of the Khalsa Panth of keeping uncut hair, not smoking, wearing of the comb, underpants, kirpan and bangle. According to the contemporary source Macauliffe, Guru Govind Singh specifically prohibited his followers from any kind of social intercourse with Guru Ram Rai, his followers or descendants. Upon Ram Rai making his abode at Khurbura he soon attracted several followers and devotees and the town which developed around his settlement came to be known as "Dera" Doon ("Dera" meaning abode and Doon as already mentioned meaning valley). This was later to be known as Dehradun and envelops the present city. Raja Fateh Shah of Garhwal also had a gurudwara built at Srinagar where he would often go and stay. A compromise with Guru Govind Singh then staying in the nearby town of Poanta Sahib was attempted by Ram Rai, but of no avail. Guru Ram Rai used to go into a trance during long periods of meditation and shut himself in his room during such periods. In one such period in September 1687, when he did not come out for a long period the Masands of his entourage forced his wife Punjab Kaur to open the door, and he was found dead on the bed in the room. After his death a system of Mahant administration was arranged for the gurudwara and his followers. The Mahants have to take a vow of celibacy for life according to the wishes of Guru Ram Rai, as he had willed this. The Mahants were to be named from their chelas or successors. In the early days the selection was guided by the Chiefs of the Sikh states of the Punjab but later the successor was named by the head Mahant from his chelas. The system prevails till today. Even though not recognized by mainstream Sikhism the Ram Raiya Sikhs have a large stream of devotees among the Hindus particularly in Dehradun. It is a fact however, that Guru Govind Singh assisted Ram Rai`s widow Punjab Kaur to get rid of some of the Masands who created some problems for her. Maharaja Ranjit Singh apprehensive of his life ebbing out in the near future sent an offering of Rs 500/- to the gurudwara of Ram Rai.

Every year at Dehradun, five days after the festival of Holi, is held the "Jhanda Ka Mela"or fair of the flag. This is to commemorate Ram Rai`s birthday. The Gurudwara Nishan or flag is changed every year, thus the name "Jhanda Ka Mela". Upon coming to know of Ram Rai`s death, Aurangzeb ordered the building of the mausoleum in memory of Ram Rai built on the lines of the architecture of Jehangir`s tomb in Lahore. On the top of the south gate to the mausoleum is embedded a large marble slab of which are inscribed 66 lines in Persian. They begin with the line, "Praise be to God whose attribute is mercy, and by whose grace man has received life" and goes on to give the description of Guru Ram Rai`s life and his association with Aurangzeb. The Shri Guru Ram Rai Education Mission runs 122 schools at subsidized rates in Uttarakhand and western Uttar Pradesh.

Another landmark in the narrative of the region of the Doon Valley, is the advent of the Gorkhas and their regime ending in the battle of Kalunga. Bahadur Shah the de facto ruler of Nepal had an expansionist policy vis-à-vis neighbouring states, Garhwal being one of them. He made the ruler of Garhwal a vassal of Nepal by 1792. Subsequently on an attack by the Nepalese forces the ruler of Garhwal Pradyuman Shah fled his capital Srinagar and took refuge first in Saharanpur and then in Haridwar as Saharanpur had come under the ambit of the East India Company. Shah took refuge with his family priest at Kankhal in Haridwar. By 1804 Amar Singh Thapa the Nepalese general, slayed Pradyuman Shah at Khurbura in the Doon and this resulted in a total rout of the Garhwali army. Amar Singh then returned to Srinagar leaving a Gorkha Governor to administer the Doon. The Gorkha administration was as autocratic as those of the Garhwali rajas but much more severe where the question of punishment was concerned. They carried many women away as slaves (for a paltry amount of Rs 10/- or Rs 15/-) and these women were used to satisfy the lust of the Gorkhas soldiers and officials in a brutal way. The dread of the Gorkha taking away their female child once she grew up, forced parents to strangle them at birth. However, some of the Governors like Ranjor Thapa, were well disposed and mild rather than autocratic. Bam Shah and Hastidal were the Governors of Garhwal. The executive officers were however, severe in their conduct, in fact tyrannical in many ways. Generally life under the Gorkha administration was one abject neglect for the common people. Agriculture was virtually ruined and the countryside fell to lamentable decay. The administration of justice also followed no regular pattern and depended on officers exercising jurisdiction according to their position. Commandants of troops and their Deputies called "Becharis" held sway. Garhwal was divided into three provinces, the Doon being one of them.

The Gorkha rule came to an end after the epic battle Kalunga in 1814. The final assault was at Kalunga on Nalapani Hill on the Sastradhara road 10 kms north-east of Dehradun, where the Gorkha forces where concentrated under the leadershi p of Balbhadra Thapa. Before this an assault led by Major General Gillespie and a comparatively huge force of five companies of British Infantry with more than adequate Horse Artillery and guns under his command were repulsed by the Gorkha forces in which General Gillespie was also slain. He had shown a great act of gallantry by leading the charge himself. Gillespie was known as the hero of Vellore (South India), Cornellis, Palimbang (in the West Indies) and Djoejocrata (in Indonesia). Ultimately, on November 30, 1814, the British troops under the command of Major Kelly took possession of Kalunga fort. The siege laid by the British troops proved to be the proverbial last straw to break the camel's back. It is felt by contemporary historians that "thirst not might of arms forced the Gorkhas to withdraw and leave the bastion." The determined resolution of a small party to hold out against such a large force of the British speaks volumes of the unsubdued courage of the Gorkhas.

The camp of the withdrawing Gorkhas were attacked and defeated by the British troops on the night of December 1/2, 1814. Balbhadra Thapa escaped via Sirmur to later join the forces of Mahraja Ranjit Singh. This warrior of great dauntlessness ultimately fell to the Afghan artillery while fighting for Ranjit Singh. The fort of Kalunga was unfortunately razed to the ground by the English troops. On the southern end of the spur on the road to Sahasthrdhara stand two small monuments in the shape of twin obelisks which were erected by the victorious British Army. One is to the memory of General Gillespie and his men who fell and the other to Balbhadra and his Gorkhas. It is according to the Archeological Survey of India, the only occasion in military history that a victorious army has raised a memorial to the vanquished one, and is a tribute to the indominatable fortitude of the Gorkha forces. Thus from the fateful night of December 1/2 , 1814, when they proved triumphant in the historic campaign at the Kalunga fort the British Union Jack fluttered over the Doon till August 15, 1947.

By a resolution the East India Company annexed the Doon to the British District of Saharanpur on November 17, 1815. During the Anglo-Gurkha war a military officer called Lieutenant Young had been captured by the Gorkhas.

They were impressed by his gentlemanly conduct of not trying to escape and he by the Gorkhas' manliness. He obtained from the Company permission to raise a battalion of Gorkha troops known as the "Sirmur Battalion" as it was first stationed at Nahan which was the principal town of Sirmur State. Later the battalion was stationed at Dehradun and came to be known as the 2nd Battalion of the Gorkha Rifles. Subsequent to this Young was appointed Superintendent of the Doon which encompassed both offices of District Magistrate and Revenue Collector. He held the office for 15 years from 1826 to 1841, probably the longest anybody held this post.

The Christian Cemetery came up in Dehradun about 1819. The oldest marked grave is in the name of John Graves, and the tombstone reads, *"Sacred to the memory of John Graves son of*

John Graves Sgt Major, Sirmur Battalion who died on April 9, 1820 aged 25 days." This grave is in the shape of a toy Noah`s Ark at the plinth. Some of the inscriptions can be quite intriguing like this one on the tomb of a wife`s grave *"Weep not for me husband dear, But prayer and think of me; As I am now you must be, Prepare yourself to follow me."* Among those buried in Mussoorie is a survivor of the "six hundred" from the "Charge of the Light Brigade" of the Crimean War made famous by Alfred Lord Tennyson in the poem of that name. Dehra also has a vast Muslim graveyard and a Paris one. The Hindus and Sikhs are cremated at the Lakhibagh cremation ground in the vicinity of the Railway Station.

A word about the neighbouring resort of Mussoorie which is today one of the choicest hill tourist spots of northern India, may not be out of place here. The first house was established in 1823 in this station. The salubrious climate and good sport obtainable proved to be an attractive draw for the Europeans. In 1827 a convalescent depot was established for British soldiers in Landhaur which later became the cantonment area. By 1829, many houses had come up in Mussoorie. How this mountainous town got its name is an interesting story. It has been named after the *Mansur (Coriaria nepalensis)* shrub which grew in abundance in the area. On being asked by a Britisher about the name of the locality, the native thinking that he was asking about the name of the plant growing here replied, "Mansuri". The officials later dropped the 'n' from the name calling it Mussoorie. In the Hindi dialect it is still often referred to as "Mansuri". In May 1833, Sir George Everest, FRS, CB, Kt came to Mussoorie and established his office as Surveyor General and Superintendent of the Great Trigonometrical Survey.He was the first departmental head to have direct access to the Company`s Government at Kolkata. He purchased a property called "The Park" at Hati paon (which means elephant foot) area in Mussoorie. At this estate one gets one of the most breathtaking views of the Doon Valley on one side and the Garhwal Himalayas on the other. Everest continued his operations till 1843 and was touring various parts of the country on survey work. "The Park" was his residence-cum-office. He also established an office at Dehradun. Once Everest took exception to an application wherein he was addressed as "Compass Wala Sahib" and protested to the District Magistrate saying that no correspondence with this familiar appellative be forwarded to him as the vernacular title of his appointment was "Surveyor General Kishewar Hind!" The whole conception of the Survey of India as it existed in those days was the creation of George Everest`s brain.He provided to India a grid survey even before Europe. It is after this great surveyor that the highest mountain of the world, Mount Everest is named.

The Mussoorie Munici pal Board came into being in 1842. Later on came up "The Savoy" Hotel which was to be one of the most famous watering holes for the British in north India. The Mussoorie Library came into being in 1843 and is one of the landmarks of the town. It was founded by Major Swetenham one of the well known figures of Mussoorie of that era. The funds for the Library was collected through subscri ptions and a sum of Rs 2500/- was collected in the first year. The Library is located on the flat below the Savoy Hotel and the band stand. Some shops were constructed here to provide income for the Library. Bands of the British regiments used to play here on Wednedays and Saturdays. The upper verandah of the Library on these evenings was hired out to the Savoy on these evenings and many Sahibs and Memsahibs savoured cucumber sandwiches and tea while the band played.

Outside hung a board with the legend "Dogs and Indians not allowed". After a mighty tug of war of protest from a visiting High Court Judge of Madras it was changed to "Rights of admission reserved". The Library is at the beginning of The Mall, the main thoroughfare of Mussoorie, behind which the panoramic "Camel`s Back Road" is located. One of the most scenic buildings in this part of Mussoorie just above the Savoy Hotel, is "The Chateau" built in the French style by H.R.H. Jagatjit Singh Bahadur, G.C.S.I. the Maharaja of Kapurthala who was a frequent visitor to the hill station. He was also responsible for the construction of the band stand mentioned above, in 1915.

During the Mutiny of 1857, the Doon remained largely unaffected though the Sirmur Battalion of Gorkhas was used to quell the incursion of about 600 revolutionaries from Jalandhar who attempted to enter the Valley but did not find much support from the local populace. Tea estates began on a big scale from the 1850s onwards in this area, and by 1857 100,000 acres of land were under tea cultivation but the industry declined and by 1947 there were only 22 tea estates covering an area of about 5500 acres. The industry has diminished further since and tea gardens in the vicinity of Dehradun are few and far between, the rapid urbanization of the city being the main cause.

G.R.C. Williams of the Bengal Civil Service, was appointed Assistant Superintendent of Dehradun in 1871. In his book *Memoir of Dehradun* published in 1874, he dwells on the climatic conditions of the valley which make an interesting read. Williams mentions that the Doon has climate which has a *"resemblance to that of lower Bengal"* this mainly on account of being moist, and also makes mention of the absence of the scorching heat of the plains. Another point he refers to is the substantial amount of snowfall in Dehra, where in February 1814, it lay on the ground for two whole days so thick was the snow cover. Dehradun or at least the upper part of it was known to have snowfall till the mid-twentieth century. All this is a distant dream now as air-conditioners abound in the town.

The year 1878 marked the coming into being of the Central Forest School, which was then in an impressive building along the southern boundary of the parade ground in the heart of the city, which was later to become the Imperial Forest School for the training of foresters at the all India level. Later it moved to the Chandbagh area, where the Doon School now stands. Presently known as the Forest Research Institute it is housed majestically on the Chakrata road among avenues of forestry. Dehradun can be called the capital of forestry as far as India is concerned. Also it would not be out of turn to mention the Rangers College of northern India which has been running courses here since 1935.

Lady Dufferin then the Vicerene and wife of Lord Dufferin who was Viceroy and Governor General of India, from 1884 to 1888, maintained a meticulous journal of her visits to the Doon Valley during the years 1885 and 1887. The Viceroy's party stayed at the "Body-Guard Estate" which is on the upper part of Rajpur Road, and is now the "President's Body-Guard Estate" or "Rahtrapati Ashiana" as it is known in official terminology. Lady Dufferin notes, *"It really is much nicer to look up at moderate hills, and to move about on a level world, than to be perched on a high peak and look down upon a range of gigantic mountains. A river too is a refreshing sight, and the Jamuna is a very rapid one. We crossed it on a pontoon bridge, which had been expressly built for the Viceroy. We lunched half-way, and then drove onto Dehra Doon, the country getting prettier at every step. It is a sort of table land between the two last ranges of the Himalayas, and its climate is quite pleasant to live in all the year round. In sight of it is Mussoorie, another hill station at a much more reasonable distance from the world in general than Simla is."* Of the flora and fauna she witnessed in the valley, Lady Dufferin writes, "*Our way lay through different kinds of wood and jungle and in many parts the lovely little rose, which is so abundant in Dehra covered the forest trees, and fell in pink cascades from all the branches. Then we saw the tall grasses......some of them grow twenty feet high, and are yellow and and dried up now with black marks on them."* Describing her visit to a tea garden she says, "*He (the Manager of the tea garden) gave us some home made beverage before we left and we walked all over the gardens which are very pretty. The tea bushes are neat looking shrubs, and there are some good trees in the place and a lovely view of the mountains from it."* Evidently, the Britisher's penchant for detail was not lost on the Vicerene.

In 1922, the Prince of Wales Royal Indian Military College was inaugurated by the Prince of Wales himself, who was later King Edward VIII. The institution was to be a feeder to Sandhurst, and is still a feeder to all the Defence Training Institutions of India, now known as the Rashtriya (National) Indian Military College. It has a sprawling campus, a part of the cantonment. Among the first batch was K.S. Thimayya who was not only a great Chief of the Indian Army but also made a name for himself internationally as a force commander of the United Nations. By the year 1932, it was necessary to have the officer cadre of the army Indianized and the estate of the Railway Staff College was taken over and the Indian Military Academy was established in Dehradun to train the Indian army's future officers. While inaugurating this Academy, Field Marshal Sir Philip Chetwode, GCB, GCSS, CCMA, DSO Commander-in-Chief of the Indian Army briefed the cadets about the army they would be joining, *"no better material exists in the world, and they have proved it on many stricken fields."* He also gave the Academy its credo, which says, *"the safety honour and welfare of your country come first always and every time, the honour, welfare and comfort of the men you command come next, your own ease, comfort and safety come last always and every time."* Twice every year about 600 cadets are commissioned from here in a ceremonial Passing Out Parade, which is a spectacle to behold. In the first batch of the Indian Military Academy in 1932 was Smith Dun of Burma, Mohmmad Musa of what later became Pakistan and Sam Manekshaw, of India. All three rose to be Chiefs of their respective armies. Sam Manekshaw the famous victor of the 1971 Bangladesh War, became India's first Field Marshal. The Academy received the Viceroy's colours in 1934, and the President's colours in 1962 and 1976 respectively.

The Doon School based on the public school concept of Harrow and Eton keeping in view India's tradition enriched soil, was established in 1935 at Chandbagh by S.R. Das who was an eminent barrister and a member of the Executive Council of the Viceroy. It has produced many eminent alumni among which former Prime Minister Rajiv Gandhi is the most prominent. It's sister school, the Welham Girls School was to come up in 1957, and was founded by Miss H. Oliphant, a retired English Headmistress and is named after the little Welsh village from where Miss Oliphant hailed. Located in the Dalanwala residential area, its former students (known popularly as Welhamites) include media personality Madhu Trehan, politician Brinda Karat, film actress Kareena Kapoor and Priyanka Gandhi. Apart from these two premier institutions, Dehradun and Mussoorie are home to many excellent schools like the St Joseph's Academy, Convent of Jesus and Mary, St George's College, Waverly Convent, Wineberg Allen School, Oakgrove School run for railway employees and Woodstock School, to name a few. A description of Dehradun without mention of the litchi orchards and basmati rice would be akin to writing of Beethoven and not mentioning his total loss of hearing. The litchi orchids which used to cover large parts of the valley in its magnificent bright red colour is slowly diminishing as property sharks convert the lush orchards into concrete jungles. The fruit is grown mainly in tropical countries like China, Burma, Thailand, and Pakistan to mention a few places in the world apart from India of course. It first appeared in Burma in the 18th century, but is said to have been brought to Dehradun by the British from China. The Basmati rice was brought here by the former Afghan ruler Dost Mohmmad who was kept in exile at Barlowganj near Mussoorie in 1840. He had brought the rice seeds from Kunar in Afghanistan. The word Basmati means "smell of the earth."

Many celebrities of our nation have visited the Doon and some indeed, have made it there home. Raja Mahendra Pratap, the famous revolutionary, M.N. Roy the Communist mastermind who later propounded the ideology of "radical humanism,"and Vijaya Lakshmi Pandit the diplomat "par excellence" are in the roll of honour of those who made the valley their abode. Among the recent residents are Nayantara Seghal, the well known writer who has won many international awards in literature. Also Dr Subramaniam Swamy the Harvard Professor turned politician who played the role of the "scarlet pimpernel" during the internal emergency of 1975-77, owns a house here. He and his wife Roxana Swamy are often seen in the valley and mix with like-minded friends and intellectuals. Pandit Jawaharlal Nehru had a great fascination for Dehradun. He spent quite a few years in the Doon gaol during the freedom struggle in the 1930s and early 40s, his last incarceration ending in December 1941. A large part of the book *Glimpses of World History* was written during these periods. On his transfer from Bareilly Gaol on June 10, 1932, Panditji writes to his daughter Indira *"and so here I sit in the little gaol of Dehradun and it is better here than at Bareilly. It is not quite so hot, and the temperature does not rise to 112 degrees as it did in Bareilly. And the walls surrounding us are lower and the trees that overlook them are greener. In the distance I can even see, over our wall, the top of a palm tree, and the sight delights me and makes me think of Ceylon and Malabar. Beyond the trees there lie the mountains, not many miles away perched up on top of them sits Mussoorie. I cannot see the mountains for the trees hide them, but it is good to be near them and to imagine at night the lights of Mussoorie twinkling in the far distance."* Panditji's alluring prose gives a wonderful description of the valley he loved so much. As Prime Minister he came to Dehra on many occasions and fate so willed that he spent the last full day of his life in this town. His last holiday in Dehradun was from May 23-26, 1964 and he stayed as usual in the Circuit

House (the present residence of the Governor of Uttarakhand) and on the evening of 26th May, he drove to the nearby heli pad on the Polo ground to board the helicopter to Sarsawa near Saharanpur from where he would emplane for Delhi. As he drove to the Polo ground he waved to the crowds gathered on either side of the road, who knew then that it was to be his last interaction with the Indian people. Early on the morning of 27th May he would fall unconscious and by noon the gentle colossus would pass away. Mahatma Gandhi came to the valley on various occasions. In 1944, upon his release from the Agha Khan Palace at Pune, he came to Mussoorie to recuperate as he was in poor health at the time and stayed at the Birla House in Happy Valley. Every evening he would visit the Kulri Area (lower Mall) and hold his prayer meetings in the tennis courts in the compound of the Sylverton Hotel, opposite the "Picture Palace" cinema house.

Dehra was the centre of many activities during the struggle for independence or the "weaponless war for freedom" as Mahatma Gandhi called it. During the Non-Co-operation movement of 1921-22, many volunteers (the number of which reached a thousand by January 1922) enrolled. It was decided by the Indian National Congress to boycott the visit of the Prince of Wales to the city in March 1922, and on March 13, 1922 when he alighted at the Railway Station he was greeted by black flags which promptly led to the arrest of the protesters. It may be stated that officially his reception was a glittering one, with school children from the European schools lining the route from the station to the cantonment. In the same year a meeting was organized at a place called Doiwala which lies on the Dehra – Haridwar road and was addressed by Pandit Jawaharlal Nehru and Swami Shankaracharya. Nehru urged the people to use Swadeshi (Indian-made) textiles, abstain from violence during the agitation against the government, refer their legal disputes to arbitration and work for national unity. The Khilafat movement led by Maulana Mohmmad Ali and Maulana Shaukat Ali known commonly as the Ali brothers, was to find support in Dehradun. Provincial Legislative Council elections were held in 1926. Several meetings were held and those luminaries who visited the town for this election campaign included Motilal Nehru, Hakim Ajmal Khan, Maulana Abdul Kalam Azad, and Devdas Gandhi, who was the son of the Mahatma. The Congress candidate Thakur Manjit Singh, son of Thakur Mitrajit Singh, a well known Arya Samajist and social worker was victorious defeating the sitting member Rai Bahadur Ugra Sen. During the 1930 Salt Satyagrah of Gandhiji made famous by his march to Dandi, Dehradun also witnessed hectic activity as people made salt at public places and compounds of government offices like the District Courts and the Municipal Office. On August 29, 1931 a bomb of the size of a cricket ball was thrown into the house of the city`s Kotwal (Police Chief) injuring many people. Loknayak Jayaprakash Narayan, Ram Manohar Lohia among others while moving around as leaders who had gone underground in 1942-43, stayed in the basement of the house of a prominent resident of Mussoorie who was known to be a British toady to the outside world, but was at heart a nationalist.

In August 1942, following the arrest of Mahatma Gandhi and virtually the "who`s-who" of the Congress leadership upon the launching of the "Quit India" movement, Dehradun was not far behind in the struggle. Shopkeepers downed the shutters of their shops and people took out processions in violation of prohibitory orders. More than 300 people were arrested and various fines levied. In August 1942 a procession of students from the local DAV College was taken out in support of the Congress agitation. Upon arriving at the school called St Joseph's Academy,they urged the Principal to close down the school. The Principal being an Irishman whose own country had fought against the British had sympathy for the cause of India's independence, and instead of closing the school he took the processionists to the senior classes and told the students that they could join the protest march if they so desired and would not be marked as absent from school. Some boys joined the procession and were later let off by the police with an admonition. Mahant Inderesh Charan Das who was later head of the Guru Ram Rai Mission was also arrested in this movement as a student in Allahabad, but later released as the presiding Mahant died and Inderesh had to take over as head of the organization. At one stage the Police Chief of Dehra, an Englishman called C.P. Luck wanted to fire on a peaceful procession but the District Magistrate an Indian, Hifazat Husain, I.C.S. saved the town from calamity by refusing permission as it was a peaceful assembly of people. The Doon like the rest of the country celebrated Independence on August 15, 1947 with great fervour.

Post-independence as a result of partition Dehradun saw the influx of several refugees from West Punjab. They were put up in the Premnagar prisoner war camp which had housed the Italian Army prisoners of war during the Second World War. These refugee families have largely taken to trade and some to government service and other activities. A large number re-migrated to Delhi and neighbouring cities in the mid-1950s. The Lal Bahadur Shastri National Academy of Administration (earlier known as the National Academy of Administration) was moved to Mussoorie from New Delhi (where it was known as Metcalfe House) in 1959 and located in the Happy Valley Area. It trains officers selected for the prestigious Indian Administrative Service and gives basic training to officers of the Indian Police Service and other Central Government Services. The Oil and Natural Gas Commission established in 1959, has a massive infrastructure set-up between the Cantonment and the Forest Research Institute Campus at Dehradun. It is primarily engaged in Oil Exploration and has made notable strides in this direction in the last five decades of existence. Apart from these two institutions it is worthy to mention the Indian Institute of Petroleum which came up on the Haridwar Road in the years after freedom. The "Raphael" Home started by Lord Leonard Cheshire in 1959, has also done commendable work among physically and mentally challenged people and is located in the wooded groves across the Rispana River adjoining the Dalanwala residential area. It has a full-fledged Tuberculosis Hospital and a total of about 300 residents, apart from organizing various programmers and day centres for the "children of a lesser God." A branch of the "Cheshire Homes" is also in Dehradun.

On the intervening night of November 8-9, 2000, the State of Uttarakhand (then known as Uttaranchal) was inaugurated at the Parade Ground of Dehradun in the heart of the city. Dehradun from a District town of Uttar Pradesh now became the temporary capital of the new hill province. Being a state capital has meant a rush of urbanization and also development of the metro culture in the once quiet and tranquil little town. The first elected assembly of Uttarakhand State was constituted in 2002 and Mr Narain Dutt

Tiwari, the veteran Congressman became the first elected Chief Minister. It was during the term of his government which lasted till 2007, that the State Infrastructure and Industrial Development Corporation of Uttarakhand, was formed and has a large estate located at Haridwar. Among his other handiwork was providing good impetus to the industrial hub of Selaqui on the Dehra-Poanta Sahib Road, the concept of Ring Road connecting the Haridwar-Mussoorie bypass on one side and the Saharanpur bypass on the other, the setting up of the IT Park on Sahstradhara Road, and the Doon University Campus well located on the Saharanpur by-pass to mention a few. His successors are also continuing a fairly level pace of development in Dehradun and in the new state.

Dehradun as seen today, in the year of the Lord 2011, is a bustling, busy town bursting at the seams and a far cry from the once serene paradise like city of the green valley known for "green hedges and grey heads." As the well known writer Ruskin Bond writes of the Dehra of yore, *"Dehradun was a much smaller, greener, considerably less crowded town; sleepier too, and somewhat laid back, easy going; fond of gossip, but tolerant of human foibles. A place of bicycles and pony drawn tongas. Only a few cars and you could walk almost anywhere at any time of the year, night or day."* The author Ramachandra Guha now living in Bangalore, dwells on the Dehra of his childhood thus, *"Still although, I think of it seldom, in my dreams my other (and original) home town pops up every so often. Its dense and crowded bazaar figures, but more often I dream of the valley in which the town is set; of its pine forests, its swift running streams, its views of the hills, and its birds beautiful and grand from the Paradise Flycatcher to the Red-billed Blue Magpie."*

Dehradun the city as is known to the world and the Doon Valley surrounding it, have a glorious history immersed in tradition and the exquisite charm of mother nature. One only hopes that the city and valley retain it in the years that lie ahead so that it makes its date with eternity.

□

36

For the Honour of India and Beyond

"For the Honour of India" is the motto set by Lt General S.S.P. Thorat, DSO when he (then a Major General) was deputed as commander of the Indian Custodian Force in Korea in the year 1953, the first UN peacekeeping effort by the Indian Army. Lt Gen Satish Nambiar has had a celebrated career in the Army, and has among other things been 'in action' during the 1965 and 1971 operations. He is a recipient of the Veer Chakra and was this year awarded the Padma Bhushan for his contribution on National Security Affairs.The "feathers in his cap" include being a graduate of Australian Staff College, being with a Training Team in Iraq, Military Adviser in the U.K., Director General of Military Operations, First Commander and head of the UN Forces in the former Yugoslavia, and Deputy Chief of the Army Staff. Post reitirement he was for more than 12 years Director of the well known think-tank on Defence Affairs, the United Services Institution of India.

The foreword of this treatise is by Lt General Mathew Thomas, a distinguished General who was Commandant of the Indian Military Academy and partici pated in Independent India's first peace-keeping mission in Korea. The author has spread out his work in the following sections: East and South East Asia, West Asia, Central and East Africa, Southern Africa, West Africa and Regional Peace Keeping. It also includes a section devoted to distilling thoughts about the challenges facing India in the areana of international peacekeeping in the years to come.

In the environment of international politics, "collective security" and "peace-keeping" often tend to be inter-mingled in commonplace reference. The former is a punitive process designed to be carried out with some degree of discrimination but not necessarily impartially, the latter is politically impartial and essentially non-coercive. This is pivotal point on the matter, exteremly relevant for scholars of the subject. Nambiar`s book makes this distinction in its introduction, itself.

One finds for good measure interesting pen-potraits of the eminent figures who have represented India at the United Nations.The late General Kodendra Subbayya Thimayya is one of the most renowned peace-keepers from the Indian Army.Both in Korea as Chairman of the Neutral Nations Repatriation Commission (NNRC) which involved the repatriation of 120000 Chinese and North Korean Prisoners of War. Ironically, General Thimayya died while commanding the United Nations forces in Cyprus in 1965, an assignment for which U Thant, the United Nations Secretary General had personally requested him for. Other personalities covered include were Lt General Dewan Prem Chand who was the army peacekeeper who remained with the UN for the longest stint, Ms Vijaya Lakshmi Pandit the diplomat par excellence who was President of the 8th session of the UN General Assembly in 1953, Lt General Prem Singh Gyani who was the second force commander of the UNEF 1 for 5 years in Sinai, Mr K.P.S. Menon who was of the nine member United Nations in Korea. Some more worthies from India figure in this section, which the discerning reader will take note off.

Of the missions which the book covers, it is of significance to touch upon those in Korea and Congo. In the event of the Korean armstice coming into effect from July 1953, a large number of Prisoners of War from North Korea and China refused to return to their respective countries causing a great deal of astonishment to their home governments. However, the UN stood by its resolve that choice repatriation be left to the individual soldier. The Neutral Nations Repatriation Commission (NNRC) was proposed by India, and therefore an Indian officer Lt General K.S. Thimayya was chosen for the appointment of chaiman, and Major General S.S.P. Thorat was chosen to head the Custodian Force India. After many ups and downs the force completed its assigned task within the stipulated period of 90 days. Most of the prisoners were handed back to the UN Command and some to the Red Cross representatives of China and North Korea. The mission ended successfully by April 1954, 88 prisoners were brought back to India and their final fate announced after ascertaining their choices. Major General Thorat and Lance Naik Thakur Singh were awarded the Ashoka Chakra Class II and III respectively for conspicuous bravery.

The mission in the Congo in 1960-63, was a vexed tangle. Congo is was a country extremely rich in mineral resources and was a colony of Belgium having gained independence in June 1960, but Belgium continued administrative control through a treaty of friendship. Through UN intervention the UN Peacekeeping Force (ONUC) was deputed to assist the Congolese Government in maintaining law and order till their own security forces were able to handle it. India's participation began in July 1960 with the deployment of supply, technical and medical personnel. Following the shocking assassination of Congolese Prime Minister Patrice Lumumba on January 17, 1961, India hiked its troop deployment to Brigade level. 99 Infantry Brigade under the command Brig K.A.S. Raja, the troop rotation took place in May 1962 and a new Brigade group under Brig R.S. Narohna took over. The groups were able bring to an end the Katangese secessionist struggle (Katananga) was the most mineral rich province). The mission fulfilled its main objectives and Congo did not descend into an all out civil war, political stability was achieved by the end of 1963. The Indian contingent returned in the spring of 1963.

The book also pieces together the UN peacekeeping missions done by the armed forces be it Gaza, Sri Lanka, Ethiopia and Eritrea, Rwanda, Sudan, the second mission to Congo and much else. It is produced on art paper and has a wonderful pictorial spread, it is obvious that a great deal of painstaking research has been undertaken to bring out a work of this nature for which the author and his team deserve well earned kudos.

(For the Honour of India: A History of India in Peacekeeping by Lt General Satish Nambiar, PVSM, VSM, VRC (Retd) published in Defence Watch October 2009)

□

37

Another "Daughter of the East" Rises

At the outset let me make a prediction. Irrespective of the fact whether she is going to make her mark on the public life of the strife torn state of Pakistan or not(she has vehemently denied any political ambitions) Fatima Bhutto will go down in history as a woman of letters. To do this she has to do two things, she has to show a sense of objectivity in her writings without unnecessarily becoming emotional, and has to show a sense of history. I would lay more emphasis on the former than the latter. If she achieves this she has the potential to go on to be one of the great wordsmiths of the sub-continent.

The book opens with the tragic assassination of the author's father, Mir Murtaza Bhutto, virtually at the gates of the of the family house of 70, Clifton, Karachi on the fateful evening of 20 September 1996, (for which she quite unequivocally blames the present President of Pakistan Asif Zardari),and then goes on to trace the history of the Bhutto's, who originated in the deserts of Rajasthan before migrating to Mitho Jo Mikam a small hamlet in the vicinity of Gharhi Khuda Bux which in the province of Sind still remains the abode of the Bhuttos of Larkana. Fatima notes, "Bhuttos very rarely, even then died natural deaths. Many of them died violently and before reaching middle age." Zulfi Bhutto the debonair son of Sir Shahnawaz Bhutto, Sindh's well known bureaucrat and fabulously rich land-owner, attended Berkeley in the US followed later by Oxford. It must be pointed that the elder Bhutto (Sir Shah Nawaz) was diwan of Junagadh State when the problem arose there and it is a known fact that it was he who had advised the Nawab to unilaterally declare accession to Pakistan.

Zulfi climbed the political ladder quickly, taking the right decisions and turning the right corners, and at the young of 30 had become Minister for Fuel, Power and Natural Resources in General Ayub Khan's government. Here he was eminently successful, and it was when he was at the helm of this Department that the Indus River Sharing Accord was signed with India. This accord is still in force and has stood the test of time. Later in the Foreign Office where he reigned supreme for several years, against Field Marshal Ayub Khan's better judgement he went on to develop a Sino-Pakistan relationshi p destined to upset the balance of power in the subcontinent. Though Fatima puts it di plomatically it was Zulfi more than anyone else, who persuaded Ayub Khan to go in for the conflict with India in the early autumn of 1965. The result was diasterous and the Tashkent Accord was to herald Z.A. Bhutto's departure from the government. In a well known anecdote, on the morning of Prime Minister Lal Bahadur Shastri's tragic death at Tashkent, Bhutto was told by an aide, "the bastard's dead" to which he immediately replied, "which one?" such was his contempt for the Field Marshal. None of this forms part of the author's eulogizing account of her grandfather. She is, however, right when she concludes that Bhutto was the main catalyst for Ayub Khan's downfall in early 1969, after he had formed the Pakistan People's Party in 1967. The events of 1970-71, are well known and have been well documented by contemporary historians of which Prof. Stanley Wolpert stands out. All of them have stated that Zulfi refused to accept the verdict of the 1970 elections and succeded in taking President Yahya Khan for a ride as it would have meant accepting Mujib-ur-Rehman as the Prime Minister of undivided Pakistan, so much so that he stated that any delegate who went to Dhakka to attend the proposed session of the National Assembly would have his "legs broken!" Again, this does not appear in the book.

After the dismemberment of Pakistan,Zulfi Bhutto was first President and later Prime Minister of Pakistan.The book throws light on the successful conclusion of the Shimla Accord, (she mentions that an oil portrait of the signing ceremony adorns her grandfather's study in Karachi) Bhutto's comprehensive land reforms, his successful foreign policy vis-à-vis China and other countries, the hosting of the second Organization of Islamic Countries Summit in 1974, socialist policies like bank nationalization which she terms as a "short term solution". She is critical of his crackdown in Baluchistan in the mid-1970s. All this can be described as a correct evaluation of these years of Bhutto at the helm. One would have liked to hear something however, about Husna Sheikh, a woman of extraordinary beauty,who was rumoured to be Zulfi's mistress. Prof Stanley Wolpert has quoted her extensively in his biography of Zulfiqar. The volume then covers the coup of 1977, when the long night of the Generals under Muhmmad Zia ul-Haq,the ruthless dictator who would rule Pakistan for 11 years began, the end-game for Zulfiqar, and the final march to the gallows in the early hours of April 4, 1979.

The coverage given to Mir Murtaza Bhutto, Shahnawaz Bhutto and Benazir (upto her 2007 assassination) as well as the other Bhuttos is exhaustive and gives extensive information related to Fatima's late father, his loves and his life as well his violent bent on politics. The chicanery, deceit and corruption described here sometimes leaves one stumped. The book is already in some controversy on certain statements pertaining to her father's basing himself in Afghanistan on the "final directions" of Z.A. Bhutto from the death cell and some other statements attributed have been challenged by Sanam Bhutto,Zulfiqar's sole surviving child and Tariq Islam a nephew of the late Prime Minister published in *The Dawn* newspaper of Karachi. Fatima lives with stepmother Ghinwa Bhutto and half brother Zulfiqar Jr in Karachi.

On the whole this treatise will be well appreciated for its comprehensive coverage and excellent prose. For Fatima, obviously it has been a labour of love. This you can detect from every line. The reference to the song of the mynah birds in her garden in Karachi, at the end of the book, the reason she cites as never wanting to leave Pakistan is ample proof of her having an "intelligent heart and a kind brain." This Bhutto has the capacity to be heard of for a long time to come, provided the dice of destiny is loaded in her favour.

(*Songs of Blood and Sword: A Daughter's Memoir: Fatima Bhutto published in Defence Watch June 2010*)

□

38

The Battle of Dograi and Batapore by Brig Desmond E. Hayde, MVC (Retd)

It shall long be debated in the military history of the post-independence period as whether it was appropriate to follow the UN-sponsored initiative on the cease fire in 1965, when our troops on Amritsar-Wagah axis were on the outskirts of Lahore. Some historians feel that possibly India went in for the right option as the effect of getting into street fights would have been disastrous for any army given the hostile feeling of the local populace of the city. Brig Desmond E. Hayde's account of the epic battle of Dograi and Batapore shall remain a sturdy reference treatise on the successful advance of the Indian Army by the third battalion of the Jat regiment of which Hayde was the skipper. His Battalion had moved to Khasa on August 4, 1965, just about a month before the operations began when no inkling of the oncoming war was available. Hayde made some sound decisions and used the ability of his experienced JCOs in strategic positions rather then the exuberance of his young officers whose drive he used elsewhere. He rightly notes "a unit becomes formidable when there is confidence in its leadership." These are hallmarks of a good commander at the helm.

The action at Dograi took place a few miles out of Lahore and though the fighting was severe the redoubtable Jat soldier proved to be more than a match for the vastly superior, well entrenched 16th Pathan Battalion of the Pakistani Army. Hayde gives a vivid narrative of the battlefield in the Punjab plains during that crucial

September. He himself was struck by shrapnel in the small of his back and was saved by his water bottle from what could have been a fatal attack!

The strategy for the attack, the actual execution of the plan and the final capture of Dograi and Batapore as well as crossing of the Ichhogil canal comes alive in your mind's eye as you read this history of the Indo-Pakistan conflict of 1965.As Lt Gen S.K. Sinha (Retd), Governor of J&K says in his foreword, "Brigadier Hayde led his men and wielded his carbine with marked comptence at Dograi. For the benefit of his readers, he has now wielded his pen with equal competence in this book, vividly recreating for us the sound, the smell, and the scene of this great battle."

The author has certain grievances about awards and battle-honours which he has every right to express. But in a democratic country this has to take this in one's stride.

(Published in Defence Watch)

□

39

Leaders in Olive Green

What makes a leader out of a man? Vision, boldness, courage and honesty no doubt but more than that he must have a certain charisma and an aura around him to come to be rated a true leader. Also let it be pointed out that most of the leaders of repute, at least in the military sphere, were not exactly paragons of virtue or flawless characters in their personal lives. It is a fact of life which history has borne out time and again. V.K. Singh has not dealt about the military celebrities in his book in this vein and glossed over the negative aspects of their lives. This is a serious flaw in a work of this nature. For example, Thimayya's philandering was legendary. He did not pursue his resignation in 1959, because he was informed by the powers that be that some embarrassing evidence would be released publicly which related to some of his "flings" (Militarism in India: The Army and Civil Society in Consensus by Apurba Kundu) Prem Bhagat's love for the bottle was more than well known. So was Sam Manekshaw's "evenings at the Oberoi".

V.K.Singh's book it must be said fulfils a long standing gap as to the best of my knowledge no other work has been published with profiling military leaders of the post independence period. Interesting anecdotes will enlighten the reader and it will be grist for the mill to students of military history.

Among the highlights are descriptions of Sam Manekshaw being demoted as a cadet in the Academy for over-staying, the night in Mussoorie, his rather embarrassing advice to nurses while visiting a military hospital, his role in the 1971 war, the denial of the post of Chief of Defence Staff for petty reasons, Prem Bhagat's humility and strength of character, his action in East Afica of unparalleled bravery and inspiring leadership which won him the Victoria Cross, Brig Mohmmad Usman the hero of the battle of Jhangar who won the Mahavir Chakra posthmously, K.S. Thimayya the leader among generals whose mere visit to a unit was enough to provide a tonic to raise flagging spirits, Nathu Singh a fearless nationalist who did not hesitate to clash with Nehru, S.K. "Mannah" Sinha the thinking man's General who was unjustly superseded for the post of Chief of Staff and now ably serves the country as Governor of Jammu & Kashmir, SSP Thorat who did valuable work during the Korean crisis, K.M. Carriappa the first Indian to be Commander-in-Chief who was a stickler for propriety, ZC "Zoru" Bakshi who was India's most decorated general, Sagat Singh one of the hero's of Bangladesh, R.N. Batra who streamlined communications in the army and Hanut Singh, a battle scarred veteran who never hesitated to call a spade a spade. Some omissions in Singh's list of leaders are Generals J.F.R. Jacob, Ranjit Singh Dayal of Hajipir fame, Kulwant Singh the hero of Kashmir and Gen K. Sundarji. One wonders why he did not expand his description of these veterans.

On the whole an important addition to the library of "matters military"

Leadership in the Indian Army: Biographies of Twelve Soldiers
by Major General V. K. Singh (Retd.)
(Published in 'Defence Watch')

□

40

The Herbert Fieldman Omnibus

The Herbert Fieldman Ominibus covers in encyclopedic detail the events occurring in Pakistan starting from the coup of 1958 which brought Ayub Khan to power resulting in the first declaration of martial law in that country, till the dismemberment of Pakistan following the Bangladesh War in 1971, first published as three volumes.

Major General Iskander Mirza President of Pakistan issued a 1400 word statement on October 7, 1958 deriding the ruthless power struggle of and exploitation of the citizenry of Pakistan by professional politicians which had ensued during the past two years preceding the declaration of Martial Law and announced the appointment of the Supreme Commander of the Pakistan Army Gen Mohammad Ayub Khan as Chief Martial Law Administrator.. It was a familiar theme to be repeated on many an occasion whenever a military takeover has occurred in Pakistan during the 55 years of its existence, the latest being by Parvez Mushharaf in October 1999. Iskander Mirza was put on the shelf before the month of October 1958 was over, and Ayub had ascended the Presidency.

During the early part of his regime Ayub Khan ensured a system of fixed prices for essential commodities and took stringent measures against black-marketeers. Martial Law regulations were also issued with the object of gathering taxes on undisclosed income. Ayub Khan coined the slogan "Austerity is our national style" but in substance it was nothing but a naïve piece of self-deception. Ayub, like most men of eminence was a man in whose life destiny had played a major role. Had Lt General Iftikhar not been killed in an air accident, he would probably never have been Chief of the Pakistani Army. It must be said that Ayub could establish a warm rapport with his audience and people at large. Rajeshwar Dayal, India`s ambassador to Pakistan immediately after the 1958 coup has put on record that Ayub(whom he knew well before partition) told him that he was willing "to do anything to sort out Indo-Pak relations in the first six months in power, before politicians hold me in hock". It is a tragedy that such opportunities were wasted. On more than one occasion he proposed a joint defence pact with India.

The system of Basic Democracy on the basis of 'tiers' and 'unit' could not by any stretch of the imagination be called a genuine democracy. Ayub ushered in fairly good economic growth for Pakistan during his regime and is brought out in the book, he powerfully stimulated the private sector, GNP went up from Rs 3014 crores in 1958–59, to Rs 4828 crores in 1967-68. The 1965 Presidential election was quite controversial against Fatima Jinnah. Ayub was led to believe that Kashmiris would rise in revolt against the Indian government in the event of hostilities with Pakistan which in turn led him to plan Operation Gibraltar and Grand Slam. Also he was confident about the creation of a China-Pakistan-Indonesia axis. The author gives graphic details of these events and those of the 1965 war, followed by the Tashkent Accord. There is talk of a secret protocol of `status quo` on Kashmir which was to be repeated at the Shimla talks of 1972. Ayub allowed corruption to grow and was surrounded by fawning courtiers. His sons and relatives enriched themselves phenomenally. The agitation against his government which began in the autumn of 1968, masterminded by his former Foreign Minister Zulfikar Ali Bhutto proved fatal, and on March 25, 1969 Ayub bid adieu to the Presidency of Pakistan.

Yahya Khan who succeeded Ayub was a bizarre character. The book details the initial period of his rule, leading to his holding of elections to the National Assembly in December 1970, on 'one man one vote' in which the Awami League of Shiekh Mujibur Reham scored a thumping majority sweeping all the seats of East Pakistan. Playing the evil genius, Bhutto caused one of the worst genocides in human history at the hands of Yahya and Tikka Khan.

Yahya Khan on the eve of his departure from Dacca told Tikka Khan with regard to the Bengalis, "Sort them Out". How cavalier could one get! Feldman has chronicled the events following the massacre of 25 March in great detail giving the hijack of the Forker Friendshi p aircraft as the moot point which from which the hostile situation began to deteriorate. Also well catalogued is the Yahya – Bhutto relationshi p in the post–March scenario with the migration of 714300 refugees to India. Bhutto`s last ditch attempt to woo China is of special interest as also the events of the Bangladesh war from the Pakistani angle. On the whole this trilogy will go down as essential reading for any researcher of the period.

(Review Published in USI Journal)

□

41

How the Vaishno Devi Temple was Reformed?

Jagmohan has been an active and able administrator. He has proved his mettle in various capacities as a bureaucrat, in gubernatorial office or as a cabinet minister in the central government. The book under consideration is partly about his tenure in Jammu & Kashmir State as the Governor in the mid 1980s and partly on the topic of Hinduism from a historical perspective as well as contains some ideas for reform in Hindu religion.

It was just a matter of chance that Jagmohan as Governor of J&K happened to visit the Vaishno Devi Shrine in the Jammu region of the state in June 1985. The sight that confronted him on the pilgrimage was hardly edifying. Here is what he has to say, "Unbearable filth too, seemed to come out of the same junk store. Most places stank of urine. Excreta of horses and mares and uneven walkways, added to the insufferability of the conditions. Beggars had their own detestable hovels in whatever niches they could locate among the rocky mounds along the path." Apart from all this he also discovered that unhygienic food was being served to pilgrims during their journey, a large number of whom contracted gastro enteritis, he witnessed people falling and sustaining injuries and even an old woman collapsing fatally at the beginning of the cave. All this brought home the massive discomfort suffered by the pilgrims as also the plunder by the local custodians of the temple known as *baridars*, so much so that the spiritual peace he experienced inside the sanctum was negated by the cesspool which existed outside.

Jagmohan came to the conclusion that a massive effort was required to reform the shrine and he was willing to undertake the same in the form of "firm action when opportunity came my way." On March 7, 1986, the province of Jammu & Kashmir came under Governor`s rule as per Section 92 of the Constitution of Jammu & Kashmir. As soon as this was done, Jagmohan gave paramountcy to the takeover and reform of the Vaishno Devi Shrine. He, with the help of capable and experienced officials drafted a law which would secure the purpose of takeover of the shrine without infringing any of the sections of the Constitution. On the night of August 30-31, 1986, the shrine was taken over and the work began in real earnest. Apart from a dedicated team of local level officers Jagmohan got on deputation some officers who had worked with him in the Delhi administration as well. Soon a proper road was built with lighting facilities of 1000 sodium vapour lamps, 15 lakh tiles were fixed, 5000 parapet walls were constructed and 2000 metres of protective railings installed at dangerous points. Shelters and allied aspects of bedding were also taken care of. Hygienic and cheap food was made available at restaurants which were well equipped. In short the route was transformed into a place of cleanliness and great convenience to the people undertaking the journey. The happiest beneficiaries were the common pilgrims who expressed joy over the takeover and new developments. Jagmohan has given ample examples of the responses received in the book. He also wanted to undertake a similar reform for the Amarnath Yatra and had prepared a comprehensive plan for it, but the duration of Governor`s rule was not long enough, and the popular government which came to power later took no interest in this scheme.

Part 2 of this volume deals with "A case for reformed reawakened and enlightened Hinduism". In this section he deals with the question "Who are the Hindus?" The author debunks the theory of Arayan invasion on the basis of various contemporary historical studies along with recent genetic research in this field, and gives a fairly detailed research on Harappan Civilization and the Sarasvati river which may have disappeared. Gandhi had once said that "Hinduism is a relentless pursuit after truth". The opus in its concluding pages deals with some suggestions of reform, where the writer dwells on neo-Vedanta, practical Vedanta, the position of women, sati and the caste system of which he is justifiably critical. In this context he quotes Swami Vivekananda who observed "India`s doom was sealed the very day it coined the word 'Mlechaa'." The book also contains as an appendix Sister Nivedita's account of Swami Vivekananda's journey to the Amarnath shrine in 1898 which will be of interest to the discerning reader.

On the whole this publication will be well accepted by the thinking public of our country, who has the interest of the future of the nation at heart.

(Reforming Vaishno Devi and a Case for Reformed, Reawakened and Enlightened Hinduism by Jagmohan published in the Himachal Times, Dehradun, April 27, 2010)

□

42

Those Whom I Have Known

Reviwing life as a film, one looks back at the beginning and thinks of those whom one has come across in life's journey, a rich haul of memories flock to the mind even at middle age. Some celebrities have come my way and many prosaic people. I sometimes think that these 'prosaic people' are of more interest and use to society than the 'celebrities' who came my way, but that is just a thought that comes and goes on the surface of one's mind. I must add however that some of the best thoughts and ideas have come to me when I allow my imagination to go wild, often as wild as the stormy sky on a tempestuous evening when thunder makes a mighty sound and lightning strikes with its colossal fury. Rudyard Kipling wrote in *"If"*, *"if you can walk with kings and yet not lose the common touch.......If you can dream, and not make dreams your master."* These words of verse have often haunted me. In this context I must also look back to those "who met a stranger and left a friend." Sometimes one meets such people. I have found people who have treated me with great warmth and hospitality even though they hardly knew me. I remember once a kindness personified by someone who hardly knew me on a social occasion. These experiences, though not more than a few minutes long have had more powerful impact on my being than any other involvement because of their profound nature. It has ingrained in me the feeling that all the loveliness in the world can be reduced to its first syllable.

The former Prime Minister Morarji Desai, the legal genius Nani Palkhivala, India's first Field Marshal Sam Manekshaw, the

A Group photograph of 1981. L to R: Maj Gen P.E. Menon, Military Secretary to the President, Lt Gen Mohindar Singh, AVSM, Commandant Defence Services Staff College (the author's father), President N. Sanjeeva Reddi, the Author, Sadiq Ali, Governor of Tamil Nadu

artist Governor Surjit Singh Barnnala, Narain Dutt Tewari, the first elected Chief Minister of Uttarakhand, the present Uttarakhand Governor Margaret Alva are among the big names who have been kind enough to spend their valuable time with this humble soul, who doubles as a businessman and writer. I shall also later on deal with just a few of the less glitzy mortals who were by no means less consequential in providing meaning to my life.

Morarjibhai the Gandhian was somewhat different from the media image of being a hard forbidding disciplinarian when you met him personally, I must make it clear that I came into contact with him in 1982, when his active political career was long over. He still however took time off to campaign for his political outfit the Janata Party, and his gait was fairly fast for a man of his age, there was still the pink of youthfulness in his face and his cheeks were rosy. You usually entered his room in the morning hours when he was sitting cross legged on his bed and spinning (a Gandhian exercise which he undertook every day for an hour). After you greeted him and sat down on the settee beside his bed, he would look at you and say "hmmmm" in a long singsong manner. The journalist Rajinder Puri once wrote that this "hmmmm" "*is at once an exclamation, a question, a veiled accusation which meant three things, (a)There you are; (b) where have you been and what have you been doing? (c) been upto some mischief, no doubt!"* (Rajinder Puri:*A Crisis of Conscience*, New Delhi, 1971)

Then the conversation would turn to various topics, some of them current, some on his philosophy of life and spiritual matters. I must say that he was particularly knowledgeable about the Bhagavad Gita, and I knew that he had memorized the holy treatise which he would recite every day. He could be brutally frank in his comments about his colleagues, some of his own Party. I remember his stinging comments about the personal life of a politician who later became Prime Minister. While speaking to him in his apartment 'Oceana' on Mumbai's scenic Marine Drive, one could not but get the impression that the lion was in his den. Outside stretched the Arabian sea in all its regal glory. Pritish Nandy while interviewing him for *The Illustrated Weekly of India* entitled his story "*The Old Man Beside The Sea"* Nandy however made no apologies to Ernest Hemingway! Often in our conversation his dose of auto urine therapy would come up. He was convinced that it had done him a world of good. May be there was something to it. He lived upto the age of 99 years. I also think of the time when we discussed his being accused of being a CIA mole by the American writer Seymour Hersh. He was rightly dismissive about it as beneath contempt. He hinted that Hersh was a communist ideologue and this may have had something to do with the affair. I felt sad that a veteran political stalwart of the nation had to face these unfounded accusations in the autumn of his life. Some years after Morarji had passed away, a friend and I had a long conversation with the former Governor B.K. Nehru at his residence in Kasauli. On my bringing up the CIA issue Nehru (who had known Morarji well and had worked with him in the Finance Ministry) said immediately, "it was not him, but M.J. Desai, who was Foreign Secretary during the Indo-China war who could have been the person involved. He was beholden to the Americans for certain reasons." On my asking him if he had some ground to think that way, B.K. Nehru was emphatic and said, "I am convinced about it, poor Morarjibhai was a victim of mistaken identity." B.K. Nehru had been ambassador in the United States for a considerably long period and must have been talking on the basis of some inside information.

Morarji would stand out in any group. His hallmarks were a well chiselled handsome countenance and this combined with a fine sense of dress. Self-confidence oozed out of him when you met him, I think it took him a long way in life. A certain deliberation was a hallmark to his way of talking; it did make an impact on you when you sat face to face with him. It was the voice of a man born to command. His eyes also penetratingly looked at you as he gave you his views. He also took a long time to give you an exhaustive explanation of any topic you brought to his notice particularly if it was philosophical in nature or concerned a question of significant political relevance. I remember a long discussion on the Kamraj Plan and how it came about. He had a great feeling of destiny which he said had played a great part in his life. An ordinary school teacher's son had become the chief executive of this country. Even his emergency detention in Haryana State was his destiny he believed. Thrice destiny had denied him the prime ministershi p,on the fourth occasion destiny was kinder,thanks largely to the anti-Congress mood of the country in the aftermath of the emergency in 1977. He had been nurtured in the ashram culture and was given to using the Mahatma as a yardstick for judging issues. People who knew him often say that administration was his forte. He could seize a file from its head and tail as well and ask the right questions drawing upon the right conclusions when required. His words once uttered to me at one of our first meetings, "*in life you may lose everything, but if you have not lost being true to yourself you have lost nothing*" act as great solace to me while one (as everyone must) encounters worldly storms as one traverses life's path.

Nani Palkhivala was humility personified. Exchanging preliminaries with him led you to feel that you were shaking hands with grace and diginity itself. He first met me in the company of my father and with the enthusiasm of a school boy I quizzed him with various questions. When he met my father alone nearly a year later, the first question he asked him was, "How is your son?". So photographic was his memory. To look at there was nothing unduly impressive about him. It was only when he spoke that you realized that this was an extraordinary man. When he mounted the podium and began speaking to his audience you remained dazzled with his words. When he spoke on the constitution, it was as if dry written words were coming to life. He conjured up before you the historical atmosphere when the constituent assembly first met and when at that first meeting the American jurist Joseph Story's famous words were used in the context of the Indian Constitution on the anvil, a document *"which has been reared for immortality, if the work of man may justly aspire to such a title."* Before you were portrayed the drama of the constitutional crisis witnessed during the internal emergency of 1975 to 1977 when at great personal loss and at the risk of indefinite imprisonment he waged often a lone battle against the all powerful establishment. If he took a liking to you, you were treated like a member of his larger family. On a number of occasions on arrival at Mumbai, I would ring him only to be told "*have potluck with us tonight, or the next afternoon.*" It was of course hardly potluck and would be a four course meal which would start with drinks and interesting conversation. The other guests used to be a sprinkling of people from various walks of life, sometimes Tata employees, sometimes some NRI friends and other people or his nephews and nieces. His wife Nargesh was an excellent hostess. Those get-togethers at 'Commonwealth' (the Palkhivala residence in Mumbai) will remain imprinted in my mind as long as I live. Palkhivala had a gift with the written word. *An open letter to the Prime Minister* written in *The Illustrated Weekly of India* dated April 17, 1977 was one of his finest pieces written within a month of the lifting of the Emergency on March 21, 1977, addressed to the new Prime Minister, Morarji Desai. Inter alia he said,

> *The gruesome nightmare is over. It is your great destiny to lead the nation after its second liberation to the broad sunny uplands. The people – one sixth of the human race have given you a generous and confident*

mandate. Only one man in a billion is born with your destiny." Of Jayaprakash Narayan the patriarch of the movement he mentioned in the same article, "*Not since the time of Gandhiji has moral force – personified by a frail invalid – triumphed so spectacularly over the forces of evil. He changed decisively the course of history. One life transformed the destiny of 620 millions. His epoch making work must be carried on and the process of public education must never cease. Others will have to continue to propagate the great values which Jayaprakash has taught the nation – a lesson which our people may not always remember but which they will never wholly forget.*

A soul stirring expression by any standard and that was what he was, a human being, humane in every way.

Nani was very prompt in replying to letters and one always received a speedy reply. For example on March 7, 1996, he wrote to me "I am deeply touched by the generous sentiments you have expressed......It was a pleasure meeting you in Delhi and I look forward to meeting you in Dehradun." After the Dehradun visit he thought it fit to write again, on March 26, 1996, "Nargesh and I are grateful to you for your kind courtesy and great friendliness during our brief stay in Dehradun......with every good wish and renewed thanks for the trouble you have taken over us." The death of my parents and brother in quick succession in 1998, resulted in my not sending out new year cards that year, but simply letters of greeting explaining the reason why. Nani was touched, and said in his reply of January 4, 1999, "Last year was a sad year for you and we share your sadness and sorrow." In March 1999, a lively evening at "Commonwealth" had taken place on my visit to Mumbai that month (alas! it was the last time we broke bread together) and the conversation had somehow turned to Dehradun and its famed *basmati* rice. On return home, I sent him some which he acknowledged on April 9, 1999, "We are grateful for the delicious basmati rice you sent us. We are always happy to have you over, whenever you are in Bombay." In September 1999 his book *Selected Writings* was out, which I read with interest resulting in my conveying my comments to Nani about it. His letter of October 6, 1999, refers to this, "I am so glad you liked the book of my selected writings. I hope you will visit Bombay in the near future. Nargesh and I look forward to meeting you again." Sadly, I was never to see Nargesh again, though I met Nani a few times in the year 2000 who was by then a pale shadow of his former self. It left me feeling immeasurably downcast at that time.

I remembered occasions when he took me with him in his car for a public meeting introducing me to his hosts as a close friend of his. I also remembered being with him on the train when he visited my hometown Dehradun in March 1996, having a long talk about the disci pline and glorious traditions of the Indian Army. Knowing my army background he was seeking me out on the subject.

Palkhivala's life, particularily in the context of his role during the emergency, can well be summed up by the famous speech of Douglas Macarthur, the illustrious general of the United States of America at West Point in 1962,

> *Duty-Honour-Country. Those three hallowed words reverently dictate what you ought to be, what you can be, what you will be. They are your rallying points: to build courage when courage seems to fail; to regain faith when there seems little cause for faith; to create hope when hope becomes forlorn.........humble and gentle in success; not to substitute words for actions, nor seek the path of comfort but to challenge; to master yourself before you seek to master others; to have a heart that is clean; a goal that is high; to learn to laugh and yet never forget how to weep; to reach in to the future yet never neglect the past; to be serious yet never take yourself too seriously; to be modest so that you will remember the simplicity of true greatness; the open mind of true wisdom; the meekness of strength.*

Although not a military man,this code of conduct and descri ption of a righteous life given in the preceding paragraph was followed by this eminent personality to the tee. He knew more than anyone else that I have met yet showed the simplicity of true greatness and the meekness of strength, and practised it in letter and spirit.

On the intervening night of November 8–9, 2000 the State of Uttarakhand (then known as Uttaranchal) was inaugurated at the Parade Ground in the heart of Dehradun city. Sardar Surjit Singh Barnala, a veteran Akali leader who had already occupied the post of Union Minister, Chief Minister of Punjab and Governor of Tamil Nadu was sworn in as the nascent state's first governor at the same venue where the state was inaugurated. But I must take the reader back to the time when I had my first meeting with Barnala in the year 1996. His extremely interesting book *The Story of an Escape* was published that year, and I had enjoyed reading it. It told the story of his life in an out of the ordinary way engrossing the reader. Barnala had some years previously, disguised himself as a Sikh farmer and gone in a truck through the length and breath of the country and this was combined with the autobiographical narration. In the summer of 1996 he had re-entered parliament after a long gap and I met him in Delhi at the Punjab Bhavan where we discussed his book and some commonalities. A few other meetings followed, but I left it at that, wondering if I would meet Barnala again. Destiny however had other plans. Soon after he became head of our state, I went to call on him again. He greeted me in a hearty manner, "I have been here a considerable time, and now you call on me!" I had to mutter something about being out of town and reminded him of our conversation in 1996 when he had praised the ambience of Dehradun's Circuit House. He laughed at this and said "Yes, we could not imagine then that it would one day be my residence" (the Dehradun Circuit House became Uttaranchal's Raj Bhavan or governor's house). After this I took to meeting him almost every month when he was our governor for about two years. We also met at functions across the town from time to time; I was also to be at many functions at the Raj Bhavan.

When you met Barnala, one thing you could not help noticing was that he was totally focused on you. You held his complete attention during that period and he was able to convey to you that your presence in his chamber was of fairly significant importance to the head of state. He asked searching questions and was equally substantive in the answers he gave to your queries. Not a whiff of snobbishness or arrogance was traceable. I remember how he wanted to know everything about my childhood physical difficulties and how I overcame them. That day he was really showing a rare sensitivity which was something to cherish. When a governor assumes office he takes an oath "to devote myself to the service of the people of the state". Barnala took his oath seriously. In the Raj Bhavan those days one found common people lined up in the corridors, seated in the verandah or in the waiting rooms. I also realized soon that he was a bit of a workaholic. He could continue to meet people and give interviews late into the night, often well past 10 pm during Dehradun's cold winter. He remained fresh at whatever time you met him. Painting has been a thing of passion with him; mention it and his face lights up. I often think that his physical and mental equipoise have a lot to do with the fact that he has been an artist for so many years now. At the age of 85 he is acquitting his duties as Governor of Tamil Nadu with all the energy required. He was the only governor appointed by the NDA Government who was given a second term by the UPA Government in 2006. His autobiography contains a lovely and emotional story when he was in detention in Panchmari in 1984–85. A jailor called Sohan Lal was his 'guardian angel'. Writes Barnala in his narration, *"I found that Sohan Lal was a drunkard and would drink any liquor that came to hand at any time....... He one day showed me a photo of a small lovely girl. "This is my daughter Gauri's snap. Two years back she died in an accident; a truck hit her cycle when she was going to school," he said. She was studying in the seventh class and was a bright student and it was after her death that he had started drinking as he did. I took the picture from his hand and examined it more carefully. As I was looking at it he asked me, "could you paint her picture for me?" I agreed. The next day I started working on the portrait. Sohan Lal would come at intervals to see the progress and I found that he was sober throughout the day. It took me four days and I felt that I had succeeded in portraying her innocence and beauty to my best satisfaction. After finishing it I placed the painting on the table standing against the wall. Sohan Lal came early with some flowers and placing the flowers on the table took the portrait in his embrace. He was sobbing when I helped him up. "Aap ne bitiya ke shakshat darshan karwa diyen hain." (you have brought her to life), he said.*

On a few occasions I visited him and stayed with him at the Raj Bhavans in Hyderabad, Chennai and Ooty. He is always an excellent host making his guest comfortable. Once while leaving for Chennai, I had finalized my itinerary with his ADC when the phone rang again, "His Excellency would like to speak you," the ADC said, and Barnala was on the line checking up my flight details and other aspects of my stay. It was obviously an act of etiquette by a person who values the feelings of other human beings.

My recollections of Sam Manekshaw are from my adolescent days. The Wellington Cantonment is a quaint little dwelling nestled in the Nilgiri Hills in Tamil Nadu state. Here I remained for nearly four years since 1978, as my father headed an institution called the Defence Services Staff College; Sam had also headed the Institution many years earlier and was often a guest at our residence since he had made the neighbouring township of Coonoor his home. His personality was undoubtedly awesome, he would command the attention of those present as soon as he entered a room, particularly of the fair sex.

He would joke with many of the guests present and make many a ravishing maiden blush. I heard that he had once told a beautiful lady at a party, "you are wearing a lovely sari sweetie but you would look much better in a state which I shall not describe!" Another of his witticisms while addressing the Defence Services Staff College was, "My wife and I sleep in separate rooms; she says I snore but I say no other woman has complained!" Thank God there were no 24X7 TV channels in those days otherwise the army would have been buffeting from controversy to controversy given his loquacious nature. Whatever his faults, he was a born leader of men and his mere appearance could cause a ripple among a gathering. I last met him in December 2002 when he came to take the salute at the Passing out Parade at the Indian Military Academy at Dehradun. I was invited to the dinner night hosted by the Commandant of the Indian Military Academy. His daughter Maja Daruwala whom I had known through a common friend, introduced me saying, "Here is Arvindar, he has written on you." "Nothing scandalous I hope," was his ready response.

Narain Dutt Tiwari had had a long innings at the Centre and

the undivided state of Uttar Pradesh before he came to Uttaranchal (as the state was so named at the time) as chief minister in March 2002. I remember a function in his early days as chief minister in a fairly large hall with a good seating capacity. Tiwari did not climb the podium but went to the last row and began shaking hands with the audience. Within a short time he had won the hearts of those present. Tiwari, when you meet him personally always shows you utmost courtesy. It is obvious that he has feeling for those he comes into contact with and is one of the last of the old school politicians. Talking to him in the quiet atmosphere of his drawing room however, Tiwari is on a different plane. What is perceptible as daylight is that he is an extremely well read person. He could hold forth about the freedom struggle and his tours abroad as foreign minister with equal ease. Even at the age of more than eighty-five he has a razor sharp mind.

Mrs. Margaret Alva was appointed Governor of Uttarakhand in August 2009. I wanted to meet her in order to interview her for the local press. She gave me an appointment and I was duly ushered into the main drawing room of the governor's house. After the pleasantries were over, she came directly to the issue, "you want an interview, but as you know, as a rule, Governors do not give interviews." "Yes, Ma'am," I replied. "But if you see my questions you will find them of a neutral nature, and since the State formation day is around the corner, I thought that it would be only appropriate if the head of state's views are duly represented in Uttarakhand's oldest English daily. Also in Uttarakhand some of your illustrious predecessors often have given interviews many times to me. So a tradition to this effect prevails in the State. "Life's experience has taught me that some people are more amenable to your arguments if they have logic behind them and have the flexibility to alter their views. I could clearly see that Margaret Alva was one of those people. She thought for half a minute, and replied, "Have you sent the qestionnaire?" "I said that I had. "But I have not received it," she said. Soon she had gone into this issue with her staff and told me, glancing at the questionnaire I had with me, "You will receive the reply shortly, now let us have a cup of tea and tell me about yourself and the newspaper you represent." An interesting conversation followed in which she showed particular interest when I told her that I belonged to a family where my father was in a transferable service. "My father was also in government service and we moved often," she said. "It gives you a broader outlook on life." Margaret Alva was true to her word. In about a week I got a typed copy of the interview and it was published.

In the time that has since elapsed I have met her on many occasions and each interaction has been rewarding. She combines a kind of dignity and grace which is not commonplace. A believer in efficiency in work; no letter to her office goes unanswered, no communication unattended. She is a highly accessible governor concerned with people's problems and solutions to them.

A mention of some others I have come across in the course of my life, who have been co-travellers in this odyssey would be befitting here.

One person who played an edifying role in my life was Lt Gen R.K. Jasbir Singh, a doyen of the Indian Army whom I had known since childhood. However it was after the loss of my parents that we came into close touch in a manner which was to be long sustaining. I could almost read his mind and reactions on many occasions. 'Gen Jasbir', as we, close friends of his, often referred to him in private conversations,was an aristocrat to his finger tips. I doubt if ever any bad thought towards anybody entered his mind. His twinkling green eyes and handsome presence was dominating in the positive sense of the word. Somehow in his company one felt a kind of reassurance not easy to describe.

Jasbir Singh belonged to the erstwhile royal family of Jind State, hence the prefix 'RK' meaning Raj Kumar to his name. He was fond of angling and the great outdoors. He played the role of an officer and a gentleman in the true meaning of the term. He had served the Indian Army with distinction having been in the UN Missions in Korea and the Congo. Also he had seen action both in 1965 and1971 wars. In the Chamb action he was unduly blamed for the reverses suffered by the army but had the moral courage to stand up for his subordinates and clearly brought to the fore the issue of wrong planning at the higher level of command which resulted in converting an obvious defensive position in battle to an offensive action which resulted in the setbacks.

He was a graduate of the National Defence College and

commanded an Infantry Division as well as the National Defence Academy at Pune. He had also been Corps commander in Jammu and Kashmir retiring as Military Secretary at the Army Headquarters in 1983. Right till the winter of his life he retained all his goodness and was alert till the very end. When you met him during this period it was as if he was articulated the following lines,

> *The twilight is here. My days of old have vanished tone and tint; they have gone glimmering through the dreams of things that were. Their memory is of wondrous beauty watered by tears, and coaxed and caressed by the smiles of yesterday. I listen vainly for the witching melody of faint bugles blowing reveille of far drums beating the long roll. In my dreams I hear again the crash of guns the rattle of musketry, the strange mournful mutter of the battlefield.*

A word about my parents would not be out of place before this chapter draws to an end. Both were exceptional people in their own right, and were complementary to each other; a real 'made for each other pair'. Both were an exceptionally handsome couple during their prime. Both exceedingly caring and loving. My father was a thorough professional and excelled in his career, rising to the second highest rank in the Indian Army(as mentioned in the separate chapter on him and his regiment). My mother was a person whose dedication and love knew no bounds. She worked tirelessly during my childhood infirmity, achieving a near miracle for my recovery with rare resourcefulness and prayer. I saw in her the likeness of a tigress fighting for the health of her child.

The Gallery of personalities is complete. I hope later to write more about those I have known otherwise, appropriately. Morarji Desai spinning the charkha and holding forth about the momentousness of spirituality was as relevant as Surjit Singh Barnala talking of his passion for painting and art. Nani Palkhivala's wonderful voice and choice of words behind the microphone was as significant as Margaret Alva's courtesy and accessible approach. Sam Manekshaw's fondness for wisecracks gave a new dimension of leadership qualities to me. Narain Dutt Tiwari's humility and Gen

Jasbir Singh's charm may have been as contrasts to each other as chalk and cheese, but both have had a powerful impact on my way of thinking. The role of my parents, sublime in their own way, has also been recorded for good measure. It has been said that the hall of fame is mixed company, from my understanding I have found this to be true to a large extent, yet "those whom I have known" have mirrored the various aspects of a fruitful and well furnished life in every way. I hope the readers find this chapter as interesting as I did while writing it.

□

43

Complicated Situations Analysed

Webster's Dictionary defines the word "simulation" as "the imitative representation of the functioning of one system or process by the means of the functioning of another."

Edited by Radha Kumar who is Director of the Mandela Centre for Peace and Conflict Resolution at Jamia Millia Islamia University and also one of the three interlocutors, appointed by the Government of India, on the Jammu and Kashmir issue, this book gives the reader an unreserved and thorough version of various trouble spots, the world over with a simulation exercise on each dispute. The regions covered include Northern Ireland, Bosnia-Herzegovina, the Naga Conflict as well as Jammu and Kashmir. The contributors apart from Radha Kumar include John Doyle, Adrian Guelke, Anjali Puri, Udayon Mishra and Ellora Puri.

The Irish problem, as is well known, began after establishment of British control over Ireland by a series of invasions. However, after much struggle Ireland gained a measure of Independence in 1922. This was followed by the division of the country into the northern and southern parts which was predominantly catholic in the south and protestant majority in the north. Years of armed struggle was followed by the Sunningdale Agreement in 1973, which was a non-starter. The IRA ceasefire in 1994, in which Bill Clinton's administration played a leading role, resulted in the Belfast (Good Friday) Agreement of 1998 which finally brought down the curtain on the 700 year dispute wherein both the British and Irish governments agreed to give up their competing claims to Northern Ireland and the Protestants as well as the Catholics agreed to establish joint political and administrative institutions. The breakup of Yugoslavia, a federation of six republics of Serbia, Croatia, Montenegro, Bosnia-Herzegovina and Macedonia which was created in the early nineties. By early 1992, this strife torn area particularly Bosnia was engulfed in war on two fronts: in the west between Croatians and Muslims and in the east as well as the north between the Serbians and Muslims. The Vance-Owen Peace Pact which aimed at decentralization of the functioning units proved to be a non-starter. The Dayton Peace Accord, signed at Paris in December 1995 which was in many ways the brainchild of Serbian President Slobodan Milosevic, resulted in enduring peace.

Nearer home, the volume deals with the Naga problem which began in as a conflict for a Naga homeland in the 1940s. The demand for 'Greater Nagalim' ('lim' in Naga language means 'land') included unifying those who lived on the Myanammar side of the border and belonged to Naga ethnic origin to be brought under one administrative unit along with Naga populated areas of Assam and Mani pur which resulted in one of the longest surviving armed struggles in the Sub-continent. The formation of Nagaland State in 1963, did not bring about a lasting solution to this imbroglio. The Naga National Council (NNC) first led by A.Z. Phizo and later by his daughter Adino Phizo. Issac Muivah and Swu broke away from the NNC of Phizo and formed the National Socialist Council of Nagaland (NSCN) in 1980 which further split into two in 1988 called NSCN (I-M) and NSCN (K), which are till today involved in negotiations with the Government of India.

The last chapter deals with the Jammu and Kashmir issue, the dispute which seems to elude being disentangled by successive governments since independence. In the last more than sixty years no issue has cost us more materially and spiritually as a nation than Kashmir. The events of 1947, the delay of Maharaja Hari Singh in signing the instrument of accession; the invasion by the tribals; the fight back and repulsion of the Pakistani attack; declaring a cease-fire when we had a upper hand; going to the UN, an ill advised blunder; the passage of Article 370; the wars of 1965 and 1971; the accord with Shiekh Abdullah in 1975; the election of 1987 which was widely believed to have been rigged; the unleashing of militancy since 1990 which seems to be an ongoing and unending nightmare comes before one in meticulous detail as one goes through this piece.

On the whole a stimulating, thought provoking book, and the "simulations" in exercise form will be of great use to academicians and students of these quandaries as well. One wonders however why the learned authors or the editor did not devote a section on the Punjab issue which was at one time one of the most intense terrorist movements this country has witnessed.

Negotiating Peace in Deeply Divided Societies:
A Set of Simulations edited by Radha Kumar
(Published in 'Defence Watch' June 2011)

□

44

Morarji Desai: In the Right Perspective

In his column entitled "Encore" published in an English daily of March 6, 2011, under the heading "My Spat with Morarji Desai" former Foreign Minister K Natwar Singh has held forth against Morarji Desai who was Prime Minister of India from 1977 to 1979, during which period Natwar Singh represented the country as High Commissioner to Zambia.

Natwar Singh records that when Morarjibhai died in April 1995, "No comets were seen, no thunder, no hail, no storm happened." I would advise Natwar Singh to go through the newspaper files of April-May 1995, particularly those of Maharashtra and Gujarat. He will find them full of touching tributes written straight for the heart about an able administrator and true Gandhian for whom hypocrisy was miles away from his personality. HY Sharda Prasad, who served as Desai's press secretary, wrote in a tribute to him, "He was a first rate administrator one of the best in free India. He could seize a problem or file by its head and its tail. He asked the right questions and came to the right conclusions. He had too much common sense and knowledge of rules and precedents to be fooled by the bureaucracy." Clearly Sharda Prasad's apposite comments should lay any doubts at rest about the rather subjective picture that Natwar Singh has chosen to paint.

Natwar Singh holds that Desai's knowledge of African affairs was abysmal. Again here we are unable to fathom on what basis he jumps to the conclusion. That a person of Morarji Desai's proficiency and calibre should raise questions on state funding of terrorist by the then Zambian government and the fact that Natwar Singh was heaping undue praise on the Zambia administration only goes to show that all was not well in our High Commission at Lusaka. Singh also takes umbrage of the fact that Desai pulled him up for coming to New Delhi with a Zambian delegation without MEA approval. Undoubtedly, Singh is quite right when he states that a delegation headed by the Zambian Prime Minister should have been accompanied by the Indian High Commissioner, however, he should have made proper efforts to get MEA approval, which would not have been denied if ample notice had been given. Natwar Singh could have also obtained telephonic approval from Foreign Minister AB Vajpayee or Foreign Secretary Jagat Mehta.

Another aspect or Natwar Singh's piece is personal. He bemoans the fact that when arrived at 1, Safdarjung Road (the then Prime Minister's residence) "elegance and style had departed". For those raised in the ashram culture and who are votaries of the Gandhian philosophy of simple living and high thinking, "elegance and style" exist but of a different variety. This may not suit the author's aesthetic tastes, but I feel it is a matter of pride when a Certain type of Gandhian simplicity manifests itself at the abode of the Chief Executive of the country. I must confess that I never visited 1, Safdarjung Road when Morarji was the occupant, but I had visited his residences in Mumbai on many occasions, and I never found them lacking in either "elegance or taste". Natwar Singh might feel that I lack "elegance and taste". Maybe as an earthy Jat Sikh I could plead guilty of the charge!

Natwar Singh was busy as High Commissioner getting testimonial from foreign dignitaries like Kenneth Kaunda, the Zambian President, and expected the Prime Minister of India to give detailed replies to these testimonials! Morarji was obviously on the beam, when telling him not to be "needlessly sensitive" over the matter.

In the concluding part of his column, Natwar Singh states that Morarji Desai asked him to bring his wife (who was waiting for him in the car) inside to join them. This he stubbornly refused to do, on the pretext that his was an official and not a social call. This infuriated the Prime Minister who curtly told him to leave his residence. Natwar now states in retrospect that this was "quite improper". Natwar Singh's mother-in-law, the dowager Maharani of Patiala, Mohinder Kaur had been a member of Morarji Desai's party since the time of the Congress split in 1969. She remained a loyal supporter of him throughout the rest of his life. Therefore, it was only natural that he wanted to exchange pleasantries with the daughter of a senior party colleague who was also a Member of Parliament at the time.

A close up with Morarji Desai, Bombay, 1984

Morarji Desai had a long innings as a freedom fighter and an administrator of high repute. He had his blind spots like prohibition to some extent, but he was a hard taskmaster and great believer in moral values and high principles. He had worked for 12 years as a Provincial Civil Service Officer in the Government of Bombay before joining the Independence movement in 1930. Throughout the Emergency he remained in solitary confinement in Haryana state, not once appealing for parole, in fact turning down the offer for a conditional release, point blank. "I knew I would be free only the day the elections are announced," he often said. Thus, he successfully withstood the hideous fury of dictatorship which was prevalent during those years. In the parliamentary elections held in the aftermath of the Emergency, he led the combined opposition under the label of the Janta Party to victory and was named Prime Minister on March 24, 1977. His government will be remembered for its sound economic policies and foreign policy, particularly the well-grounded relations he sought to build with our neighbours especially Pakistan. A political coup in the summer of 1979 brought about the demise of his government. He is the only Indian recipient of the "Nishan-e-Pakistan", the highest civilian honour of that country.

NA Palkhivala, the eminent jurist, once described him (quoting Milton) as a person who remained "unmoved, unshaken, unseduced, unterrified" throughout his life. Most of his countrymen will view him similarly. Unfortunately K Natwar Singh stands a in minority.

(The writer is the author of the book, ***Morarji Desai: A Profile in Courage*** *a biography of the late Prime Minister).*

(Published in Uday India 2 April, 2011)

□

45

An Encounter with Orhan Pamuk

The wintry morning sun-rays shimmered softly on the dew-dappled grass carpeting the lawns of Jaipur's famous Diggi Palace. Like me there were scores of lovers of literature basking in the warmth of mellow sunshine ruminating over Dr Karan Singh's soft voice discoursing on the importance of translators.

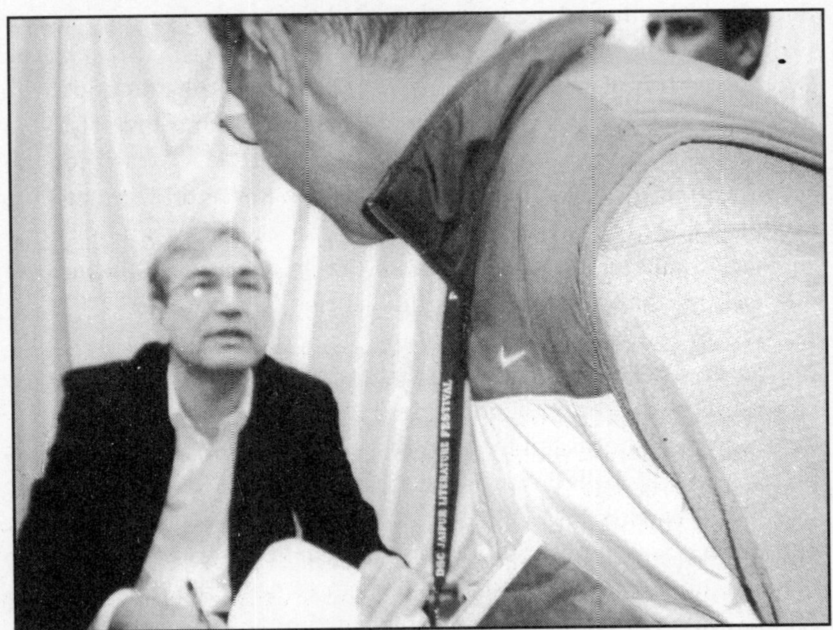

The author (back to the camera) with Nobel Laurette Orhan Pamuk at the Jaipur Literature Festival 2011

Great works like Tolstoy's *War and Peace,* Dumas's *Three Musketeers,* and Mann's *The Magic Mountain,* reached other shores and soil, "only because of selfless dedication of translators." Dr Singh emphasised, adding an afterthought, "I personally have around 25,000 volumes in my library in Jammu." To this a listener, flushed with the cool dawn breeze added: "Love them, support them and turn them into literature."

Even as the ominous warnings of Dr Singh was sinking and permeating into the psyche of the participants of Jaipur Literary Festival, Sheldon Pollock, Professor of Sanskrit and Indian Studies, Columbia University reiterated a similar concern over the fast disappearance and demise of languages as species: just as plants and animals are disappearing from the history of nature never to be seen again. Dr Pollock emphasised the importance of the preservation of indigenous languages–as the death of languages is a warning signal to the worldwide evaporation of cultures from the history of civilisation.

As the sun traversed across the skies, everybody flocked to the talk of the day–An hour with Nobel Laureate, Turkish novelist Orhan Pamuk. Though I had read his novel *The Museum of Innocence* (published in 2009) I was still eager to listen and swim in the poignant mesmerizing waves of this touching love story.

When Pamuk won the International IMPAC Award for *My Name is Red,* British supernatural fantasy writer and historian Tom Holland declared: "We in the West can only feel grateful that such a novelist as Pamuk exists to act as a bridge between our culture and that of a heritage quite as rich as our own."

After the publication of *Snow,* Canadian poet and novelist, Margaret Atwood, simply stated that the novel should be made "an essential reading for our times". *Istanbul* a memoir of his life in the city was shortlisted for the BBC Channel Four Samuel Johnson prize, and was called "an irresistibly seductive book" by Welsh writer Jan Morris. *Other Colours*, a personal selection of essays and writings was published in 2007. The year 2010 saw the publication of non-fiction work–a compilation of lectures delivered in the Charles Eliot Norton Series at Harvard University, under the title *The Naïve and Sentimental Novelist.*

Ironically, earlier in the same year, Pamuk (who had divorced his first wife Aylin in 2001) was in news for quite some time, but it was not for any literary reason. Rumours were then making rounds of his dalliance with a female novelist. Pamuk gave rest to the grapevine by admitting to his relationshi p with the Man Booker Prize winner novelist–Kiran Desai.

Pamuk's prime concern in almost all his work–revolves around the collective unconscious psyche of the people and a region's cultural memories. And even as he began his talk in reference to his novel, *My Name is Red,* he came to the basic premise which haunts all his novels–What is my Culture?

The concern for the evaporation of varied and multi-hued cultural patchwork quilt that once covered the earth rankled most of the speakers in the feast. And Pamuk also expressed concern over the cultural hegemony of the America-churned out global monoculture which like an oil slick is fast spreading over the planet engulfing, gobbling and suffocating every other culture underneath its surface.

Dwelling on his desperate attempts to brush and etch out his visions and emotions on empty canvases early in his career, Pamuk jocularly added that his cameo appearances in his novels was akin to Hitchcock making appreences in films. "There is no need to delve into or indulge in any psycho-analysis on his effort of mine, except that I like to be a part of the effort. Finding publishers in my native (Turkish) language was one Herculean effort," and probably, that maybe, one of the reasons that Pamuk confessed, "I kept taking pocket money from my father till the age of 31."

In his Nobel lecture in 2006, Pamuk had stated, "What literature needs most to tell and investigate today are humanity's basic fears: the fear of being left outside, and the fear of counting for nothing, and the feelings of worthlessness that come with such fears; the collective humiliations, vulnerabilities, slights, grievances, sensitivities and imagined insults, and nationalist boasts and inflations are their next of kind... Whenever I am confronted with such sentiments and by their irrational, overstated language in which they are usually expressed, I know they touch on a darkness inside me..."

Harping on his basic premise circling on the issue of love, Pamuk pointedly said, My novel *The Museum of Innocence* was an answer to my feminist critics. Love is not to be put on a pedestal there is nothing to be embarrassed about love."

And as if to silence the votaries of Victorian prudishness, Pamuk to a query (raised by this writer) on the dichotomy of treatment in *The Museum of Innocence* towards the concept and depth of love, simply shot back, "You mean the sexual and philosophical aspect of love? Since you have used the word depth...both require a great deal of penetration!" The audience roared, and the Delhi press gloated over the one-line answer.

Later in a relaxed atmosphere, I asked him, "Did you like my question?" The answer was: "Did you like my answer? Your Stress on depth brought it out of me. I just could not help it."

The day-session drew the curtains down. And the sinking orange orb slowly ushered in the gloaming darkening radiance with shafts of rays playing with the glimmering swaying mirrors shooting out flecks of rainbow lights, patched on the clothes of the folk dancers.

Sipping my Vodka tinged with a dash of Coke, as I watched the dancers dancing out universes of human evolution and shared memories of culture and humanity in sheer ecstatic rhythmic steps, Pamuk's words delivered in his Nobel Prize speech came flashing to me, "I believe literature to be the most valuable hoard that humanity has gathered in its quest to understand itself. Societies, tribes and people grow more intelligent, richer, and more advanced as they pay attention to the troubled words of their authors... But literature is never just a national concern. The writer who shuts himself up in a room and first goes on a journey inside himself, will over the years, discover literature's eternal rule: he must have the artistry to tell his own stories as if they were other people's stories, and tell other people's stories as if they were his own, for this is what literature is. But we must first travel through other people's stories and books".

(Published in Uday India 5 March, 2011)

□□□